The Role of Birds in
the Second World War

The Role of Birds in the Second World War

How Ornithology Helped Win The War

Nicholas Milton

Foreword by Chris Packham CBE

PEN & SWORD HISTORY

First published in Great Britain in 2022 by
Pen & Sword History
An imprint of
Pen & Sword Books Ltd
Yorkshire – Philadelphia

ISBN 978 1 52679 414 7

Typeset by Mac Style
Printed and bound in the UK by CPI Group (UK) Ltd,
Croydon, CR0 4YY.

Pen & Sword Books Limited incorporates the imprints of Atlas,
Archaeology, Aviation, Discovery, Family History, Fiction, History,
Maritime, Military, Military Classics, Politics, Select, Transport,
True Crime, Air World, Frontline Publishing, Leo Cooper, Remember
When, Seaforth Publishing, The Praetorian Press, Wharncliffe
Local History, Wharncliffe Transport, Wharncliffe True Crime
and White Owl.

For a complete list of Pen & Sword titles please contact

PEN & SWORD BOOKS LIMITED
47 Church Street, Barnsley, South Yorkshire, S70 2AS, England
E-mail: enquiries@pen-and-sword.co.uk
Website: www.pen-and-sword.co.uk

Or

PEN AND SWORD BOOKS
1950 Lawrence Rd, Havertown, PA 19083, USA
E-mail: Uspen-and-sword@casematepublishers.com
Website: www.penandswordbooks.com

Contents

Foreword

The brambles tremble. It's almost imperceptible but in the still morning the shivering leaves betray a bird, hopping invisibly through the shiny veil of green tiles. Then it's calm … and all my focus is on the frond that last quivered. The rest of the tangle, that part of the hedgerow, the lane, the woods, the world itself all vanish and all I can see and feel is that sprig of prickly plant. Such is my concentration and such is the power of nature to command it.

The briar rocks again, a series of jerks which conclude in a veritable shaking in one spot, and when I sneak up I glimpse the blackcap slipping away like a quick mouse, and when I crane down and peep I see its grassy nest cup and the four brown waxy eggs with little hair squiggles of black which look like cracks in their perfect shells, and my heart misses a beat, and I smile, and in this tiny microcosm of all space and time I am happy. Happy in a very unhappy world, not a world at war but a world warring with a disease which has just invaded our lives and cells with diabolical consequences. And my escape, my respite, my moment of comfort, of solace, is framed by my passion for birds. And this is nothing new, across the whole world in the spring of 2020 people escaped extremes of anxiety, fear and stress by finding nature.

I try hard to imagine war. I've always felt I owe that at the very least to those who fell or whose lives were irrevocably transformed by its horrors. So as well as just building the Airfix Spitfires, I've watched, listened and learned about what it was like in the cockpit of the most beautiful aircraft ever built: not as a nostalgic icon of resistance, but for the young, fragile and frightened pilot in that cramped and lonely weapon. I've watched and rewatched *The World at War* throughout my life along with just about every other TV documentary and have read many accounts, biographies and stories about the conflict; that cataclysm which has undeniably shaped and informed so many of our lives. So it's no surprise that I was drawn to this extraordinary book which explores two of my greatest interests at once: birds and the wartime experience.

And it is remarkable. Because through the terrible darkness the passion of its diverse protagonists shines so very brightly, their determination to unite with their feathered spirits is so strong and the results so important. In times that we can, in fact, only struggle to imagine, these men and women went to nature to escape the terror of war, to find some sanity, some hope – just as many of us did in the Covid spring. What is also so joyously uplifting is that the intensity of their relationships with birds then shaped and fulfilled their post-war lives. Their lives' work went beyond securing a world without fascism, because in the aftermath so many became formative and influential conservationists, the very people who helped ensure that our seasons have been as well populated with birds as they were, and are.

But now we are in real trouble. We continue to fight with each other, but we have also been at war with nature. We have ravaged the richness of life on earth and destroyed its habitats. We have assaulted the very air that we breathe, and, just as in 1939, our planet is spinning on the edge of ruin. We need to act, and quickly, to repair, restore and recover nature. And as I read of some of the terrible trials these characters endured, and how hard they tried to teach us to cherish and protect the natural world, I couldn't help but feel we have failed them, forgotten their legacy, and how much their love of birds gave us.

So please read. Admire, be shocked and awed by their endeavours and encounters, respect their sacrifices and conclude with some of their resolution to put the world right for people and for wildlife. And given our ongoing predicament, maybe learn their most important lesson.

In the hell of war, these people found refuge and beauty, and that refuge was life-saving, and that beauty was made of birds.

Chris Packham
New Forest, 2021

Acknowledgements

Writing a book on birds in the Second World War has really opened my eyes to how much nature means to people during the most testing of times. The lockdowns due to Covid-19 were my generation's equivalent of the war-time restrictions placed on the country in 1939 and it was fascinating to see how once again birds played such an important role in maintaining our morale. One person who truly championed nature during the pandemic was Chris Packham. I have known Chris for over thirty-five years since we worked on the *Really Wild Show* together and I am grateful to him for writing the foreword. I would also like to thank Helen Wright, who proofread the draft and gave me a lot of useful feedback. Fenella Madoc-Davis provided background information on her father's time in Changi prison and his unique book, *An Introduction to Malayan Birds,* bringing to life his truly amazing story. I would also like to thank Tan Swee Hee from the Lee Kong Chian Natural History Museum in Singapore, and Bonny Tan, an independent researcher living in Vietnam, for their help with the chapter on birds behind barbed wire. Claire Rees from WWT Slimbridge kindly allowed me access to Sir Peter Scott's office, and Chris Moore, a volunteer at the Scott House Museum, was extremely helpful in providing information on Scott's life. Chris Gomersall generously provided the pictures of the avocet and black redstart used on the cover. Finally, my thanks again go to my wife, Andrea, and daughter, Georgia, for putting up with me writing this book at all hours of the day and night.

Preface

This book was started in March 2020 during the first lockdown to contain the spread of the Covid-19 virus as Britain faced the gravest threat to its survival since the Second World War. Not since war was declared in September 1939 had any government imposed such severe restrictions on people's lives by seeking to control where they went, who they saw and what they did. Yet the similarities between the response of people and communities to the pandemic in 2020 and the Blitz in 1940 were striking.

Just like in the dark days of the Blitz, people during the Covid-19 crisis had little choice but to keep calm and carry on. Communities came together to support each other in ways that would have made the Second World War generation proud. However, just like in the Blitz, society now faces a mental health crisis, the impact of which we are only beginning to understand. One of the most famous people to suffer from depression during the war was the prime minister Neville Chamberlain. To help him cope, he put up nest boxes in the garden of 10 Downing Street and nearly every day went birdwatching in nearby St James's Park. Similarly, in 2020, in order to cope with being confined to our homes, millions of us turned to the nature on our doorsteps for our mental wellbeing, just like people did throughout the long war years.

Wild birds, perhaps more than any other wildlife, gave us all hope during the pandemic because they carried on visiting our homes, gardens and local parks where, during lockdown, we developed a new appreciation for them. In response, the Royal Society for the Protection of Birds, Britain's largest nature conservation charity, organised its Breakfast Birdwatch online, while the naturalist Chris Packham started the Self Isolating Bird Club which soon was being watched by eight million people. Similarly, during the Second World War birds played their part in maintaining the nation's morale by providing escapism, entertainment and solace during truly momentous times.

A love of birds has always been an important part of the British way of life, but in wartime birds came into their own, helping to define our national identity. Birdwatching as a hobby flourished, one of the most popular bird books ever, *Watching Birds*, was published in 1940 while songs like '(There'll Be Bluebirds Over) The White Cliffs of Dover' and 'A Nightingale Sang in Berkeley Square' soon epitomised the 'Blitz spirit'. Real birds also benefitted; the avocet made a remarkable return as the result of flooding along the coast to prevent a German invasion, while the black redstart found an unlikely home in our bombed-out buildings. Birds even featured in wartime propaganda movies. Seagulls had a leading role in *The First of the Few*, released in 1942 and starring Leslie Howard, where they inspired R.J. Mitchell to come up with the legendary design of the Spitfire. In the 1944 film *Tawny Pipit* an injured Battle of Britain pilot finds a very rare pipit nest and when it's threatened he brings together the village community in defence of the birds. A ringed ouzel even had its own wartime storyline in the hugely popular *Just William* books by Richmal Crompton, where it helped to defend the country from invasion.

Birds at the front featured in every theatre of war, providing hope in the face of adversity. One of the most systematic seabird surveys ever took place during the Battle of the Atlantic. On the home front, great crested grebes were the inspiration for the ground-breaking Mass-Observation survey. Pigeons carried top-secret messages back to Britain from Nazi-occupied Europe, winning more Dickin medals for outstanding gallantry than any other animal. The animal equivalent of the Victoria Cross, this bronze medal issued by the People's Dispensary for Sick Animals (PDSA) was inscribed with the words 'PDSA; For Gallantry; We Also Serve'. In marked contrast the pigeon's perceived enemy, the peregrine falcon, was shot indiscriminately by order of the government and almost disappeared from large parts of our countryside.

As interesting as the birds were some of the people who watched them. Max Nicholson, a senior civil servant, was one of the chief planners for D-Day, but would stop meetings whenever he heard a black redstart singing outside his offices in London. Richard Meinertzhagen, an ex-soldier, also monitored black redstarts on a patch of waste ground during the Blitz, but was an attention-seeking fraud who used ornithology for self-aggrandisement. Matthew Rankin, a surgeon, surveyed seabirds from the bridge of his destroyer escorting convoys, while his pilot colleague,

Eric Duffey, flew over the ocean counting the same seabirds when looking for U-boats. Tom Harrisson, a polymath, was the mastermind behind Mass-Observation and watched people 'as if they were birds', but was also proud to call himself 'the most offending soul alive'. Despite these characteristics, he played a key role in defeating the Japanese in Borneo.

In the Far East, Carl Alexander Gibson-Hill, a doctor and the curator of Raffles Museum, remained studying his bird books when a Japanese officer pulled a gun on him after the fall of Singapore in 1941, living up to his reputation as the 'Wildman of Malaya'. While incarcerated in the notorious Changi camp, he met Guy Charles Madoc, who produced a truly unique book on Malayan birds, typed on paper stolen from the Japanese commandant's office using a commandeered typewriter. While inside, Gibson-Hill also met a seventeen-year-old girl called Sheila Allan and the two formed an unlikely friendship, she christening him 'Shakespeare' because of his love of the Bard and he treating her ill father. This relationship helped them survive over three years of brutal treatment at the hands of the Japanese. When they were transferred to an outside prison, Gibson-Hill made a detailed study of the long-tailed tailorbird and the spotted munia as a way of surviving the appalling conditions and boredom in the camp. Similarly for E.H. Ware, an RAF wireless mechanic posted to North Africa, birds enabled him to while away the long hours on duty and make sense of his time in the service.

For one of the most important figures of the Second World War, birdwatching became an escape from the immense pressures of responsibility involved in his job. Field Marshal Alan Brooke was Britain's top soldier and filming birds was his way of coping with the continual demands of Winston Churchill, a man he loathed and admired in almost equal measure. For the young Peter Scott, birds provided a lifeline while serving in the Royal Navy on destroyers. Afterwards, they were the inspiration for creating the Wildfowl and Wetlands Trust at Slimbridge. Before the war, Scott was seduced by Adolf Hitler and was a passionate wildfowler who craved adventure, but afterwards the veteran hunter turned conservationist, going on to become one of the greatest naturalists of his generation.

When, in 1945, the church bells finally rang out to mark the end of war and celebrate victory, it was a dove holding an olive branch that was used to proclaim the peace. From companions in the field to comrades in arms, birds served throughout the conflict and more than did their bit to help win the war.

Chapter 1

Bluebirds, Nightingales and Black Redstarts

At the outbreak of the Second World War the Avicultural Society, who counted among its membership many prominent British and German ornithologists, ran an editorial in its monthly magazine.[1] It said: 'A war has now broken upon us bringing untold misery and suffering – a war which no one wants and which we have done our utmost to avoid. It is not a war against a country, but a war against a system which has already brought persecution, destitution, and despair to countless members of the German nation itself.'

In response, the Society also published an article, 'Care of birds in war-time'[2] in October 1939, appealing to its members with bird collections to contact London Zoo. The notice read: 'Many aviculturists who are called either to military or national service are finding it difficult to provide for their collections of birds, also those living in areas more vulnerable to air attack are anxious to transfer their rarer birds to safer quarters. Owners of birds are earnestly requested not to have their birds destroyed without inquiry as to the possibility of their being suitably cared for.'

The Avicultural Society had been founded in 1894 to promote the keeping and breeding of non domesticated birds in captivity. During the First World War the society's magazine editor, Hubert S. Astley, had published an article about the German contribution to aviculture.[3] It was his attempt to unite the warring nations, but he faced a vitriolic backlash and had to resign. The new editor of the *Avicultural Magazine*, Phyllis Barclay-Smith, faced a similar dilemma, writing: 'The future is uncertain and obscure, but in the end right must prevail. In the dark days that are before us we must never give way to the inclination to assume that there is no future at all and that all culture is lost for ever.'

Like many others, Barclay-Smith had painful memories of a generation massacred in the First World War. So, as editor, she had invited foreign contributions from 'scientific institutions and societies' across Europe. It was, she wrote, her 'sincerest hope' that 'we are [not] cut off from the

German aviculturists', and assured them that her 'friendly regard' would remain. To prove her point, Barclay-Smith said she would publish articles from German contributors and over the next year did exactly that. Unlike her predecessor in the First World War, she did not have to fall on her sword.

The start of the war was also marked by Henry Douglas-Home (1907–1980, brother of the future prime minister Alec Douglas-Home), an ornithologist, broadcaster and Colonel in the Scottish Command of the British Army. He wrote 'September 2, 1939, had been a lovely day but at dusk a thick mist closed in. The next morning I could sense that extraordinary feeling that those of us who had felt the rumble of war for so long would not have long to wait before the storm broke. I went down and opened the french windows to the garden and the dense mist came floating into the room. I turned on the wireless, but before it operated, very close by but invisible came the delicate, haunting song of a willow warbler from the complete silence outside. Almost immediately the sombre voice of Chamberlain announced that we were at war. Somehow I felt that while the willow warbler sang, one day there would be sunshine and peace again.'[4]

As well as bringing hope, birds brightened up the dark days of the Blitz. In November 1940 a little paperback, *Watching Birds*, appeared in bookshops at the height of German bombing of British cities. It was written by the Secretary of the British Trust for Ornithology, James Fisher (1912–1970), who was also working for the Ministry of Agriculture on the impact of pests on crop production. Educated at Eton and Oxford University, before the war Fisher was a curator at London Zoo. Despite his academic background he believed passionately that birdwatching should be accessible to everyone, so, in his spare time he wrote the book, trying to make it as up-to-date and scientific as possible while appealing to the widest possible audience. In the preface he wrote:

Some people might consider an apology necessary for the appearance of a book about birds at a time when Britain is fighting for its own and many other lives. I make no such apology. Birds are part of the heritage we are fighting for. After this war ordinary people are going to have a better time than they have had; they are going to get about more; they will have time to rest from their tremendous tasks; many will get the opportunity, hitherto sought in vain, of watching wild creatures and making discoveries about them. It is for these men and women, and not for the privileged few to whom ornithology has been an indulgence, that I have written this little book.[5]

The egalitarian and eccentric Fisher believed that birdwatchers were drawn from every political party, class and walk of life. To prove it, he came up with his own rather bizarre list of birdwatchers he knew. They included 'a prime minister, a secretary of state, a charwoman, two policemen, two kings, one ex-king, five communists, one fascist, two labour, one liberal and six conservative members of parliament, the chairman of a county council, several farm labourers earning 30 shillings a week, a rich man who earned four or five times that amount in every hour of the day, and at least 46 schoolmasters.'[6]

Fisher didn't name anyone in his list but the prime minister was Neville Chamberlain, a well-known ornithologist, and the secretary of state was Edward Grey, the foreign secretary at the start of the First World War. The reference to '46 schoolmasters' was a jibe at his father who was one, Fisher commenting wryly that when it came to birds they were all 'grimly scientific about them and will talk for hours on the territory theory, the classification of the swallows, or changes in the bird populations of British woodland during historic times.'

The reasons why people watched birds fascinated Fisher. He wrote that some had no explanation, they just liked them, while for others it was 'their shape, their colours, their songs, the places where they live'. Others painted, wrote prose or created poetry about them. According to Fisher birdwatching was 'a superstition, a tradition, an art, a science, a pleasure, a hobby or a bore'. Fisher's own motivation was to get people excited by the science of birdwatching and he succeeded spectacularly. His book, published by Penguin, proved to be amazingly popular, with ordinary people reading it on the bus, in their air raid shelter and even on fire-watching duty during the Blitz. Just how popular birdwatching became during this time can be judged by the fact that Fisher's 'little book' would go on to sell over three million copies (among the many people who bought a copy was Carl Alexander Gibson-Hill, who was to contribute to a truly unique bird book while incarcerated as a prisoner of war by the Japanese).[7]

As well as featuring in bestselling books, birds also found their way into the songs that would come to define the 'Blitz spirit'. One of the most famous songs of the war was '(There'll Be Bluebirds Over) The White Cliffs of Dover'. It was recorded by many artists, including the big bandleader Glenn Miller (1904–1944), but it was immortalised by the forces' sweetheart Vera Lynn (1917–2020) in 1941 when she was aged just twenty-four. The song was written to inspire a war-weary nation to carry on the fight when all seemed at its darkest. The full song includes two verses rarely found in recordings:

I'll never forget the people I met
Braving those angry skies
I remember well as the shadows fell
The light of hope in their eyes
And though I'm far away
I still can hear them say
Thumbs up!
For when the dawn comes up
There'll be bluebirds over
The white cliffs of Dover
Tomorrow,
Just you wait and see
There'll be love and laughter
And peace ever after
Tomorrow, when the world is free.
When night shadows fall, I'll always recall out there across the sea
Twilight falling down on some little town;
It's fresh in my memory.
I hear mother pray, and to her baby say 'Don't cry,'
This is her lullaby.
There'll be bluebirds over
The white cliffs of Dover
Tomorrow,
Just you wait and see
There'll be love and laughter
And peace ever after
Tomorrow, when the world is free.

The song was recorded in 1940, just after the RAF had won its historic victory in the Battle of Britain, and released the following year when Adolf Hitler was still threatening to invade. The music was composed by Walter Kent (1911–1994) and the lyrics were written by Nat Burton (1901–1945), both of whom were American. Kent was an architect by training who wrote music as a hobby until he had his first success with 'Pu-leeze, Mister Hemingway' in 1932. This was a big hit for the famous bandleader Bert Ambrose and his orchestra and the English vocalist Elsie Carlisle, who was better known by her nickname, 'Radio Sweetheart Number One'.

Afterwards Kent penned other hits and soon found himself in demand by the film industry, moving to Los Angeles where he worked in Paramount studios, producing the music for several westerns. With the onset of war Kent was asked to produce music to accompany the morale-boosting propaganda movies coming out of the studios. It was there he met and collaborated with the lyricist Nat Burton to produce '(There'll Be Bluebirds Over) The White Cliffs of Dover'. Burton was a Jewish New Yorker of German origin whose real name was Nat Schwartz. Like Kent, he had never been to England, but because of his roots was determined to do whatever he could to defeat the Nazis.

So Burton penned the immortal lines about bluebirds over 5,000 miles away in his studio in Los Angeles. As he was separated by the Atlantic Ocean from any English ornithological influence, there has been much speculation about the reference to bluebirds in the song. What bird was Burton referring to? And was there a hidden meaning in the wartime verse?

The most common 'blue bird' in Britain is the blue tit, but the species is more associated with woods and gardens than majestic white cliffs. The lines of the song conjure up a picture of bluebirds soaring over the imposing cliffs whereas blue tits tend to flit from tree to tree. The other more plausible candidate is the swallow, whose metallic, glossy, blue plumage and acrobatic flight would certainly fit the bill. The species is common around the white cliffs of Dover, spending much of its time on the wing catching invertebrates in mid-air. In Britain the word 'swallow' is used to mean the barn swallow, but it is also the name for a family of birds that are found throughout the world, including America. But if Burton had been referring to swallows why would not call them by their name rather than highlighting their colour?

While bluebirds do not occur in Britain, they do in North America where they belong to the thrush family. There are three species: the eastern bluebird, western bluebird and the mountain bluebird, each with distinctive blue, or blue and red plumage, which gives them their name. Bluebirds had already featured in many popular songs from the era, including 'Bluebirds in the Moonlight' from the film *Gulliver's Travels*, 'Bluebird Sing me a Song', and 'A Bluebird of Happiness'. In each of them bluebirds were synonymous not with real birds but with joy and love. The best-known song featuring bluebirds was 'Over the Rainbow' from the 1939 film *The Wizard of Oz*. Sung by Judy Garland (1922–1969) in her most celebrated role as Dorothy Gale, it won her an Academy Award for Best Original Song and became her signature anthem.

So did Burton plagiarise one of the most popular songs of the era? Or did he refer obliquely to the swallow or base the song on the American bluebird? The charge of plagiarism seems more likely as Burton was not known for his knowledge of birds, British or American. But perhaps the bluebirds in the title aren't feathered birds at all but war birds. After the Battle of Britain, the entire underside of the Spitfire, the most iconic plane of the Second World War, was painted a duck-egg blue colour called 'sky' to camouflage it from the ground. At the time America had not entered the war and public opinion was still strongly against it being dragged into the conflict. So Burton may have been using the bluebird to try to bring America into the war on the side of the Allies, or showing solidarity with his fellow Jews suffering under Nazism. Or he may have simply been saying that Britain would prevail in the war because a Spitfire would always fly over the white cliffs of Dover. Whatever his motivation, the song became hugely popular with the troops at the front and proved to be one of the most successful songs of the war.

Another song immortalised by Vera Lynn featuring birds was 'A Nightingale Sang in Berkley Square'. Produced in 1939, it conjures up the magic that happens when two lovers meet in the heart of London, expressed through the song of nightingale. The song was written by Eric Maschwitz (1901–1969) and the accompanying music produced by Manning Sherwin (1902–1974), but when it was first performed in the summer of 1939 by the duo in a local bar, it proved to be a flop.

Maschwitz was a writer and lyricist who, in 1926, had joined the BBC where he edited the *Radio Times*, receiving an OBE in 1936 for his services to broadcasting. In 1937 he started working for the British office of Hollywood's MGM Studios where he penned the screenplay to several successful movies including *Goodnight Mr Chips*, for which he received an Academy Award nomination. Like Burton, he had German roots but tried to hide his ancestry by working under the memorable pseudonym 'Holt Marvell'.

When war broke out, Maschwitz wanted to do his bit and got a job as a postal censor, checking any European post for secret messages from fifth columnists. By the time he wrote 'A Nightingale Sang in Berkeley Square', he had been recruited by the security services and went on to have a successful career in the clandestine Special Operations Executive.

Maschwitz's musical partner, Manning Sherwin, was an American composer who had settled in Britain in 1938. Sherwin had already had an earlier wartime hit with 'Who's Taking You Home Tonight', a song also made famous by Vera Lynn. It was about a stranger winning over a girl's heart on the dance floor. However, reflecting the morals of the time, the 'lucky boy' only got to kiss the girl goodnight on the doorstep.

Maschwitz got the inspiration for the song while on holiday in the village of Le Lavandou in Provence. There he had an apartment and every evening would go for a walk among the lavender fields. One night, he heard the unmistakable virtuoso sound of the nightingale, emerging as if by magic from a nearby thicket. Like other great writers and poets before him, Maschwitz was mesmerised by the loud whistling crescendo which seemed to emanate from the darkness (the word nightingale is derived from the words 'night' and the Old English 'galan' or 'to sing', reflecting the habit of the male singing at night to attract a mate). Returning home, he looked up one of the most famous poems about the bird, 'Ode to a Nightingale', by John Keats (1795–1821):

> My heart aches, and a drowsy numbness pains
> My sense, as though of hemlock I had drunk,
> Or emptied some dull opiate to the drains
> One minute past, and Lethe-wards had sunk:
> 'Tis not through envy of thy happy lot,
> But being too happy in thine happiness,

That thou, light-winged Dryad of the trees
In some melodious plot
Of beechen green, and shadows numberless,
Singest of summer in full-throated ease.
O, for a draught of vintage! that hath been
Cool'd a long age in the deep-delved earth,
Tasting of Flora and the country green,
Dance, and Provençal song, and sunburnt mirth!
O for a beaker full of the warm South,
Full of the true, the blushful Hippocrene,
With beaded bubbles winking at the brim,
And purple-stained mouth;
That I might drink, and leave the world unseen,
And with thee fade away into the forest dim.

Maschwitz was inspired by Keats' line about the 'Provençal song', a reference to the nightingale being a common bird in the south of France. Britain has always been on the northern edge of the nightingale's range, although Maschwitz, not being a birdwatcher, probably didn't know this. What mattered to him was not that the song was ornithologically accurate but that it would be a hit that people could sing along to. And what better way, he reasoned, to signal the romantic chemistry which happens when two lovers meet at night and 'magic was abroad in the air', than the beautiful song of the nightingale?

The final title of the song came from an anthology of short stories, *These Charming People*, by Michael Arlen (1895–1956), published in 1923. One of the stories was called 'A Nightingale Sang in Berkeley Square'. So Maschwitz lifted the title, transporting the nightingale from the Mediterranean to Mayfair and substituting the obscure village of Le Lavandou for the more glamorous Berkeley Square.

According to Maschwitz's autobiography, *No Chip on my Shoulder*, the song had its first public performance in his local bar. He sang the words, glass of wine in hand, while Manning Sherwin played the piano accompanied by a saxophonist. The locals listened politely but 'nobody seemed impressed'. Despite this, the song was published on 11 April 1940 and was performed in the London revue *New Faces* by the actress Judy Campbell (1916–2004) where it received rapturous applause. It went on to become one of the biggest hits of the war and would be recorded by all the major artists of the time, including Vera Lynn, Glenn Miller and Bing Crosby.

Reviews of the song, both at the time and since, have made much of the unlikelihood of a nightingale ever singing in central London. The square is now totally unsuitable for the species, being composed of London plane trees and a manicured lawn. In contrast, nightingales are secretive birds that are found in thick scrub or dense woodland where they sing from deep cover. But contrary to popular belief, from mid-April until early June the males also sing in the early morning and out in the open. Some ornithologists have speculated that Maschwitz mistook the sound of a robin for a nightingale as robins also sing at night and in the early morning. That seems unlikely as he would have been familiar with the song of the nightingale from his holidays in the south of France.

During the war, 20 Berkeley Square was home to the Royal Air Force 'Comforts Committee'. Their mission was to recruit volunteers to knit a range of garments for serving air men and women including scarfs, socks, gum boot stockings, pullovers, mittens and gloves. To do this they encouraged 'Working Parties' of at least ten knitters to apply for ration coupon-free wool on the strict understanding that all the garments would be sent directly to the Comforts Committee. In return, each volunteer received a chromium and enamel badge in recognition of their contribution. A small army of volunteers was soon raised who knitted to support the troops at the front. With the garments an acknowledgment slip was included so service personnel could say a personal thank you to their benefactors. In 1939 the Comforts Committee produced an official book of instructions called *Knitting for the RAF*. With an introduction by Archibald Sinclair, the Secretary of State for Air, it featured patterns and thanked the knitters for their efforts. On the back of the booklet, reflecting the squares most famous resident, was a picture of a nightingale. Sat on the bough of a darkened tree, it is singing 'knit, knit, knit!' in the moonlight.[8]

Today, Berkeley Square supports little in the way of birdlife, and when in 2019 a concert was held there in honour of the nightingale, a recording of the bird's song was used. However, recently nightingales have been reported as raising their young just six miles from Berkeley Square, their song having to compete with the sound of London traffic.[9] Back in 1939 the square would have looked very different and been shrouded in darkness due to the blackout. At the outset of the war many parks and gardens in London were left to go wild, the gardeners having been called up or redeployed to support the war effort. So the habitat then may have been more suitable for nightingales, and by the end of the war could have been quite overgrown. So maybe, just maybe, during the war a nightingale really did sing in Berkeley Square.

Nightingales not only featured in Maschwitz's and Sherwin's song but were also the only bird during the war that could boast its own annual radio programme. In 1924 the BBC's first live-to-radio broadcast featured the accomplished cellist Beatrice Harrison (1892–1965) playing a duet with a nightingale, amazingly recorded in her garden in Surrey. As a result, Harrison released records of her playing with nightingales and also accompanying the dawn chorus, both proving very popular with the public. The BBC continued this annual ritual until 1942, when the broadcast was famously abandoned on air after the microphones picked up the sound of Wellington and Lancaster bombers flying overhead on a raid. The radio engineers, suddenly realizing the sounds could be picked up in Germany and forewarn the Luftwaffe, quickly cut the live broadcast. The nightingale continued singing over the sound of the bombers for the rest of the war, but sadly today its song has disappeared from much of the British countryside, and so a reprisal of the wartime duet seems unlikely.

As well as songs, birds also made their contribution to the war effort in other surprising ways. The most famous service personnel named after birds were the Wrens, who served during the First and Second World wars. In 1917, in response to severe shortages in manpower, the Women's Royal Naval Service (WRNS) was founded, the Royal Navy becoming the first of the three services to officially recruit women. It was not long before those serving were being nicknamed Wrens or 'Jenny Wrens' in naval slang.

The ornithological wren is one of our most common birds and in comparison to its diminutive size has one of the loudest calls of any species. Unlike many birds, they call all year round, their 'machine gun rattle' often emanating from the depths of a hedge, even in the middle of winter. These small birds with their russet plumage and big voice are always busy and energetic, their small, stubby and cocked tails being a defining feature. Females become particularly vocal when their nests are threatened, hence their nickname, the 'Jenny Wren'. So when the WRNS adopted the nickname Wrens they were in good ornithological company.

The WRNS was disbanded when the First World War ended, but was resurrected in 1939 with the outbreak of the Second World War. This time, women had a more prominent role from the outset, although one of their first recruiting campaigns still had the slogan 'Join the Wrens today and free a man to join the Fleet'. However, as the war progressed new roles were offered to them including radio operators, meteorologists, cypher officers and boat crew. Wrens would go on to serve with distinction throughout the war, over one hundred making the ultimate sacrifice and dying for their country.

The wren also featured on one of the Second World War's most iconic coins, the farthing. This, the smallest value British coin ever produced, was first minted in 1860 and was worth approximately a quarter of a penny. The name farthing is derived from the word 'fourthing' or 'feorling', the very first farthings being made from pennies cut into four pieces. These were forged in the days of Oliver Cromwell and were originally made of silver. The coin featuring the wren was first introduced in 1937, replacing Britannia for the first time in over 250 years, after Edward VIII had asked the Royal Mint for the redesign, not liking their reliance on 'ancient heraldry'. The designer chosen was Harold Parker, a British sculptor brought up in Australia, whose work had been shown at the Paris Salon, the Royal Academy and the Australian Academy of Art.

To meet the royal wish, Parker prepared a series of coin designs based on 'royal animals' including the eagle, dove, stag, sturgeon, swan and the wren. The wren was eventually chosen, and although a few coins were pressed with Edward VIII's head and the year 1937 they never entered circulation following his abdication in December 1936. So the first coin to feature the wren had instead George VI's head on it with the inscription 'GEORGIVS VI DEI GRA BRITT OMN REX FID DEF IND IMP', or by 'George VI the Grace of God, King of all Britain, Defender of the Faith, Emperor of India'. However, despite all the titles, the symbolism of using a wren was historic. Britain's second-smallest bird had replaced Britannia, the might and power of the British Empire, who had first appeared on coins back in the Roman era. The farthing featuring the wren design remained in circulation until the end of 1960, the peak number minted during its hundred-year lifespan occurring at the height of the Second World War in 1943 when over 33 million were produced.[10]

As well as birds supporting the war effort in books, songs and coins, the emergency measures put in place to prevent invasion by the Germans had some surprising benefits for real birds. The most famous example is the return of the avocet, one of our most graceful wading birds, to the coast of East Anglia. The species is famous for its porcelain-white and black plumage and its long, slender and upturned bill which it continuously sweeps from side to side as it feeds.

Prior to the Second World War the avocet had been extinct as a breeding species for more than a century, its old rural names such as 'crooked bill', 'scooper', 'shoohing horne' and 'cobbler's awl' fading into folklore (an awl is long, sharp tool used by shoemakers to punch small holes through leather). Its disappearance was due to the widespread draining of its wetland habitat and relentless persecution. In Victorian times, like many other elegant and colourful birds, its ornate black and white feathers were prized as adornments to women's hats. When this practice was finally outlawed, the birds were then shot by fishermen in large numbers, despite in theory being protected, because their feathers made very good flies. By the early nineteenth century, they had been reduced to a small population on the North Norfolk coast where they were targeted by egg collectors, avocet pudding and cake being a popular local delicacy. In 1843, the final pair were killed when they were shot on a Norfolk marsh.

With the onset of war and a German invasion imminent, the Ministry of Defence ordered that all low-lying, vulnerable land along the coast of East Anglia should be flooded. This included land at Minsmere in Suffolk, which before the war was farmland owned by the Ogilvie family. To protect the area, extensive military defences were built along the coast at Minsmere and neighbouring Dunwich, including pillboxes, anti-aircraft defences, anti-tank traps and lines of horizontal scaffold tubes that were anchored along the beaches to prevent landing craft coming ashore. The surrounding heathland was also fenced off for military manoeuvres, the army using it to practice repelling an invasion force.

Not to be outdone, the RAF also did their bit to help the avocet when a plane from a nearby military base at Boyton dropped its bombs by accident on Havergate Island, blowing up the sluice and breaching the seawall. The result was that the sea flooded the low-lying land at both Minsmere and Havergate Island, creating shallow brackish lagoons which proved to be the ideal habitat. In the Netherlands, avocets had bred successfully throughout the war and in 1947 birds from a colony there turned up for the first time in Minsmere. Their appearance galvanised the RSPB into launching an almost military-style operation to protect them from egg collectors. The next year, avocets also turned up at Havergate Island. Such was the secrecy surrounding both sites that they were assigned code words which covertly referred to the bird's piebald plumage – 'zebra' for Minsmere and 'zebra island' for Havergate. The RSPB then bought both Minsmere and Havergate Island, managing them for the avocet, and in acknowledgement of its remarkable return adopted the bird as its official logo in 1955. Eight years later, in 1963, all their efforts were crowned with success when the first pair of avocets successfully bred at Minsmere.

Another very rare bird to benefit directly from the war was the black redstart. As the Blitz raged and large parts of London were reduced to rubble or razed to the ground, the bird found an unlikely home among the bombed remnants of people's houses. Remarkably, the rubble resembled the scree slopes of the birds' favoured Alpine habitat, and despite the destruction going on all around them, the species thrived. Black redstarts are summer visitors to Britain and get their name from the plumage of the male bird which has a charcoal grey back, black face and a striking crimson chest and tail. They are highly energetic birds, constantly bobbing up and down, and in Britain are found almost exclusively in urban areas.

The first successful breeding record in London was at the Wembley Exhibition Centre in 1926 (the species had first bred in Britain three years earlier in Sussex). A decade later, there were regular reports of birds in the city, but they had failed to raise any young. However, with the start of the German bombing raids on the capital in 1940 a pair successfully reared two broods in the confines of Westminster Abbey and did the same the following year, despite the abbey being severely damaged by enemy action on 11 May 1941. The ornithologist C.B. Ashby, who made a detailed study of the birds, reported that they 'spent the summer of 1941 in Westminster [and] inhabited an area of private gardens and fair-sized buildings which had been damaged by air raids.'

To monitor the spread of the species, the London Natural History Society made a direct appeal to the capital's birdwatchers to send in records. Members in peacetime would normally have carried out a detailed survey, but this was impossible under the restrictions of wartime, so instead it published any records in the London Bird Report and the prestigious journal *British Birds*. They showed that by 1942 the number of singing males in the capital had increased considerably, twenty being present from April to September. In 1943 three pairs successfully nested, one in Temple, another off Fetter Lane and a third in Charterhouse. Among the records the Society received were ones from a truly eclectic range of ornithologists. They included an organiser of D-Day, a brigadier, a teacher, a wildlife photographer and an infamous intelligence officer, a roll call that read like a 'who's who' of conservation.[11]

A regular recorder was Max Nicholson (1904–2003) who was in charge of organising convoys during the Battle of the Atlantic and went on to become one of the chief planners of D-Day and 'Operation Overlord', the invasion of Hitler's fortress Europe. A friend of Edward Grey, the First World War Foreign Secretary, he was also a very keen birdwatcher, and in 1932 he founded the British Trust for Ornithology. Confined to London for the duration of the war where he worked in the Ministries of Shipping and Transport, Nicholson took a particular interest in the black redstart, recording it singing from tall buildings near his office in Marsham Street. One day he noted that the male bird would fly at least 600 yards between song posts after he heard one singing outside Marsham Street tube station. He then spotted the same bird again when he emerged from St James's Park station. Nicholson would even break off from important war meetings if he heard the black redstart's song, as he recalled in a 1995 episode of Radio 4's *Desert Island Discs*:

Our headquarters was in Berkeley Square House and it so happened that almost at the [same] time the popular hit 'A Nightingale Sang in Berkeley Square' was loosed on the world. We were having a very difficult meeting with about 20 people which was deadlocked on some shipping problem. Suddenly there was a slight pause in the meeting and Hercomb [Lord, 1883–1975], who was in the chair and I both got up and left the meeting hurriedly. [We] went over to the window and listened to one of the first black redstarts to sing. It wasn't a nightingale, it was a black redstart, but we listened to it and just made sure of it. We came back to the table, everyone was dumbfounded and this difficult argument immediately came to an end. Everybody agreed within two minutes, so never underestimate the power of a bird![12]

After the war Nicholson went on to write a number of very influential ornithological books, founded the World Wildlife Fund with Sir Peter Scott, became the first chair of the Nature Conservancy and the President of the RSPB.

Other contributors to the survey included Brigadier H. Christie, who was in charge of the 307th Infantry Brigade, but when not on duty monitored a black redstart nest he found in a fireplace in a bombed-out house in Wandsworth, a nesting record he sent in two years running. Another recorder was Desmond Nethersole-Thompson, a teacher, who submitted a record of a bird singing from Mincing Street in London. After the war he became a great ornithologist, writing monographs on the greenshank, snow bunting and pine crossbill. The world-renowned wildlife photographer Erik Hosking (1909–1991), who lived in south London, was another recorder. He would regularly explore bombed-out buildings in the capital in search of the birds. However, the most infamous black redstart contributor was Colonel Richard Meinertzhagen (1878–1967) who faithfully monitored a pair of birds breeding on waste ground in Notting Hill, noting how they fed their three young on ants.

Meinertzhagen, whose surname derived from the German town of the same name, was an intelligence officer during the First World War, serving in East Africa and the Middle East. His claim to fame was being the brains behind the Haversack Ruse, a hoax which involved planting a bag of false battle plans behind enemy lines in the Mesopotamia (Middle East) campaign. These deceived the Ottoman Turks into expecting an attack at Gaza, leading to the famous British victory at the Battle of Beersheba in 1917. The battle opened the way for General Allenby to capture Jerusalem, famously getting off his horse to enter the city in deference to Jesus who had entered on a donkey. The ruse also inspired Winston Churchill in the Second World War to form a secret department called the London Controlling Section. This was responsible for planning some of the greatest deceptions of the war, including Operation Mincemeat, which tricked the Germans into moving their troops to Greece prior to the Allied invasion of Sicily in 1943.

After the war Meinertzhagen went on ornithological expeditions to the Middle East and Africa, collecting a vast number of specimens which he left to the Natural History Museum in London. However, his illustrious war and bird record unravelled after his death when the author Brian Garfield revealed in his 2007 book *The Meinertzhagen Mystery* that he was an attention-seeking fraud who didn't invent the Haversack Ruse, and that many of his bird specimens were stolen from other collections.[13] Meinertzhagen remains a controversial figure in the conservation movement, but one whose black redstart sightings in the war nevertheless helped to confirm the species as a breeding bird in Britain.

Outside London, the black redstart was reported in a number of cities, most of which had been bombed. In Cambridge it bred in 1940 and again in 1941 when it was reported nesting in Christ's College. In the summer of 1942 three pairs and three single birds were present in the city – one pair nested in a hole in the wall of the chemistry laboratories in Downing Street, another in St. John's Trinity College and the third pair in Queen's College. The black redstart was clearly an adaptable and erudite bird, flourishing in both the rubble and the historic buildings of Britain's great university town.

All the black redstart records during the war were collated by the naturalist and author Richard Fitter (1913–2005). He initially started compiling them in a private capacity before formerly launching *The Black Redstart Inquiry* in 1944. In 1940 Fitter joined the Mass-Observation social research project, where he worked with Major Tom Harrisson investigating civilian morale during the Blitz for the Ministry of Information. He later worked at the Operations Research section of RAF Coastal Command, but spent two hours every evening writing a book about the black redstart and other London wildlife. This was published in May 1945 as *London's Natural History*, the third in the acclaimed *New Naturalist* series. Fitter was aided by one of the great ornithologists of his era, Harry Forbes Witherby (1873–1943), up until his death in 1943. Witherby served during the First World War with the Royal Naval Reserve and was made a Member of the Order of the British Empire for his work as an intelligence officer in Dunkirk. A talented research biologist, Witherby was the editor of the journal *British Birds* and a founding member of the British Trust for Ornithology, which was created in 1932. He was also the author of the prestigious five-volume

Handbook of British Birds, published from 1938 to 1941, a seminal work on British birds to this day.

In *London's Natural History*, Fitter summed up why the black restart was so important to both ornithology and morale during the war: 'It is not often that London acquires a new breeding bird, and still less often that the newcomer elects to breeding in the heart of the built-up area,' he concluded. 'Yet this is what has happened since 1940, when a pair of black redstarts brought off two broods in the precincts of Westminster Abbey. The story of the black redstart is quite the most remarkable in the annals of London ornithology in the past half century.' While noting that colonisation of the capital had begun before the Blitz, Fitter nevertheless acknowledged the part that bombing and the war had played in its success: 'The most that can be said for the "blitz" theory is that the bombing provided many more nesting sites than would otherwise have been available, and also ensured an abundance of the waste spaces which the bird requires to provide it with the necessary insect food. The war may also have made identification easier, for there is greater audibility due to less traffic, and greater visibility due to the destruction of buildings.'[14]

By the end of the war the *Black Redstart Inquiry* had recorded six to eight pairs breeding in Britain. Fitter concluded: 'It seems certain that the bird is still extending its range, and but for the restrictions on observation due to the war many more would probably have been reported. It is desirable that as soon as military conditions make it possible, all the towns on the south and east coasts of England should be thoroughly searched for black redstarts.'

Chapter 2

Spitfires, Tawny Pipits and Ring Ouzels

As well as being celebrated in song during wartime, birds also made it onto the big screen. In 1942 a black and white film, *The First of the Few*, came out celebrating the Supermarine Spitfire and its revolutionary designer Reginald Joseph Mitchell (1895–1937). The lead role of R.J. Mitchell ('Mitch') was played by the Hollywood film idol Leslie Howard (1893–1943) while the suave David Niven (1910–1983) played the part of an out-of-work test pilot, RAF Squadron Leader Geoffrey Crisp. Howard had previously starred in a string of successful films including *The Scarlet Pimpernel* and *Gone with the Wind* while Niven was also a household name. When it was released, the film was a big hit with cinema audiences, the title being inspired by Winston Churchill's famous speech about the pilots in the Battle of Britain.

The story of most famous plane in the world was an obvious choice for wartime film makers. However, the challenge was how to tell the tale in a way that would appeal to a mass audience. The film did this by coming up with the intriguing theory that Mitchell based the iconic design of the Spitfire not on the results of aerodynamic trials but on the shape of a seagull. Is there any truth in the story or was it just patriotic wartime propaganda?

The lead role in the *First of the Few* required a versatile actor who could play the part of Mitchell from his early twenties right up to his death at the young age of forty-two. At the time Leslie Howard, despite his 'boyish good looks', was already forty-nine. However, it was a film that he was determined to make so Howard decided to produce and direct it, casting himself in the lead role with the help of some good make-up artists and sympathetic lighting. However, to make the film he needed to not only raise a lot of money but also to get the active co-operation of RAF Fighter Command. To do this he decided to approach Churchill directly. The prime minister enthusiastically supported the idea, issuing him with a 'To whom it may concern' letter. After that the door of the RAF was always open, Howard receiving both the finance and the fighter planes he needed.

Howard had more reason than most to want to play his part in the war effort. Born Leslie Howard Steiner in London in 1893, he was of Jewish-Hungarian descent and grew up in Vienna, and like many Jews hated everything the Nazis stood for. He had fought in the First World War, serving with the Officer Training Corps and the Northamptonshire Yeomanry until he was discharged with neurasthenia, a nervous condition. Changing his name from Steiner to Howard by deed poll in 1920 to disguise his roots, Howard developed a glittering acting career playing stiff-upper-lipped and genteel Englishmen.

To get into the role Howard had studied in detail the life of Mitchell, but had struggled with the storyline until he was lucky enough to get an invitation to visit the Vickers factory which made the Spitfire. The author Ian Colvin, who in 1957 published a book about Howard's life called *Flight 777*, wrote:

> Leslie went into the story of R.J. Mitchell rather more deeply than is usual for a film director. The official material was dry, the story of the widow insufficient, but through a determined young woman in the theatrical world whom he met by pure chance over a drink in London, he found himself whisked out into the country and introduced to one of the Vickers top scientists, then working on cathode-ray tubes and other scientific advances. They sat and talked for hours. From him he heard the amazing story of Mitchell, the £6-a-week draughtsman who became absorbed in aerodynamics and studied the shape of birds in flight in search for the plane that could outfly the new fighters that Germany would build.[1]

From this conversation, Howard decided that the inspiration for the Spitfire should come from Mitchell lying on his back on a clifftop watching the seagulls floating past. So he asked the screenwriters to produce some suitable ornithological dialogue for transforming a seagull into a Spitfire. To reflect the dark days in which they were living, Howard also added in some real footage of the Nazis' *Blitzkrieg* on Europe and the Battle of Britain, and included excerpts of speeches from Lord Haw-Haw, Churchill, Hitler, Goebbels, and Goering.

After the speeches the film then cuts to an airfield where David Niven, playing the RAF Station Commander, is talking to a group of pilots about the Battle of Britain and their remarkable plane, the Spitfire. One pilot says, 'Can't see a Spit in the air without getting a kick out of it,' and a conversation then ensues about its designer, Mitchell, who is described as a 'wizard'. The pilots argue among themselves where he is now, each quipping, 'Inverness, Canada with MI5, working at Vickers or dead'. One pilot then comes out with the memorable line that 'Mitchell invented the Spitfire in two hours at a golf club.' Niven corrects him, saying, 'No he didn't. It wasn't as easy as that. Yes, a lot of things had to happen before that miracle came to life, and it all began a long time ago, it must have been 1922.'

The young pilots featured in the opening sequence were not actors but real airmen from local squadrons who had fought in the Battle of Britain. The scene was filmed in the summer of 1941 at RAF Ibsley in Dorset, which doubled for the fictional airfield of 'Seafield'. Here, and at other bases, footage was also shot of Spitfires coming in to land and a mock dogfight was staged with a captured Heinkel bomber which provided the climax for the film. While critics pointed out that some of the acting by the pilots was quite wooden, their bravery in real life was shown by the fact that several of them did not live to see themselves on the screen when the film was released a year later.[2]

At the outbreak of the war Niven, even though a leading actor, had been determined to do his bit. So he had joined the commandos and had been given special leave to star in the film. All the filming was done between combat operations and Niven was so impressed with the young pilots that at the end of the shoot the wealthy actor paid for them all to have a weekend away at the Savoy. He also made sure that all the advertising for the film credited them, the posters stating: 'Starring ... Leslie Howard, David Niven and Pilots & Other Personnel of The RAF Fighter Command.'

After the conversation at the dispersal hut the film cuts away to clouds and the sound of seagulls, the film makers using this to introduce the 1922 'flashback scenes'. These feature a much younger Mitchell (played by Howard with a different hairstyle) lying on the grass on a clifftop looking up at the birds through his binoculars. The first birds that come into his view are seagulls, probably herring gulls, circling around the cliff edge, before the film makers cut away rather unexpectedly to a close-up of a gannet, a seabird normally found out at sea. Then Mitch's charming wife, played by Rosamund John (1913–1988), appears in his binoculars. The scene ends with the two enjoying a romantic picnic, with Mitch engaging in small talk while puffing contentedly on his pipe.

After its release *The First of the Few* was faithfully recreated in the fortnightly fanzine *Picture Show and Film Pictorial*. This featured the film as their 'complete short story' in the issue dated 12 September 1942. 'The seagulls swooped and dived in the sunshine, their strong, curved wings outstretched, every movement a poem of controlled speed and unconscious grace as they screamed and fought, shot steeply upwards, hurtled to the waves, skimmed the surface of the sea and soared again to join the wheeling crowd in the air,' the magazine journalist breathlessly wrote. 'Far below them a man lay flat on his back on the cliff top, intently watching their flight through a pair of binoculars, glorying in their swiftness and sureness, longing to probe the secret of their flight.'[3]

The clifftop scene that introduced the link between the seagulls and the Spitfire was shot at Polperro cliffs in Cornwall, the closest stretch of coastline that the crew could find without beach defences and barbed wire in the shot. Ironically, the binoculars used by Howard in the film were almost certainly made by the German firm Zeiss, their distinctive shape and leather carrying case being prominently displayed. (Under the Nazis, Zeiss manufactured optical instruments for all kinds of weapons, and to cope with the huge demand created by arms orders, controversially employed foreign workers and forced labourers from virtually every occupied country in Europe.)

The fanzine writer from *Picture Show and Film Pictorial* breezily continues with the story, recreating the dialogue from the film where Mitchell gets his inspiration for the Spitfire by marvelling at the way that herring gulls wheel and glide above the cliffs.

'If we could fly half so well,' he said at last, half to himself, half to the girl who lay beside him. 'Look at them! Those curved wings – what a beautiful line! We've got to learn from the birds if we want to fly properly, and faster – always faster – and the world gets smaller and places closer. Places halfway across the world not strangers but neighbours. Distances, frontiers, wars – we can do away with them.

We will, too, some day, otherwise there's no meaning to progress – and there must be a meaning – .' He broke off, again enraptured by the gulls' flight, 'the way they turn and bank and glide! Perfect. All in one! Wings, body and tail – all in one.' This rather remarkable tribute to the physiology of the seagull might have sounded queer to the casual hearer who might take it for granted that a one-piece seagull was quite normal, but Diana Mitchell only smiled as her husband continued: 'When we try, we build something all sticks and struts and wires.' He sat up excitedly, 'You wait! Some day I'll build a plane that will be like a bird – like that seagull.'

The analogy between bird and plane was, in fact, a very old one, birds having been an inspiration for the design of aircraft since Leonardo da Vinci (1452–1519) first published his *Codex on the Flight of Birds* in around 1505. According to Steven P. Wickstrom, the author of *The Sea Gull Who Was Afraid to Fly*, who has studied the relationship, when a gull flaps its wings there is a down-stroke to provide thrust followed by an up-stroke to provide lift. This, Wickstrom states, creates an action which 'causes the wings to act like the propeller on an airplane to pull the gull forward.' The reference in the film to the building of planes using 'sticks, struts and wires' alluded to the biplanes which then still dominated the Royal Air Force, such as the aptly named Supermarine Seagull produced by the company in 1922. Now Mitchell was going to build a plane that not only looked like a seagull but was able to soar and dive like one, too.

The opening shots of the birds circling overhead in the film finish with Mitchell, like Da Vinci, doing his own sketch for a plane based on the flight of the gull. The writer for *Picture Show and Film Pictorial* magazine again enthusiastically recreated the story: 'He pulled a piece of pasteboard and a pencil from his pocket and began to sketch. Diana sat up and looked over his shoulder. It was a rough sketch of a seagull in the act of alighting on the water, wings and legs outstretched, and as she watched, his pencil transformed the feet into floats – it was a strange looking aircraft, not a bird at all, that she was seeing.'

Mitchell's sketch may have only been loosely based on the anatomy of a seagull, but researchers have recently been doing a lot of computer modelling of gulls' wings as a way of improving aircraft design. The research, carried out at the University of British Columbia, has been looking at how a single elbow joint enables gulls to adapt their wing shape to different climatic conditions. Douglas Altshuler, senior author of the study published in the *Journal of the Royal Society Interface*, writes: 'While we know birds frequently alter their wing shape, this is the first empirical evidence demonstrating how that wing morphing affects avian stability. And in this case, the gull's wing design points to a novel, and fairly simple, avian-inspired joint that may enable aircraft to adjust dynamically to challenging conditions.'[4]

The idea that gulls inspired the design of the Spitfire was not just confined to Mitchell. The artist Raymond Sheppard (1913–1958), who illustrated stories for Enid Blyton, Jim Corbett and Ernest Hemingway, wrote a book called *How To Draw Birds* which was published at the height of the Battle of Britain in July 1940. In the introduction he said 'Those big aeroplanes which fly overhead look rather like great birds, don't they? You, see the men who design them have been studying the shape and flow of lines of a bird, which they call its streamline, and they have tried to adapt these shapes to the designs because they know that birds are the most perfectly streamlined creatures in the world. But I'm afraid man has got a long way to go before he produces a flying machine as efficient as some of the birds. Look at the sea-gull, how easily he floats on effortless wings. Throw a piece of bread in the air and he swoops with the precision of a Spitfire.'

Gulls often encounter a lot of turbulence when flying near buildings, above water or over cliffs, and to compensate can change the angle of their elbow joint to pull their wings in and back. This flexibility gives them more control over their flight through turbulent air, in comparison to a fixed-wing aircraft which often has to ride out any air currents. As a result, engineers are now trying to produce aircraft wings that can dynamically adjust their wing shape to cope with any flying conditions. So Mitchell's idea of building a plane around the anatomy of a gull was not far-fetched, instead it was ahead of its time.

Seagulls don't appear again until near the end of the film when Mitchell is dying in his garden, the result of overwork on the Spitfire (in real life Mitchell died of rectal cancer and was working on lots of aircraft; not a good ending for a film designed to inspire a war-weary audience). Just before he passes away, Mitchell is told that the Spitfire has officially been put into production and there is a cut away to the clouds with the sound of seagulls calling. Mitchell's Spitfire saves the day, the writer for *Picture Post and Film Pictorial* again capturing the dialogue:

When the Spitfire prototype passed its final tests Mitch was gravely ill. Then one summer afternoon Geoffrey brought the news that they had all been waiting for so anxiously. The Air Ministry had adopted the Spitfire – hundreds of them were to be made. 'So you were in time after all, Mitch,' said Geoffrey as he saw Mitch's eye shine. Mitch nodded. 'Yes,' he said – 'but we cut it pretty fine.' After Geoffrey had left, Mitch lay very still, filled with peace and thankfulness that he had not worked in vain. Then his eyes closed. Near by a solitary seagull screamed, then soared higher and higher into the cloudless sky until it was lost to sight ...

The Spitfire has gone down in history as our saviour in the Battle of Britain (although the real credit should go to the Hurricane, which was the workhorse of the battle) and was the only fighter produced throughout the Second World War. In the film Mitchell says he wants his new plane to be 'a bird that breathes fire and spits out death and destruction – a "spitfire" bird,' giving the aircraft its iconic name. When R.J. Mitchell was told about the name the RAF had given to his design, he is reported to have said, 'That's the sort of bloody silly name they would choose!'[5]

Seagulls may have had a starring role in *First of the Few* but birds did not always get the credit they deserved in the film. Interestingly for a film that clearly championed birds, the producers wrongly attributed the name of the Spitfire's unique engine, the Rolls Royce Merlin, to the fabled wizard. In fact, Rolls Royce had a long tradition of naming their piston aero engines after birds of prey. So the Rolls Royce Merlin engine, which could produce just under 1,800hp and was one of the most successful engines of the war, was in real life named after Britain's smallest falcon, the dashing merlin. Birds of prey apart, did Mitchell really base his design for the Spitfire on the seagull or was it just another example of cinematic licence in war time? Howard clearly believed he did, as the author Ian Colvin states in his book on the star: 'Blood, sweat and tears went into its making, and when the final scene was devised Leslie turned to Anatole de Grunwald [one of the screenwriters] and said, I want here just a touch of the supernatural. Mitchell's bird of omen was the seagull. He loved them and studied them. So when he is dying in the garden, don't just show the death itself, just put in a shot of a gull hovering past, and as she sees it passing, his wife suddenly understands that he is gone.'

In contrast, one of the real-life people upon whom the Geoffrey Crisp character is based was Jeffrey Quill (1913–1996), a British test pilot who served with the RAF during the war. On a DVD reissue of the restored film *First of the Few*, he comments that the idea that Mitchell was inspired by gulls was pure 'fantasy'. Yet we do know that Mitchell admired birds, and in his youth kept racing pigeons. Mitchell's own son, Gordon, who wrote a biography on him and perhaps did more research on his life than anyone else, was open-minded and certainly thought birds inspired him. He stated in his biography *R.J.Mitchell, Schooldays to Spitfire,* that 'His interest in flying increased when he started to keep racing pigeons and to send them over to France to take part in 'homing' races […] Working at Supermarine, Mitchell looked out on a different world. There in front of him was the River Itchen, widening as it flowed into Southampton Water, and over which the seagulls continually dipped and soared, replacing the homing pigeons of his earlier days.'[6] So we know birds did play a part in Mitchell's life and in their own way did contribute to the design of one of the most important fighting aircraft of all time.

A tragic postscript to the story is provided by Leslie Howard's own fateful flight on 1 June 1943. *The First of the Few* was one of Howard's last films as he was killed, eighteen months after making it, on a civilian plane shot down by the Luftwaffe while travelling back to London from Lisbon after promoting a new film. Howard and his manager had taken a commercial plane to neutral Portugal to promote *The Lamp Still Burns,* a film celebrating the work of nurses during the war. On the return flight, at about noon, the DC3 plane carrying them was attacked by half a dozen German fighters and broke up over the Bay of Biscay with no survivors. The Germans later claimed the attack was a mistake, but it has been suggested that it was really revenge for Howard making *The First of the Few* and other wartime propaganda films, notably the 1941 British anti-Nazi thriller *Pimpernel*. Howard's death certainly delighted Hitler's propaganda minister, Joseph Goebbels, who quipped, '*Pimpernel* Howard has made his last trip.'

Howard was also widely believed to be working for British intelligence and was being monitored by German spies. So the Nazis certainly considered him a legitimate target, with rumours also circulating that he was on a secret mission to see the Spanish dictator Franco (1892–1975) on behalf of Churchill. However, his death could also have been a case of mistaken identity. At the time, the prime minister was visiting Algiers and was due to fly home on the same day across the bay. Howard's balding, rotund and cigar-smoking manager, Alfred Chenhalls, superficially resembled Winston Churchill so the Germans may have shot down the plane because they thought that the prime minister was on board. In contrast, Howard's own son, Ronald, in his book *In Search of My Father*, believes Howard was the intended target.[7] Whatever the truth, Howard's death did more than any of his wartime films to help harden American public opinion against the Nazis (the premiere of *The First of the Few* was screened in the United States just days after he was killed). Howard had previously played Ashley Wilkes in *Gone with the Wind* and was very popular with American audiences. His death in an unarmed civilian aircraft confirmed everything that people already suspected about the Nazis. However, the real reason for his death remains shrouded in mystery, the British government having kept the file on the incident secret until 2025.

As well as films based on fictional birds, real birds also featured in a surreal British propaganda movie, *Tawny Pipit*. Released in 1944, it tells the story of Jimmy Bancroft – played by Niall MacGinnis (1913–1977) – a fighter pilot recovering from injuries sustained during the Battle of Britain, and Hazel Court, the nurse who treats him, again played by Rosamund John. Both are keen ornithologists and on a countryside walk they come across the quaint village of Lisbury Lea. Here, they discover a pair of rare tawny pipits nesting in a field, 'only the second pair ever to have bred in Britain'. To their horror they find out that the field is about to be ploughed up by order of the War Agricultural Executive Committee ('War Ag'), the government body responsible for bringing land back into production.[8]

To protect the pipits they enlist the help of local villagers, led by the redoubtable retired Colonel Barton-Barrington, played by Bernard Miles (1907–1991). A 'save the birds' delegation is duly dispatched to the Ministry of Agriculture to stop the field being ploughed up, but their pleas fall on deaf ears. The birds are saved just in the nick of time by the 'old boys' network' – the Minister personally intervening after being reminded he was once the colonel's 'fag' (personal servant) at their public school. The film finishes when the tawny pipits' eggs finally hatch, but not before a dastardly plot to steal them is foiled by an army ornithologist in the guise of Corporal Philpotts, played by Stuart Latham (1912–1993).

The big problem with the film's title was that the real star was not a tawny pipit at all but a meadow pipit. The reason for this ornithological ruse was simple – tawny pipits do not nest in Britain but meadow pipits do. Where they did occur – France, the Low Countries, Denmark and Poland – were all under Nazi occupation and it seemed unlikely that permission to film would have been granted by Joseph Goebbels, Hitler's highly strung Minister of Enlightenment and Propaganda. *Tawny Pipit* was instead filmed in Lower Slaughter, a chocolate-box village in the Cotswolds, on the river Eye. Up to then the village's only claim to fame was its Old Mill Museum so being cast as the fictional village of Lisbury Lea firmly put it on the map.

Tawny Pipit is not a classic film, but it was an effective piece of wartime propaganda despite its ornithological *faux pas*. Its portrayal of the stoicism of the British rural way of life in the face of officialdom provided entertaining enough viewing, although the real enemy was the Germans and not the War Ag. It featured a range of cameo wartime parts, including a Land Army girl, child evacuees and, surprisingly, a female Russian sniper on a 'goodwill tour' played by Lucie Mannheim (1899–1976). The inclusion of the Russian sniper was designed to appeal to Stalin, who the British government was trying to placate over the lack of a second front in the war. The producers even included a toast to the bravery of the 'heroic Bolshevik fighters', with all the villagers joining in a rousing rendition of the Socialist anthem 'The Internationale'. However, by the time the film was released D-Day had already happened and the Germans were transferring soldiers from the Eastern Front to the western beach heads in Normandy. So the unlikely casting of a Russian sniper in the sleepy village of Lisbury Lea in the Cotswolds did little to help the war effort.

Where the film did break new ground was in its subtle but sustained mockery of the British way of life. David Parkinson, reviewing the film in the *Radio Times*, said:

> It was almost unthinkable in wartime that a British picture should criticize officialdom and poke fun at the eccentricities of national life. But that's exactly what Bernard Miles and Charles Saunders's independently produced feature succeeded in doing. The only problem is that the satire is so gentle and the humour so whimsical

that it makes *The Last of the Summer Wine* look like a searing social statement. However, the story about rare birds that nest in a field outside a Cotswold village is not without its charm, the excellent cast is a pleasure to watch and the photography is quite exquisite.[9]

When it was released, the film proved popular at the box office despite its title being an ornithological misnomer. The shots of the meadow pipits featured in the film, which doubled up as tawny pipits, were filmed by the famous ornithologist Eric Hosking (1909–1991). In his autobiography *An Eye for a Bird*, published in 1970, Hosking revealed the reason for the substitution, 'it was quite impossible to contemplate filming an actual tawny pipit; it nests mainly on the Continent where the war was raging,' he wrote. 'It was decided to photograph a pair of ordinary meadow pipits and keep to shots which showed the back view only; the tawny has a plain breast and the meadow a speckled one, but their back plumage is very similar.'[10]

The film's title also did not go down well with the critics. *Variety* magazine said, 'If the Academy had an award for the year's worst titled film, this one would cop the Oscar without a doubt. Despite this handicap, *Tawny Pipit* has everything it takes to make a box office hit. The tawny pipit is a rare bird and this film is frankly a glorification of ornithology. With such a theme, a picture could hardly be expected to have much appeal, but it actually has.'

All of which begs the question of why feature a tawny pipit at all? Not only does the species not nest in Britain, it is also not very colourful, being the classic 'little brown job'. When it comes to plumage the meadow pipit is little better, but it is at least common in Britain. So why didn't the film makers call it *Meadow Pipit* or, even better, pick a far more colourful and exotic bird? The answer, probably, is that by focusing on a bird that occurred in Germany and occupied Europe the film makers were making a wider point about saving the continent from destruction. On top of this, the brown, boring and distinctly un-British tawny pipit perfectly suited the austerity of the times. However, the tawny pipit's propaganda value really came into its own in the United States. Although the production company initially thought the film was too parochial for American audiences, it proved a surprising hit. Rosamund John said, 'Rank didn't think they would be able to sell it to America so it was stashed away for a while. When it was shown, it was wildly popular, because it was everything the Americans thought of as being English.' The *New York Times* was even more flattering: 'Seldom does such a piece of unsophisticated charm and humor reach the screen, but this is one that is presented in such an utterly beguiling fashion that it would be a grave error not to see it.'

Birds also featured in one of the most popular series of children's books of the era, the *Just William* books. The first short story featuring William was published in 1919 and twenty years later William had firmly established himself in the heart of the nation's children. The books tell the story of an eleven-year-old schoolboy called William Brown and his gang of friends, the Outlaws, composed of Ginger, Henry, Douglas and his loyal mongrel dog, Jumble. William comes from a respectable, middle-class home but is constantly getting into mischief, his antics not going down well with his long-suffering parents or his brother and sister, Robert and Ethel.

A typical adventure involves William in a brush with authority, a clash with the neighbouring gang (known as the Lane-ites), led by Hubert Lane, and coming up with some ingenious plan that usually goes horribly wrong. At the end of the story William normally triumphs, more by luck than judgement, and the stories often finish with a moral message. The books also featured a range of female characters, most notably William's nemesis, Violet Elizabeth Bott, the lisping spoiled brat of the local millionaire, and Joan Clive, a *de facto* member of the Outlaws who William admires and who often outwits him. The books are set in the fictional village of Hadleigh and reflected the changing politics of the times as seen through the eyes of a child.

The *Just William* books were the brainchild of Richmal Crompton Lamburn, who wrote under the name Richmal Crompton. Born in 1890, she was brought up in the Peak District where her father was a vicar. Crompton trained to be a teacher, first teaching at her old boarding school in Warrington, before in 1917 going on to teach in an inner-city school in Bromley, south London. Here she started to write in her spare time before tragically contracting polio and losing the use of her right leg. As a result she was forced to give up her teaching career and instead began writing full time. The *Just William* series was an instant hit, Crompton going on to write thirty-nine books in total – all but one being a series of short stories – before her death in 1969. Despite the *Just William* series selling over 12 million copies during her lifetime, Crompton's own life was far from easy. Although she loved children she never married or had any of her own. While in her forties, just before the Second World War, she developed breast cancer and had a mastectomy. Despite her illness, Crompton was determined to do her bit and when war came volunteered for the fire service.

The *Just William* books had already reflected the rise of fascism in Europe when in June 1938 Crompton had published *William – the Dictator*. With conflict looming she followed this up in May 1939 with *William and the A.R.P* (Air Raid Precautions). When war was declared in September 1939 she published *William and the Evacuees* in May 1940. The book was designed to raise morale among the million children who had been evacuated from the city to the countryside to live in villages like the fictional Hadleigh where they were often lonely and struggled to fit in.

All her books written during the war had to be passed by the censor and had to promote government messages on everything from building air raid shelters to rationing. With people watching the Battle of Britain, which was raging in the skies above their heads, the government was particularly keen to prepare the public for an imminent invasion. Reflecting this, one of the stories Crompton wrote in *William and the Evacuees* was 'William and the Bird Man'.[11]

The story starts with William and the Outlaws deciding to put on a party to welcome and entertain the evacuees. However, they have nowhere to hold it, a problem William is determined to solve. William's first choice is a stable behind the house belonging to Wing-Commander Glover, who is serving at nearby Marleigh Aerodrome, the village adjacent to Hadleigh. The wing commander is going out with William's sister, Ethel, so William thinks he will be amenable. Despite assuring him that Ethel 'liked him a lot more than all the others', Commander Glover refuses him permission. As an alternative William has the bright idea of using a big studio in the back garden of a cottage on Marleigh Hill, commenting to the Outlaws 'that artist with a beard used to have it but he's gone now.' However, Ginger informs him that the studio is not empty, and 'A man wat's writin' a book about birds has taken it. He goes about watchin' em, an' takin' photos of them an' such like but he doesn't use that studio place at all.'

So William goes there the next morning, but the bird man is out. Sneaking up to the window, he looks in on 'A small room, with a writing-table just under the window, a lot of photographs of birds and things lying about on it, a bookcase full of books. From where he stood William could see some of the titles … *Birds of the British Isles*, *Birds of the Tropics*, Birds … Birds … Birds … Gosh! He must know a jolly lot about birds.' William finally tracks down the bird man and tells him disingenuously how interested he is in birds. Suddenly a bird alights on a nearby bush and William, faking great excitement, asks him what it is. 'An ouzel,' replies the bird man, before giving William the brush-off and going back to the studio. Surreptitiously following him back to the house, William finds the bird man working on a complicated diagram. Confronting him about what he's doing, the bird man says furtively, 'This is a diagram of a blackbird's lungs. I'm writing a book at present on wild bird's diseases.' 'Corks!' replies William 'I didn't know they had any'.

Back at home, William can't help showing off his new-found knowledge when the same bird flutters onto a bush by the window. He confidently proclaims it to be an ouzel, but the wing commander and his father ridicule his observational skills, instead identifying it as a nuthatch, his father adding, 'What on earth made you think it was an ouzel?' Shocked, William tries to recover some of his credibility by stating that he knows a lot about ouzels: 'I know that it spends the winter in England and that it makes its nest in tall trees and that its eggs are a sort of greyish white.' 'On the contrary,' corrects the wing commander, who obviously does know his birds, 'the ouzel is a migratory bird, it nests in heather and holes in the wall, and its eggs are blue-green, speckled with red.' Crestfallen, William goes back to the cottage and steals the diagram of the blackbird's lungs, slipping it into Ethel's bag, knowing she will be disgusted by it. Over tea at the Grand Hotel, Ethel opens her bag in front of the wing commander who recognises the diagram instantly for what it really is – a detailed map of the aerodrome. The story finishes with him rugby tackling the bird man who turns out to be a Nazi fifth columnist who has been using birdwatching as a cover to spy on the aerodrome.

'Well you see,' said William to an entranced audience of his Outlaws, 'I put it in Ethel's handbag when she was goin' out to tea with him so he'd see it an' get it back an' know that a spy was spying on his aerodrome.' So William saves the day (and the nation) by exposing a Nazi spy who is caught out by his lack of knowledge of birds. Following the bird man being brought to justice, William would continue to do his patriotic duty throughout the war, Crompton publishing *William Does His Bit* in 1941, *William Carries On* in 1942 and *William and The Brains Trust* in 1945.

The idea that birdwatching could be used as a cover for spying was not just a flight of fancy. During the war the Home Fleet was anchored at various points in Scotland all the way from the Moray Firth north to Scapa Flow in the Orkneys. The area was sealed off for security reasons and to enter you needed a pass and to be cleared at Scottish Command in Inverness. However, it soon became clear to army intelligence that information was being leaked about the fleet's movement to the Germans. The list of pass holders was reduced to six, one of whom was a famous London dentist and fanatical wildfowler. He had been making shooting trips to the area for 10 years, sending some birds home and taking the rest with him back to London.

A secret investigation identified the dentist as the most obvious suspect but nothing could be proved against him. So the investigating officer asked the opinion of Henry Douglas-Home, an ornithologist, broadcaster and a Colonel in Scottish Command, who told him to check the birds. Recounting the incident in his book, *The Birdman*, Douglas-Home wrote 'Next time the dentist appeared, the first hamper of game he sent back to London was secretly apprehended and checked. There were six pinkfeet, four mallard and various other ducks, all of them with their gizzards slit and resown to hide the shipping codes which had been inserted. The hamper was then forwarded to London where the German agent who collected it at Kings Cross was arrested, as in due course was the dentist. We never had any more trouble.'

Chapter 3

Convoys, U-boats and Seabirds

It was not just on the home front in films and books that birds made a contribution, the Second World War also produced some surprising ornithological research results at sea. From 1940 until the end of the war, the Battle of the Atlantic raged between convoys of British merchant ships and German submarines or 'U-boats' (Unterseeboots) operating out of bases in occupied France. Hitler was determined to cut off Britain's supply route from America and in the process starve the country into defeat. Churchill famously wrote in his memoirs that, 'The only thing that ever really frightened me during the war was the U-boat peril.'

Crossing the Atlantic by merchant boat from Britain to North America or *vice versa* was one of the most dangerous activities of the entire war. The German U-boats hunted in 'wolf packs' and were faster than the convoys; they also had the advantage of surprise (later negated by the cracking of the Germans' enigma machine by the code breakers at Bletchley Park, the development of sonar and America entering the war). The merchant convoys were relatively safe in either British or American waters when protected by aircraft cover, but were much more vulnerable in the middle of the ocean where German submarines operated with impunity in the so called 'Atlantic Gap' (the area of sea beyond the reach of land-based aircraft). During the early years of the war German U-boats enjoyed great success and sent many millions of tonnes of merchant shipping to the bottom. However, by May 1941 a system of fully escorted convoys had been developed which provided much greater protection. Despite this, the Atlantic Gap was not fully closed until two years later in May 1943 when new long-range aircraft and escort carriers were put into service.

Surveying seabirds in the Atlantic outside of the breeding season has always presented ornithologists with a huge logistical challenge. The second-largest ocean on earth, the Atlantic, with its unpredictable weather systems and currents, can be an unforgiving and hostile environment. This, combined with the ever-present U-boat threat, meant that birdwatching during the Battle of the Atlantic was fraught with danger and certainly not the time to carry out detailed ornithological research. However, that is exactly what two lieutenants from the Royal Naval Volunteer Reserve (RNVR) did, from 1942 until 1945, in the process completing one of the most comprehensive seabird surveys of the Atlantic ever undertaken.

Matthew Neal Rankin (1918–1999) was born in Belfast and before the war had trained as a doctor, later becoming a surgeon. Together with his brother, Denis, they had become an authority on the birds of Northern Ireland before signing up. During the war the two brothers published many notes and papers together in *The Irish Naturalists' Journal* and *British Birds*. They included an intimate study of the breeding behaviour of the Irish dipper, notes on the roosting habits of the British tree-creeper, an account of the status of the fulmar petrel in north-east Ireland and field-notes on the breeding of the roseate tern. While on leave in their home city, both brothers also contributed many records to the bird recorder for Belfast until, sadly, in August 1944 Denis died in a flying accident while on active service.

At the outbreak of the war Matthew had joined the RNVR where he served as the Surgeon-Lieutenant on destroyers. Here he met Eric Duffey (1922–2019) who was born in Leicester, and like Rankin, had developed a passion for wildlife early on in life. In 1941 Duffey became a founder member of the Leicestershire and Rutland Ornithological Society (which is still in existence today), volunteering for the Fleet Air Arm in the same year. Two years later Duffey trained to be a pilot at 'HMS Jackdaw', a Royal Naval air base in Fife, and at 'HMS Nightjar', an air base in Lancashire (the ornithology-mad Duffey no doubt particularly appreciated that the Fleet Air Arm's bases were named after birds). He then transferred to the RNVR where he flew with 836 Squadron on convoy support patrols from Maydown in Northern Ireland, which was known as 'HMS Shrike', and Machrihanish in Argyllshire, known as 'HMS Landrail'. This included providing support for merchant aircraft carriers, which were often converted grain or oil tankers, as part of RAF Coastal Command, where Duffey obtained the rank of lieutenant.

While serving together, Rankin and Duffey soon discovered they had a mutual love of ornithology and decided to collaborate on a research project with a view to publishing a paper after the war. So while the Battle of the Atlantic raged they counted seabirds, Rankin from the bridge of his destroyer and Duffey from a carrier or the cockpit of his aircraft. After the war in 1948 they jointly published the results of their work in *British Birds* magazine in an article called 'A Study of the Birdlife of the Atlantic'.[1]

Over a twelve-month period Rankin and Duffey spent an average of nearly twenty-eight days a month at sea – an impressive total even in wartime – stating, 'we believe we have put in a record number of sea-days during a twelve-month period.' They divided the ocean into 28 transects using Admiralty charts, their main period of research being carried out in 1943–1944 after the closing of the Atlantic Gap once the U-boat menace had declined. However, they also made one winter crossing in 1942 and five during early 1945. 'From May 1943 to April 1945, either one or the other of us was at sea during every month but February 1944', they stated in their paper. In addition, Rankin made the return journey to Murmansk in May 1945 as part of the Arctic Convoy.

Even with a reduced risk of U-boat attack, birdwatching while on duty must have been a hazardous occupation as they were both meant to be looking out for the enemy. However, searching the ocean using binoculars from the bridge of a ship or flying over it at low level in a plane in search of U-boats proved to be the ideal way to assess the vast Atlantic Ocean, an area of over 106,000,000km^2. Their research not only yielded some really interesting sightings but was also a great way to while away the time and prevent the long periods of boredom which afflicted so many naval personnel while at sea. However, the Atlantic proved to be a very challenging environment in which to birdwatch. They commented that it 'can be a disappointing ocean to one who only crosses it occasionally, and days will go by without a single bird being seen. This vast area of sea presents an ever-changing pattern of bird movements and it is impossible to grasp at any one time the whole of the myriad details that make up the composite picture.' Despite this, Rankin and Duffey persevered and eventually began to build up a picture of the seabirds that plied the ocean with the convoys, writing: 'Its secrets can only be revealed after long and close familiarity, and every additional day adds a little more to what is already known.'

Birdwatching carried out from a ship had, according to Rankin, 'its own peculiarities' and challenges, including choosing the best point from which to watch. His destroyer at least was a relatively small ship, enabling him to observe the sea through 360° from multiple points. The convoys crossing from Britain to America took on average about two weeks to complete the journey, although Rankin recorded that three weeks was not uncommon if they ran into a U-boat pack or bad weather. Either would considerably slow their progress, but both together could lead to them covering just 40 miles in a day, the storms and shadowing U-boats often persisting for days on end. To help avoid attack, Rankin's merchant ship followed a zig-zag pattern to confuse the enemy, but from a birdwatching perspective this meant he covered a greatly increased area. This was particularly the case if his ship was at the front of the convoy as it had to look out for the proceeding ships and take avoiding action.

Rankin reported that being in the middle of the convoy was the most disadvantageous position as you were most vulnerable to U-boat attack, and being surrounded by other ships put birds off. They were able to compensate for this through the air surveys done by Duffey, who noted: 'Shearwaters were more numerous beyond the outer screen of ships, and on several occasions this also applied to the fulmar. On the other hand the kittiwake was attracted, a greater density of birds being found within the convoy area than outside it.' However, in general they assumed that most seabirds were affected by the presence of a large number of ships and compensated in their research accordingly.

The use of an aircraft to cover gaps in the ocean proved particularly valuable, the authors commenting: 'During many days on the ocean and around the coast of Ireland and Irish Sea it was possible to cover a large area of sea by air at a low enough height for accurate bird-watching. Under normal conditions it was as easy to assess the avifaunal situation from the ship as from the air, but often there would arise a particular point that needed clarifying, and in such a case an aerial trip was invaluable.' Unfortunately, bad weather sometimes stopped Duffey getting airborne, but usually when he did so, it merely confirmed the sightings from Rankin on the ship.

As proof that the relationship between the two types of observation could usually be correlated, except in special circumstances, Rankin and Duffey cited an example of a fine summer day in 1944. 'On June 12th, noon position 48° 46'N. 35° 52'W., the sum total of birds for several hours watch from the ship was 17 *Puffinus gravis* [great shearwater] seen during a period of an hour,' they wrote, adding, 'In early evening an aircraft took off for a patrol in calm, clear weather and covered an estimated 300 square miles at low height watching the sea closely all the time. In this huge area only 13 birds were counted, *Puffinus gravis* and *Fulmarus g. glacialis* [northern fulmar].' When assessing the totals from ship and plane they also compensated for the respective areas of sea covered by both methods. Depending on the species they calculated that the generally smaller number of birds seen from the boat and the three-to-four-times greater number seen from the air correlated almost exactly when you took into account the area covered. For example, aircraft were particularly useful for finding large concentrations of birds feeding, which were often associated with the presence of large patches of gulfweed (floating masses of algae belonging to *saragassum* family), this being particularly attractive to fulmars and shearwaters. Rankin and Duffey noted, 'On September 27th, 1944, one flock of North Atlantic shearwaters was seen from the ship feeding over a school of cetaceans, but from the air three such flocks were seen, numbering several hundreds of birds.'

On some occasions aerial reconnaissance would reveal additional birds which could only be seen from the air; for example, when crossing the Grand Banks in January 1945 fulmars were seen from the aeroplane but not from the ship. Among the most valuable records made from the air were the spring migrations of terns across the Irish Sea and North Channel. Duffey noted: 'The locality was small and easily covered; in a few hours one could see the situation from one side to another, leaving little out of the final picture.' Despite the ship and aerial surveys backing each other up, some species of bird were very hard to see, their size and colour reducing visibility and the research results. Against the backdrop of the grey Atlantic waters, small, dark birds like the storm petrel were very hard to see, even from the air just 200ft above, whereas white birds like kittiwakes were much easier to distinguish if they were flying. However, if they were resting on the water identification from boat or plane became more difficult unless they were disturbed.

When it came to the best birdwatching position in a convoy, both authors considered the bridge of a ship, not directly surrounded by other vessels, was the ideal for assessing seabird numbers, but even this location could sometimes give misleading results. Rankin noted: 'The kittiwake, always a keen follower of ships, was usually considerably more numerous in the vicinity of them than several miles away in the open sea. A convoy was often ringed by large numbers of these birds and even a single ship had a good complement. This would give the ship observer a wrong impression of the real numbers of birds per square mile, as for miles around there might be very few indeed.' However, this was compensated for by birdwatching from the air which allowed large areas to be covered quickly. Even this method had its limitations, with Duffey noting that his aerial observations were often limited to 'a comparatively small arc and at low heights the object of interest is passed by in a matter of seconds.'

When writing up their research the authors divided their results into three distinct ecological divisions – inshore, offshore and pelagic (open sea) birds. They found the availability of food was, outside the migratory season, the governing factor in terms of numbers, and that for all pelagic species their distribution ran south-west to north-east, in line with the Gulf Stream. Rankin and Duffey surmised that the changing nature of the Gulf Steam meant that the distribution and density of seabirds altered each year with the current. They also discovered a clear demarcation between the warm waters of the Gulf Stream and the colder waters of the Atlantic. This was reflected in species like *Puffinus diomedea* (corys shearwater), a warm water species, which they surmised never crossed the Gulf Stream, and *Puffinus gravis* (great shearwater) which preferred colder waters, 'as indicated by the route taken as it migrates northward along the American coast, skirting the warm Sargasso Sea area and spreading N.E. once north of the Gulf Stream.' However, where their pioneering research really came into its own was when assessing the concentrations of seabirds in the Atlantic Gap, this area of ocean being the most scrutinized due to the U-boats lurking beneath. Here, the authors concluded, 'It is significant, however, that the mid-Atlantic gap is to a large extent vacated in the winter months by the fulmar [...] the region deserted correspond[ing] to the northward movement of the warm mass of water from the Gulf Stream in that season.'

Rankin and Duffey wrote up each species in detail and compared it with the findings of other seabird research biologists of the time. For example, in line with previous research findings they found that the gannet, a common species on the British side where it nests in huge colonies on isolated rocks, rarely wandered outside of offshore waters on either side of the Atlantic, the exception being immature birds which tended to wander more widely; they even recorded one over 600 miles from land. In terms of more dispersed species such as the storm petrel, they surprisingly only came across them on one day, 9 June 1944, when 'they suddenly appeared around the ship and were common for 1½ hours.' However, their small size and dark colour may have meant that they were missed. By contrast, the leach's petrel was always to be found throughout the summer 'in a well-defined area which reaches its easterly limit about the 37th meridian', their inhabited range being about 500 miles wide adjacent to the American coast. Rankin and Duffey also recorded them during their autumn migration eastwards, on one occasion discovering them over 600 miles from their normal range following a five-day gale. It was, according to the authors, 'a most delightful bird to watch as it dances amongst the waves with what seem excessively large wings. It is worth emphasizing that the forked tail is difficult to see and therefore should not be relied on for identification. It was watched only twice feeding on refuse thrown overboard, but never actually seen following in the wake.'

During the convoys, Rankin and Duffey recorded the impact of storms on seabird behaviour. On 19 October 1944, in mid-ocean, they experienced a severe gale with wind speeds of 80–90 knots and huge waves. Not expecting to see any birds in such terrible weather, they were surprised to find leach's petrels, pomatorhine skuas (pomarine skuas), and great and North Atlantic shearwaters, all following the convoy. Caught in the very worst part of the gale, the tiny leach's petrels endeavoured to use the ship's lee-side for shelter. Rankin recorded:

> it was remarkable to see such small birds often holding their own against such powerful forces. They kept very close to the sea, hugging the wave-hollows but all the time losing ground. As long as they were able to elude the main draught they could control their movements sufficiently well to avoid disaster, but every now and again, through fatigue or just bad luck some were caught by the gale and whisked away like feathers in a hurricane at an incredible rate. Several hit the ship's side, disintegrating in a puff of feathers. In stark comparison the other three larger species rode out the storm much more easily, at times even flying well above the huge wave tops.

During their research Rankin and Duffey recorded a new species for the Atlantic and made many new observations about common species. Two days before the 19 October storm they had sighted a very rare bird, the frigate petrel or white-faced storm petrel. It was 'absolutely unmistakable in its plumage colouring, a pale-brown above with light under-parts. The white cheeks with a dark patch over the ear were also clearly seen.' Breeding on Cape Verde, the Canaries and the Savage Islands off Africa, the bird was a long way from home. Rankin and Duffey explained its presence by storms off the west coast of North Africa sweeping them across the Atlantic. They were delighted by the sighting and it was, they believed, 'a new record for the temperate North Atlantic'.

In contrast to the rarities, other common species were recorded in big numbers. In June and July 1943 they observed great shearwaters in 'huge flocks of many hundreds which passed on the water, and for three days on one transect the numbers seen daily must have reached the four figure mark.' Seeing so many shearwaters at such close range, Rankin was even able to record the varying white bands on their wings during the moult. To illustrate the different stages, he included pictures of four shearwater wings in their *British Birds* article. The kittiwake was also a 'constant companion of the sea-farer' in the North Atlantic winter; on one occasion the authors recorded it appearing '160 miles east of the Grand banks on the 45th parallel en masse almost like a plague of locusts.' It was also the most vocal of the seabirds they recorded, its shrill cry often being heard above the noise of the ship and the sea.

While both Rankin and Duffy were expert ornithologists, even they struggled on occasions to identify some similar species, particularly razorbills and guillemots, 'very favourable conditions' being needed to identify the subtle differences in their winter plumages at sea. The most common bird they came across during the convoys was the fulmar, which they recorded in both summer and winter across the ocean; they even attempted to classify the four colour phases present throughout its range. The fulmar was also the most common bird during the Arctic Convoy that Rankin completed to Murmansk in May 1945. He noted on the crossing that there was 'an abundance of the fulmar almost throughout the whole of the journey excepting that it was rather scarce at the extreme northern extent, i.e. 72°N. on both the outward and inward trip, but became common again to the east and west.'

During gales Rankin and Duffey found it especially fascinating to watch how different birds dealt with the storm-force winds and wild sea.

The little auk, as its name suggests, was one of the smallest species they encountered on the convoys. On 17 February 1944, during a howling gale with wind speeds of 55 knots, they observed a raft of them trying to make headway in front of the ship. 'Very often in rough weather it was almost a physical impossibility for them to become air-borne,' they wrote. 'Owing to their high wing loading they have to take a short run before flying speed is attained and time after time a wave would hit or break over them, bringing them into the sea again. In such weather they usually escaped by diving and swimming. To watch these birds in a raging sea almost makes one wonder whether they are not more fish than bird. Huge waves break over them continually and yet they are more concerned with the danger of the approaching ship.'

On 17 February 1945 they watched a group of puffins during another severe gale, and having an anemometer on board were able to measure the wind speed and how they coped with it. At 55 knots they found the puffins could fly fairly easily into the wind, maintaining a speed of 8–10 knots, although they could only do this for a short distance before they settled on the sea again or turned sharply with the wind and disappeared. However, during the afternoon the wind velocity reached approximately 80 knots and they recorded that 'no puffins were seen to leave the water. Occasionally a glimpse would be caught of one by the ship's side, but it would always dive.'

Rankin and Duffey also recorded in spring and autumn the bird that undertakes the longest migratory journey of any animal in the world – the Arctic tern. On 22 May 1943 on the homeward journey they were just about to enter the Irish Sea when 'parties of terns crossed the ship's bows regularly, all flying from the English to the Irish side. This was evidence of the spring movement well under way. The urge to migrate must have been new and strong, as never again from a ship were terns seen whose flight was so steady and constant.' They concluded: 'Comparing the spring and autumn migrations, it appears that whereas the former is short in duration and concentrated in effort, the latter covers a considerably longer period and is far more leisurely. This would account for the few spring pelagic records and the numerous autumn ones.'

In terms of the different bird species they came across on their convoys, Rankin and Duffey's research expanded upon the limited knowledge that was then available on the seabirds of the Atlantic (since the war much more research has been done on seabirds and we have a far better understanding of their ranges and requirements, but at the time Rankin and Duffy's research was truly ground-breaking). In total they recorded twenty-eight different species, ranging from common ones such as gannets and puffins to much rarer birds such as the white-faced storm petrel and the black guillemot (which they only saw once at sea, on 16 June 1944, about 40 miles south of Cape Race). In total, their report in the journal *British Birds* ran to over forty pages, its length meaning that it was published as a special supplement. For each species they recorded the distribution (including the exact location, date and the direction of flight the bird was travelling in) together with any defining characteristics and unusual behaviour. This resulted in copious notes, all of which had to be carefully collated and written up after the war. It was an impressive achievement, on a par with any ornithological doctorate thesis and most amazingly all done under wartime conditions.

After the war Rankin and Duffey went on to collaborate on another project together, in 1946 helping to organise the Royal Naval Birdwatching Society (RNBWS). They also produced its first journal, the *Sea Swallow*, which was published in December 1947. The Society was affiliated to the British Trust for Ornithology and they both sat on the editorial board of the *Sea Swallow* for a number of years (another early contributor was Lieutenant Commander Peter Scott). In the first editorial they wrote:

Fifteen months ago the idea of the Royal Navy having its own bird-watching society was submitted to the Admiralty. In very quick time approval had been given and the original A.F.O. [Admiralty Fleet Orders] promulgated. Since then over two hundred and fifty people have joined the R.N.B.W.S. Almost every branch of the Navy is represented and in addition we have members from the Royal Australian, Royal Canadian and Royal New Zealand Navies; from the Nautical College, Pangbourne, the Sea Cadet Corps and the American Weather Bureau [the RNBWS continues to this day, its patron for many years being the late Duke of Edinburgh who served with the Navy during the war].

In the first issue of the *Sea Swallow* Rankin wrote an article about birdwatching at sea based on his experiences on convoys during the war.

In it he discussed the challenges of watching birds from a moving vessel, commenting: 'For one thing, the observer is "fixed" in his ship and is not free to follow his quarry at will unless of course he happens to be the Commanding Officer! This means that one must make the most of the opportunity when it arrives so always carry your binoculars round your neck!'

Rankin also discussed the best location from which to watch on a ship and how to contend with the wind, spray and 'awkwardly placed bits of the ship's superstructure'. He concluded that most parts of the ship could be used for birdwatching, although in a small ship 'the bridge would be best as from here you can get an uninterrupted view through 360 degrees, unless one happens to be on duty, it is not, naturally enough, a popular move to overcrowd this part of the ship.' However, when it came to counting different species, just like birds on land, seabirds had their own habits. Rankin noted that 'the auks [...] will usually more easily be seen from the bow, while others, such as the storm petrels, gulls, albatross, which follow a ship, are best observed from the stern.'

In terms of timing and technique, Rankin recommended, 'In spring and autumn it may be advantageous to watch the southern or northern sides according to which side the migrants are likely to approach. To get the best results from your observations watching must be done at a regular time each day and should if possible be for an unbroken period of appreciable length such as a whole watch.' Repeated each day, this method enabled the observer to get a complete picture of the area traversed and, according to Rankin, gave 'a true impression of the densities of the oceanic populations as well as the number or types of species seen – remembering always that sea and visibility conditions may affect your results.' He concluded that the best way to get results at sea was to enlist your shipmates: 'In this way you will often have an unexpected observation brought to your notice and you will soon find these people will take an interest in your hobby.'

After the war Rankin left the RNVR and became a general practitioner in Hemsworth, Yorkshire. In 1977 he retired to Scotland and spent twenty happy years recording and photographing the butterflies of Galloway. He then returned to York for the last two years of his life and died in 1999. Duffey also left the RNVR in 1946 and went on to have a very distinguished career in nature conservation, becoming a regional officer for the Nature Conservancy Council in East Anglia, for which he was awarded an Order of the British Empire in 1962. In later life he became one of the world's leading authorities on spiders, publishing five books and numerous papers on arachnids. He died in 2019, his obituary in the journal *Arachnology* stating, 'He made good ornithological use of his four-year war service, recording birds observed while flying, occasionally disappearing from the radar screens much to the annoyance of the air controllers. His diaries written at that time concentrated on the birds seen rather than the tactics of flying. He made contact with an ornithologically minded naval doctor, Surg[eon]. Lt. Neal Rankin, who served on a destroyer protecting the Arctic convoys [...] these 'naturalists normally observed their birds over the sights of a gun.'[2]

Chapter 4

Great Crested Grebes and Mass-Observation

Today's multi-million-pound marketing industry owes much to the Mass-Observation project launched just before the Second World War. Like Rankin's and Duffey's seabird survey, it was organised by a remarkable birdwatcher and polymath, Tom Harrisson (1911–1976). Unusually for an ornithologist, Harrisson found watching people as interesting as watching birds. So Mass-Observation became, in his words, the 'study of Britons rather as if they were birds'. In his youth Harrisson rarely felt alive unless he was taking risks and organising expeditions to remote parts of the world. As an adult he often outraged people, being proud to call himself 'the most offending soul alive', but he could also convince them to tell him the most intimate details about their lives. These qualities made him one of the pioneering anthropologists of the twentieth century.

Like many ornithologists of his era, Harrisson came from a privileged background, attending Harrow school, where, at the age of seventeen, he took part in the first ever national census of heronries. With the help of a sympathetic house master, who also happened to be his godfather, he then wrote his first book about the birds of Harrow, which was published by the *London Naturalist* in 1930. Harrisson went on to study natural sciences at Pembroke College, Cambridge, but became disillusioned by the course and dropped out. The next year he and a friend, Phil Hollom, who had carried out a study of Surrey's water birds the year before, decided to organise the first national survey of the great crested grebe.

The changing fortunes of the great crested grebe mirrored the history of the conservation movement. Well known for its elaborate courtship display, in which birds head-shake, preen and perform the 'weed dance', grebes were widespread in central England and Wales up to the early nineteenth century. They then declined so much that by 1860 there were only around thirty-two breeding pairs left, the rest having been slaughtered to furnish the fashion trade. The bird's fine chestnut head plumes were used to decorate hats and other accessories, while their densely feathered skins were used in the clothing industry as 'grebe fur'. The eggs, which when laid change colour from white to muddy brown for camouflage, were also taken, both as food and by collectors. However, following a high-profile campaign against 'murderous millinery' by the fledging Royal Society for the Protection of Birds (RSPB), the great crested grebe was protected and by 1931 it had once again greatly increased in numbers and range. So Harrisson and Hollom decided to carry out a survey to see how much the species had recovered since its nadir in the 1860s.

The 1928 survey of heronries had been organised by the leading ornithologist Max Nicholson (1904–2003) who had used 300–400 observers to map the sites favoured by the grey heron. Herons nest colonially and use favoured sites, which are well known because they are big, raucous and very visible structures, often containing dozens of nests. However, the post-war boom in the construction industry had resulted in many new lakes being formed from former sand and gravel workings. These had greatly increased the potential habitats available in Britain for grebes, which potentially occurred on any suitable bodies of water of four acres or more. Grebes nest on a floating mass of waterweed and although easily visible, they often favour the middle of a lake or reservoir. Grebes also generally nest singly, making their nests harder to spot, although they do also occasionally occur in colonies. Harrisson and Hollom calculated that there were over 1,000 potential bodies of water where grebes could breed. This meant that many more observers would be needed than for the heron survey and that they would have to cover a lot more sites.

To attract survey volunteers Harrisson put requests for help in a range of ornithological journals including *British Birds*, *The Naturalist*, *The Scottish Naturalist* and *Bird Notes* (the magazine of the RSPB). He also advertised in sports and fishing magazines and wrote articles in local and national newspapers, including a special feature for *The Times*. Harrisson even convinced the BBC to broadcast an appeal for help with the survey at the start of the news. Hollom took on the role of writing to all the naturalists the pair knew asking them to get involved, and to landowners to ask their permission to carry out the survey. As a result over 1,300 volunteers were recruited, the largest army of ornithological surveyors then ever assembled in Britain. The results of the survey were published in five instalments in *British Birds* in 1932, a considerable achievement for a couple of twenty-year-old-ornithologists.[1] In the introduction Harrisson wrote:

> We chose this bird because it had increased to an extraordinary extent in the past fifty years, and the factors, stages, and innumerable repercussions involved in the increase of one species seemed to us a little known matter of great importance. The numbers in 1931 were to act as a standard for comparison with past and future status, having no intrinsic value in themselves. The bird was also conspicuous and unmistakable, with a limited habitat (fair sized lakes) which would greatly simplify a detailed study. For these reasons the great-crested grebe seemed ideal for our purpose.

When completed, the survey was the most comprehensive study of any breeding bird ever undertaken in Britain. It concluded that the breeding population of great crested grebes in England, Scotland and Wales had increased from just thirty-two pairs in the 1860s to around 1,200 pairs in 1931. The success of the survey established Harrisson's reputation in the bird world and generated national publicity, an article in *The Times* commenting that the report was 'one of the fullest accounts of life history which are so far available for any wild bird in any country'.

After the grebe survey in 1932 Harrisson organised expeditions on behalf of Oxford University to northern Sarawak in Borneo and the New Hebrides (now Vanuatu), a remote group of islands in the Pacific (a feat made more impressive by the fact that he did not even attend the university). There he spent the next two years studying the islands' wildlife and their indigenous tribes, including a group of cannibals. After he returned, Harrisson wrote a book, *Savage Civilisation*,[2] which soon became a bestseller.

Following its publication he came up with the radical idea of studying the people in his home town of Bolton using the same methods as he had used to observe the tribes in Borneo and the New Hebrides. Harrisson organised a small group of observers and got a job at a cotton mill where, despite his 'educated' accent, he was welcomed by the workers. Writing down his findings, he recorded that his co-workers could not imagine for a moment that 'anybody came into this heat, uproar and mechanical risk unless they absolutely had to earn £3 10s 0d a week.' After his stint at the cotton mill, Harrisson then turned his hand to driving lorries, being a shop assistant and even selling ice creams from a van, using each experience to record people's behaviour. Then he came across a letter that would change his life forever.

In late 1936, with King Edward VIII's abdication crisis looming, Harrisson sent a romantic poem to the *New Statesman* magazine to impress his new girlfriend. The poem was called 'Coconut Moon' and was published on 2 January 1937. While he was reading the poem, another letter on the page caught his eye. It was from Charles Madge of Blackheath in London and headed 'Anthropology at home'. Madge, a poet and *Daily Mirror* journalist, wrote that he represented a new group who were carrying out 'an anthropology of our own people' in reaction to the abdication crisis. The letter stated: 'The real observers in this case were the millions of people who were, for once, irretrievably involved in the public events. Only mass observations can create mass science.' Madge's letter went on to invite the 'co-operation of voluntary observers' in the study who were asked to keep a diary of what they and others around them were doing on the twelfth day of each month, starting in February 1937.

Harrisson was intrigued and sent a letter to Madge telling him about the similarities with his own observation work in Bolton. On receiving it, Madge invited him to a meeting where they decided to join forces, both men immediately starting work on a new one-shilling pamphlet entitled 'Mass-Observation'. The new organisation was officially launched on 30 January 1937 in another letter to the *New Statesman*. The pamphlet explained that Mass-Observation would carry out 'sociological research of the first importance and which has hitherto never been attempted'. To do this it would collect 'a mass of data based upon practical observation, on the everyday life of all types of people,' and would use the results for the scientific study of 'Twentieth Century man in all his different environments'. This ranged from the mundane to the surreal, including 'Behaviour of people at war memorials; Shouts and gestures of motorists; The aspidistra cult; Anthropology of football pools; Bathroom behaviour; Beards, armpits, eyebrows; Anti-semitism; Distribution, diffusion and significance of the dirty joke; Funerals and undertakers; Female taboos about eating; The private lives of midwives.'[3] Mass-Observation employed a variety of ways of collecting the data, the most important of which was a volunteer group of around 500 people who kept diaries and were known as the 'National Panel of Diarists' (from August 1939 onwards they submitted their diaries monthly). They also made extensive use of questionnaires, known as 'directives', which were used to assess controversial issues in the news.

The pamphlet on Mass-Observation received extensive coverage in the press, including a piece published in the 13 November 1937 edition of the magazine *Nature*:

'MASS OBSERVATION' by C. Madge and T. Harrisson, with a foreword by Dr. Julian Huxley, the first of a series of projected pamphlets, outlines the technique of a study of social environment and its effects on lines comparable with much bird-watching and observation of natural history, since, largely because of its empiricism, it has, like them, room for the untrained amateur as well as for the trained man of science (London: Frederick Muller, Ltd., 1937.1s. net). The three sciences most immediately relevant to Mass Observation are psychology, anthropology and sociology, and a fundamental plan for research will be evolved by the central organization as a result of suggestions from observers and scientific experts.[4]

In the autumn of 1937 Mass-Observation produced its next publication based on the diaries kept by its observers. The pamphlet detailed people's lives on 12 May 1937, when King George VI was crowned, and although it only sold about 800 copies, it again featured heavily in the press, who revelled in poking fun at the techniques employed by M-O as it soon became known. Editorials, cartoons and even music hall jokes were dedicated to lampooning the idea of 'spies under the bed' (ironically very similar images would be used in wartime during the Blitz by cartoonists such as Fougasse with campaigns like 'careless talk costs lives'). While Madge continued to organise Mass-Observation out of his home in Blackheath, in Bolton Harrisson considerably expanded his team of volunteer observers to about 250 and called the city 'Worktown' to preserve its anonymity.

The early days of Mass-Observation were difficult as, despite all the publicity, money was always in short supply. Harrisson gave paid talks and pitched articles about the new organisation but still couldn't afford to buy all his observers fish and chips, let alone pay them. However, the eclectic and sometimes scandalous information sent back by them more than compensated for the hardships. It ranged from the frequency of attendance at Baptist meetings in the town centre to the number of times people had illicit sex against the wall in the back alleys of Bolton. One of those who took part, Julian Trevelyan (1910–1988, a surrealist painter and friend of Madge's), recalls being sent out on information-gathering missions to pubs, dog races and dance halls. Here he was instructed by Harrisson to record 'anything from the contents of a chemist's shop window to an account of a service in a spiritualist church.'[5]

Harrisson enjoyed directing operations, his observers being the largest group of people he had organised since his famous grebe survey six years previously. To find out what people thought of modern art, he had Trevelyan set up his easel in the middle of the high street and paint pictures of the town in lurid, bright colours (the people of Bolton, whose lives were dominated by the bleak mills, responded very positively to the colourful images, many asking to buy a copy). The next year, 1938, Harrisson decided to find out what the average Bolton man and woman thought about modern poetry and published an article called 'Mass-Opposition and Literature' in a reputable Oxford literary magazine, *Light and Dark*. When his piece came out saying the people of Bolton cared little for modern poetry it was roundly attacked by literary critics. This resulted in a flood of letters to the *New Statesman* magazine which meant that by the summer of 1938 many people had heard of Mass-Observation even if they didn't quite understand what it was trying to achieve. Again, despite all the publicity, Harrisson soon found himself nearly broke. To make some money he published a retrospective book, *Borneo Jungle*, about his time on Sarawak six years previously. Then, just as he was despairing of how he would pay his next bill, the prime minister Neville Chamberlain came to his rescue.

In September 1938 Neville Chamberlain had flown to meet Hitler no fewer than three times, the last being on 30 September when he had come back from Munich with his piece of paper promising 'peace for our time'. Before his departure the country had come to the brink of war over the fate of the three-and-a-half million Sudeten Germans living in Czechoslovakia; after his final trip he was proclaimed as the saviour of the world. Chamberlain's flights stunned society and for weeks the British public talked about nothing else. Everyone had an opinion on whether it was right for the British prime minister to fly to meet Hitler in a last-ditch effort to secure peace.

For Mass-Observation Chamberlain's visit to Hitler's mountain retreat at Berchtesgaden in the Bavarian Alps was manna from heaven. In response to his first flight on 15 September, Madge's and Harrisson's observers reported back in droves that the public was solidly behind Chamberlain but were disappointed that the meeting was inconclusive. A week later, on 22 September, Chamberlain returned from his second meeting, this time at the Rhineland town of Bad Godesburg. Mass-Observation again reported that the British people were behind their prime minister and would prefer to let Hitler occupy the Sudetenland rather than go to war.

Just before Chamberlain's final flight to see Hitler on 30 September he made a radio broadcast to the people of Britain as the country mobilised for war. It included the line, 'How horrible, fantastic, incredible it is that we should be digging trenches and trying on gas-masks here because of a quarrel in a far-away country between people of whom we know nothing.' On his historic return, polls for Mass-Observation reflected the jubilant public mood, many observers commenting on the sheer relief felt by all classes that the crisis was over. However, as the days passed Mass-Observation began to pick up that grave doubts had set in about whether Hitler could be trusted to keep his word.

In response to the Munich crisis Harrisson and Madge together produced a short book, *Britain by Mass-Observation*.[6] This devoted a whole chapter to the prime minister's flights to secure peace. It was published in January 1939 as part of a Penguin special series and within days sold over 100,000 copies, instantly making it onto the bestseller list. In the introduction the authors set out that they were providing 'the first comprehensive and sophisticated account of British public opinion in rapid flux'. The book was widely studied in Whitehall, particularly by the War and Foreign Offices, who were keen to know what the public thought about a peace that many mandarins thought could not last. By publishing their polls promptly, Mass-Observation had done what no other survey or opinion poll had achieved – creating a 'live dialogue' between politicians and their electorate by championing what the ordinary person was thinking, saying and doing. With war looming, Mass-Observation had become an indispensable tool in policy making and Harrisson had at last got the role and recognition he craved.

For Harrisson the success of *Britain by Mass-Observation* resulted in a continual round of media interviews and radio appearances. Although it was his moment of greatest triumph, he soon became bored by the media merry-go-round. To spice things up he swapped locations with Madge, whose marriage had broken up. Madge travelled up to Bolton to be in charge of the observers there, while Harrisson took over Mass-Observation's London base in Blackheath, where he became responsible for over 1,500 observers and 500 diarists. By this time Mass-Observation had become a household name in Britain but what it still needed was another crisis to prove just how indispensable it was. On 3 September 1939 Neville Chamberlain came to the rescue for a second time when he declared war on Germany. Writing to Madge, Harrisson boasted, 'everything is blowing into our hands [...] we have got what no-one else has got, facts before the war.'[7]

The government was only too aware of the importance of maintaining morale at the outset of the war, especially as a secret report commissioned by the War Office had predicted mass civilian casualties following any bombing campaign against British cities. On 4 September 1939 the Ministry of Information was formed to 'promote the national case to the public at home and abroad in time of war' by issuing 'national propaganda and controlling the output of news and information.' Lord Macmillan (1873–1952), a Scottish advocate and judge, was sworn in as its first minister with its headquarters situated at the University of London's Senate House. The ministry was particularly keen to assess how its policies were being received by a public who remained highly sceptical of government, so it approached the founders of Mass-Observation to see if it would be willing to 'obtain information [...] from typical samples of society.'

In December 1939, Mary Adams (1898–1984) was appointed as the first director of the ministry's Office of Home Intelligence. The appointment was a stroke of luck for Harrisson, who had dated Adams at Cambridge (she was the first female BBC presenter and was instrumental in setting up their television service after the war). It was her job to monitor the morale of the nation, and one of her first acts was to hire Mass-Observation to provide her with information that she could use in a monthly report to the Minister of Home Security. Now for the first time Mass-Observation had a contract and a steady source of income. However, only too aware of the damage that could be caused if the government was found to be spying on its own people, the ministry insisted that the work remain secret.

The new Ministry of Information was particularly keen not to upset MPs, who prided themselves on knowing what their constituents were thinking. However, the ministry's first publicity campaign, a poster with the words 'Your courage, Your cheerfulness, Your resolution, will bring us victory', did exactly that. It was widely criticised in the House of Commons for its lack of inclusiveness, with many working-class people perceiving that they were the ones being expected to make all the sacrifices. Adams quickly needed a better understanding of what real people were experiencing, particularly women, who were viewed as being more anti-war than men. So she asked Mass-Observation for its first task to report back on the ministry's poster campaign, together with the public's reaction to the government's preparations for war. These included the sight of barrage balloons floating overhead, the carrying of gas masks, the erecting of air raid shelters, observing the blackout and the mass evacuation of school children from the cities to the countryside.

These observations were the basis for Mass-Observation's first book of the war, *War Begins at Home*.[8] This was published in January 1940 and covered the outbreak of the war and its impact on civilian life, particularly on women. In it Harrisson stated, 'The government should be fully aware of all the trends in civilian morale. They need an accurate machine for measuring such trends; a war barometer.' In an article on the book he wrote: 'I believe that women are bearing the brunt of this home-fronted war. I believe that the way they react to the strain may largely determine the outcome. And I see everywhere very little sign that the woman's point of view matters nearly as much as the man's. This war is being led by men and run by men, mostly old men. They are appallingly ignoring women's problems.' The report sent shock waves around Whitehall, and the Ministry of Information quickly changed its campaign messages to better reflect the needs of women.

While Harrisson was now earning a good wage working at Mass-Observation, his main client, the Ministry of Information, was still struggling to maintain morale or make any impact. As a result, Lord

Macmillan was replaced in January 1940 by Lord Reith (1889–1971, the first Director General of the BBC) who was himself soon replaced by Duff Cooper (1890–1954) after Chamberlain resigned in May 1940. Harrisson continued to send in his reports, but two months later what the Ministry of Information had been dreading most happened: stories began to appear in the press about government spies. The observers employed by Mass-Observation were soon dubbed 'Cooper's Snoopers' and weeks of negative headlines followed as the press uncovered the story. Questions were raised in the House of Commons about the competence of the Ministry of Information and its links with Mass-Observation. Surprisingly, the resulting furore, rather than damaging the reputation of Mass-Observation, enhanced its credibility and prestige. Far from objecting to their opinions being secretly recorded, the public felt that for once their views actually counted. One observer said that after a conversation a woman asked boldly, 'Are you one of Cooper's Snoopers?' When the observer admitted that they were, the woman seemed keener than ever to be interviewed.

The general trend picked up by observers during the first few months of the conflict, known as the Phoney War, was that the public understood the need to make sacrifices but resented all the regulations and restrictions. The Fall of France and then the Battle of Britain changed their opinion, many accepting that sacrifices had to be made if the Nazis were to be beaten. One of the observers was Celia Fremlin (1914–2009), at the time a waitress working in a café who later became a successful thriller writer. She recalled a typical day working for Mass-Observation. It would start at 9.30am at Ladbroke Grove station, where Harrisson would issue the daily 'news quota' and brief the observers. Fremlin would then be sent out on the streets with six questions and have to find twelve people willing to answer them. After lunch the observers would then all be set individual assignments, such as going shopping or travelling on buses, and would write down the snatched conversations they overheard about the war.[9]

Although completing the surveys was unpaid, there was no shortage of volunteers as the work was interesting and no two days were the same. Volunteering for Mass-Observation also engendered a sense of patriotic pride, many observers feeling that they were doing important war work. On 14 May 1940, after Churchill had delivered one of his famous speeches, Fremlin was sent out to record what people thought about it, noting on her answer paper that most people remembered the phrase about the 'blood and tears, toil and sweat' and that 'there was an enormously favourable response to it'. Following a particularly heavy air raid, Harrisson would ask his observers to interview people who had been caught up in the bombing. Fremlin found that a lot of intelligence could be gleaned by talking to people queuing up to enter the underground air raid shelters (these were particularly popular places to sleep during the Blitz as people felt safe in them). She discovered that those who had lost everything or were terrified of the next raid would come out of the shelter blinking at 5.00am and instantly join the queue for the next night.

The next day, Harrisson would collect the papers and would then busy himself summarising them in his report for the Ministry of Information. By the time the Blitz had started Harrisson had fifteen full-time investigators on the payroll who, as well as gauging the public's reaction to that day's news, would also have their own specialist subjects ranging from art to religion and pacifism to women working in factories. The observers were the first to survey mothers left behind doing war work in the cities when their children had been evacuated to the countryside. Despite the strength of the maternal bond, they found many working women reluctantly accepted that their children would be better off with complete strangers if it kept them safe.

The Ministry of Information found Mass-Observation reports particularly valuable after a heavy air raid as they could track which cities were showing signs of being demoralised or were being defeatist. From 7 September 1940 London was particularly targeted by the Luftwaffe in a series of raids that left great swathes of the capital in ruins. However, this time Harrisson got first-hand experience of the Blitz when the house opposite his received a direct hit, killing all the occupants. Shocked, he hastily moved his heavily pregnant wife, Biddy, his stepson, and all the Mass-Observation files out of London to the relative safety of Letchworth Garden City. There, on 29 September 1940, Biddy gave birth to a son who was christened Maxwell Barr Harrisson. Like all new fathers Harrisson adored his son and in keeping with his day job wrote a detailed observer's report on every stage of his development.

While the bombing of Britain's cities caused death and untold misery for many, for Mass-Observation observers it provided well-paid work. After years of scraping by, Harrisson now found himself able to pay his observers, many of whom were only too pleased to give up the day job and work full-time for him. They made some surprising discoveries about people's attitudes to the devastation and destruction they saw all around them. For example, observers found that people who had lost everything had a higher morale than those whose properties had merely been damaged. One observer wrote:

> [I] got the impression that people whose homes are completely destroyed seem to have a more carefree attitude to the whole situation, and to be much more optimistic and full of plans, than those whose homes were only partially damaged – windows broken, etc. A woman who has kept a little shop and finds it reduced to a heap of rubble would display quite an amount of gaiety and joking good humour about it, while one whose windows had been blown in and spoilt [...] tended to be just miserable, and sometimes full of grievances about compensation etc (about which there seems to be almost total ignorance and many rumours). It seemed that total destruction brings with it a sense of relief from responsibility.[10]

Some of the reports Harrisson received were very moving. Following a particularly heavy air raid on Coventry on the night of 25 November 1940, in which much of the city went up in flames and its famous fourteenth-century Gothic cathedral was reduced to rubble, a Mass-Observation report read: 'A group of six men were looking quietly at the Cathedral ruins. They said little, but awful and terrible were words they applied to the scene. When one middle-aged man remarked "And this is the Twentieth Century," he probably epitomized the feelings of the whole group.'

The sense of danger associated with the bombing brought out the best and worst in Harrisson. In response to media requests for articles on how 'Britain can take it' he would rush off to whichever city was being bombed that night and then walk around measuring the mood of those caught up in the raid. However, he always refused to go into a shelter himself, even when the bombs were falling all around him.

Talking to people about the depravations of war provided Harrisson with a lot of unique material for Mass-Observation's next book, *Clothes Rationing*,[11] which was published in 1941. There were sections on different types of clothes, why women had to make sacrifices and how valuable a contribution 'make do and mend' was to the war effort. Special sections dealt with frocks, hats, stockings and 'trousered women'. The Ministry of Information found the insights very useful, particularly noting women's strong desire to look glamorous occasionally so they could forget about the Blitz. As a result, in 1942 the government introduced the utility clothing scheme, offering consumers a range of well-designed quality clothes that were affordable for all.

In June 1941, just as the Blitz was beginning to wane and Hitler was turning his attention towards Russia, Harrisson's luck ran out. His old girlfriend, Mary Adams, left the Ministry of Information, soon followed by the minister, Duff Cooper. The new regime decided it could do without Mass-Observation as the war entered a new phase. However, he again fell on his feet and landed another contract, this time with the Department for Naval Intelligence who were interested in whether Communist agitators had infiltrated the naval dockyards. They were also keen to know how the Battle of the Atlantic was being perceived by the public as U-boats were taking a terrible toll on Allied shipping coming across the Atlantic. The contract again helped to keep Mass-Observation afloat financially. More importantly, it meant that Harrisson was exempted from the call-up because he was doing vital war work, protection he had also enjoyed while working for the Ministry of Information.

In March 1942 Harrisson started writing a weekly column about his work in *The Observer* newspaper, his original and humorous insights into the war soon making him very popular with readers. However, in the spring of 1942 his contract with the Admiralty ended, and lacking ministerial or War Office protection, he and all the Mass-Observation staff of fighting age were called up. Harrisson failed to put his schooling or qualifications on the call-up papers and was drafted into the King's Royal Rifle Corps where he was taught square bashing and machine gunning. However, he found the routine stupefyingly dull, so instead of taking notes about his Bren gun he used the time to answer letters about Mass-Observation, much to the annoyance of his superiors.

In June 1943 Harrisson's time as a rifleman came to abrupt end when his private-school background was discovered and he was sent to Sandhurst for officer training. After passing out he was commissioned as a second lieutenant in the Reconnaissance Corps where he soon rubbed his fellow officers up the wrong way with his opinionated views. While serving , instead of gathering tactical information, he worked on the *The Pub and the People: a Worktown Study* which was published in 1943. M-O also published to two further books – *People's Homes* and *War Factory* in 1943 (*People's Homes* focused on the task of 'rebuilding a better Britain'. *War Factory* focused on the women working in a radar factor just outside Malmesbury, Wiltshire, struggling to cope with long shifts and the demands of family life, and was researched by Celia Fremlin). Harrisson's reputation suffered further in the army's eyes when in October 1943 he was invited onto the prestigious Radio 4 programme *Desert Island Discs*. Roy Plomley introduced him not as a serving officer but as the 'anthropologist Tom Harrison'. His favourite track was not a musical record but a recording of 'English Birds' by the German pioneering nature broadcaster and sound recordist Ludwig Koch (1881–1974), his choice of a German doing little to endear him to his superiors. For his favourite book Harrisson chose *The I Ching* (a divine Chinese text meaning 'book of changes') and for his luxury item he chose a snorkel so he could survey the island's tropical marine life.[12]

Salvation from the Reconnaissance Corps came unexpectedly in early 1944. Harrisson was called to a secret meeting at a hotel in London and interviewed by Colonel E. Egerton Mott who worked for the Special Operations Executive (SOE). This covert organisation had been established in 1940 with the aim of 'setting Europe ablaze' by waging guerrilla warfare behind enemy lines. By 1944 SOE's remit had been extended to all the theatres of war and Mott was on a mission to recruit men who could lead the fight against the Japanese. As the meeting progressed it became clear to Harrisson that Mott had the wrong man, the colonel mistaking him for another Tom Harrison whose name was spelt with only one 's'. However, Harrisson was intrigued and played along, discovering to his delight that Mott needed someone with experience of Borneo to go behind the Japanese lines and cause chaos. Here at last was a chance to put all his jungle experience to good use, to birdwatch and be at the centre of a clandestine and dangerous operation deep behind enemy lines. So on 27 March 1944 Harrisson joined the SOE, ending his ties with Mass-Observation and *The Observer* newspaper. In June 1944, following a crash course in jungle warfare and parachute training, he flew to Australia. There he joined the Australian equivalent of the SOE, known as the Z Special Unit.

By the summer of 1944, the United States army was rolling back the Japanese advance in the Pacific by 'island hopping' (skipping over heavily fortified islands in order to capture lightly defended locations which could be used as a springboard for the next attack). Airfields were being built with a view to preparing airstrikes against Japan, but in the south-west Pacific the Japanese still controlled the Dutch East Indies, including Borneo and the Philippines. So the Allied Commander, General Douglas MacArthur (1880–1964) of the US Army, asked the Australian Imperial Force (AIF) to invade Borneo, which was strategically important because it gave access to the South China Sea.

The job of the Z Special Unit was to lay the path for the invasion, using a small number of highly trained troops to harass the enemy and divert their forces away from the invasion points through guerrilla action. Harrisson led an operation called SEMUT 1 (*semut* meaning 'ant' in Malay) into the mountains of north Borneo with a team of Australian commandos. His mission was to report back on the concentration of Japanese forces and the reception that the AIF could expect from the local tribes. Harrisson opted to go in by parachute because he knew the success of the whole operation depended not just on pacifying the local tribes but quickly winning them over to the Allied cause.

At dawn on 25 March 1945 Harrisson and his team took off in a B-24 Liberator and just after 7.00am local time they parachuted into Bario, a small community in the Kelabit Highlands in Sarawak. An eighteen-year-old Kelabit tribal member and warrior, Lian Labang, heard that 'strangers had dropped from in the sky' and went to investigate, recalling after the war:

> I was just a boy. We did not know if they were Japanese, if they were Europeans. But we went. And it was only when we reach Bario that we learned for the first time that they were white people. We met them. Tom Harrisson spoke Malay, and one of them named Sandy spoke Malay well. And the Kelabits all came to Bario to see Tom Harrisson. And he called the people from Kelabit area together and asked what they thought about the Japanese. He called on the Kelabits to volunteer to become guerrillas against the Japanese. So many people, including myself, decided to do it.[13]

Harrisson's small team were very successful in winning over the local tribes, and on 10 June 1945 over 23,000 Australians of the 9th Division landed on the island with minimal casualties. From there they began the liberation of Borneo. In advance of the attack, Harrisson's SEMUT 1 operation had reported that there were 17,000 Japanese troops guarding northern Borneo, more than twice the number predicted by Australian intelligence. Crucially, it had also provided their locations and unit strength, information which proved invaluable. By the end of July Borneo was free and Harrisson's war record spoke for itself – his small team had killed over 900 Japanese soldiers and captured thirty-three prisoners together with over 200 auxiliaries. In contrast only fourteen tribesmen had died and there was not a single casualty among Harrisson's team.

The dropping of atomic bombs on Hiroshima and Nagasaki in early August precipitated the Japanese surrender on 15 August. In a radio broadcast Harrisson told his Australian team, 'We have done much more – more quickly – than anyone thought possible. We provided 80% of the intelligence before D-Day [the landings on 10 June 1945] but since then we have provided a high percentage of the Japs killed […] I do appreciate the A1 job you have done, I am a pommy myself but I frankly admit that after my experience here, Australians have twice the bushcraft and five times the initiative. And they don't grumble so much.'[14]

After the war, Harrisson stayed on in Borneo and became curator of the Sarawak museum. In 1946 he was awarded the Distinguished Service Order for bravery in the war, the citation stating he had protected the flank of the Allied advance into Borneo and caused severe disruption to Japanese operations. This was followed in 1959 by the Order of the British Empire for his services to curation and ethnology. In 1966, after twenty years' service, Harrisson stepped down as curator of the Sarawak museum. Ten years later he and his second wife, the Belgian sculptor Christine Forani (1916–1976), were both tragically killed in a road accident in Thailand.

Today, Harrisson's name is synonymous with Mass-Observation and although the project was officially wound up in the 1950s, a new version was relaunched in 1982 in response to the Falklands War. The Mass-Observation archives at the University of Sussex provide a unique insight into everyday life in Britain covering some of the most momentous events of the Second World War. Mass-Observation was successful because it held a mirror up to society and it owed that success to Harrisson's ground-breaking survey of the great crested grebe.

Chapter 5

Pigeons and Peregrines

Great crested grebes may have served as the inspiration for the most celebrated survey of the war, but birds also fought and died supporting our soldiers in the field. In 2005 an animated film, *Valiant*, was released about a bunch of 'featherweight heroes'. Set against the backdrop of the Second World War, it tells the story of a group of homing pigeons in May 1944 just before D–Day. The film, a 'computer-animated epic adventure comedy', was made by Vanguard Animation and was the directorial debut of Gary Chapman who came up with the idea while working at the Imperial War Museum. A British–American film, *Valiant* was produced by John Williams, whose credits included the very successful *Shrek* films. The story was written by George Webster who also wrote screenplays for the BBC and Dreamworks.[1]

When it was released, *Valiant* received mixed reviews, Rotten Tomatoes giving it an average of 5/10, and it went quickly to DVD. However, the story that inspired the film was truly heroic. The real-life Valiant made a major contribution to winning the Second World War and was awarded the Dickin Medal, the animal version of the Victoria Cross.

Valiant was made at Ealing Studios on a 'tight budget' of £21 million and employed over 200 computer animators who completed the film in just two years. What it lacked in budget, it more than made up for in famous voiceovers, the cast featuring a galaxy of A-list actors including Ewan McGregor, Ricky Gervais, John Cleese, John Hurt, Jim Broadbent, Olivia Williams, Hugh Laurie, Tim Curry, Rik Mayall and Jonathan Ross. It was a tribute to the hundreds of pigeons who served in the war, but contained no reference to the Nazis, although the German villains were clearly based on them with subtly changed military insignia.

The film tells the story of a homing pigeon called Valiant (Ewan McGregor) who is told he is too small to serve in the Royal Homing Pigeon Service. However, after talking to Wing Commander Gutsy (Hugh Laurie) Valiant changes his mind and volunteers for a special mission to retrieve a top-secret message from behind enemy lines. He flies to sign up in Trafalgar Square in London where he meets Bugsy (Ricky Gervais), a conman pigeon on the run who joins up with him. Together with a range of other eccentric pigeon recruits, they form 'Squadron F'. After some tough training, where Valiant falls in love with the nursing dove, Victoria (Olivia Williams), Squadron F is flown into occupied France. Parachuting into enemy territory in special baskets they are met by two mice working for the French resistance who give them a secret message. However, before they can leave Bugsy is captured, along with the message, by the Germans. Interrogated by General Von Talon, a German peregrine falcon (Tim Curry), Bugsy is incarcerated in his imposing headquarters, a gun emplacement on the French coast. However, due to his small size Valiant is able to climb down the barrel of the gun, free them and retrieve the secret message.

Valiant then flies back to England with Von Talon in hot pursuit where there is a showdown at a blacksmiths. After a battle in which the feathers fly, Von Talon is eventually hoisted by his own petard after his medals get caught on the farrier's water wheel. Valiant delivers the secret message and as a result the Allies alter their plans for D-Day, successfully landing in Normandy. As a reward for his bravery, Valiant gets to enjoy rubbing beaks with Victoria and all Squadron F receive the Dickin Medal. The film ends with a message dedicated to the bravery of all the animals that fought in the Second World War and saved countless lives.

If the film *Valiant* was a flight of fancy, the premise on which it was based is surprisingly accurate. In the opening scene from the film three homing pigeons are heading for the white cliffs of Dover when they are suddenly ambushed and attacked by 'German' peregrine falcons, two being killed and the third, Mercury (John Cleese), taken prisoner. During the Second World War both sides made extensive use of homing pigeons to carry messages and also used falcons to intercept and kill them. So the opening sequence in *Valiant* shows a stylized bird battle which really was fought over the skies of Europe.

The top-secret message in the film was carried in a small pouch looped over the pigeon's back, but more commonly a small canister was used, which was attached to their leg. On it were a range of colours denoting the different services; for example, blue denoting the RAF, red the army and grey the special services. Pigeons were able to carry these messages over long distances and flew surprisingly fast. In competitive races they flew over 700 miles and averaged over 50 mph, a feat which meant they were deployed by the armed services in every theatre of war. The pigeons also had an impressive success rate, 86% of them returning with their message if unmolested, making them one of the most reliable forms of communication available to both sides.

The use of pigeons to deliver messages can be traced back to the ancient Greeks; the Romans also kept them and the French famously saved Paris from destruction during the Franco-Prussian war of 1870 by using pigeons to summon help. Homing pigeons, which are derived from the wild rock dove, were also extensively used in the First World War when the British Army Pigeon Service was formed. Pigeon racing between the wars was very popular and brought different classes together; aristocrats, bankers and miners all competed on an equal footing. So, despite some big technological advances between the wars, pigeons were still indispensable as a means of communication at the outset of the Second World War.

Although the British Army Pigeon Service had played a key part in the First World War, it had been disbanded at the end of the conflict. However, as tensions had grown in Europe during the late 1930s the International Pigeon Board based in England, who were responsible for long-distance racing and had over 120,000 members, offered to make birds available for national service. As a result, in February 1939 a new National Pigeon Service (NPS) was created. Every fancier who kept racing or show pigeons was obliged to register and obtain a licence, failure to do so being punishable by a large fine.[2]

Seven leading pigeon fanciers sat on the NPS, including Major William Hibbs Osman whose father had been in charge of pigeons during the First World War. He was the editor of the *Racing Pigeon* magazine and had successfully lobbied the War Office to create the NPS. Membership was open to anyone who had a minimum of twenty birds in their loft trained as homing pigeons, with the NPS selecting only the fastest and most reliable birds for active service. Upon joining, members were issued with a badge and a certificate of membership.

By the time Britain declared war on Germany in September 1939, it could potentially call upon one of the biggest pools of pigeons in the world. The total number was estimated at over one-and-a-half million birds, many people keeping, breeding and racing pigeons. Pigeon racing appealed to all classes, including royalty; both the Prince of Wales and Duke of York maintained teams of racing pigeons at Sandringham. However, the sport was dominated by working-class men, particularly in Wales and the North of England, where the pigeon was the 'poor man's racehorse'.

Pigeon races, both short and long distance, were normally organised around sweepstakes, and many working-class fanciers lived in cities where their birds were part of the family. Although popular, pigeon racing was not cheap: good birds typically cost between 25 shillings and £10, and the very best pedigree ones could sell for over £200. By comparison, an average man working in a factory earned about 1 shilling 2d (denarius or pence) a week.

At the outset of the war, the NPS received extensive publicity, but only a few hundred pigeon fanciers initially gave up their precious birds to the new organisation, despite the king donating all the birds in the royal loft at Sandringham. One of the first jobs the NPS did was to appoint 'Official Representatives' who worked with the local police to co-ordinate birds, some 200 being recruited (this figure rose to 1,500 as the war progressed). One representative was Mr Harding whose son recounted his father's memories of the service:

> It was decided that use should be made of the existing pigeon fanciers who had lofts nearest to the south coast, that they should be approached and checks made as to their background, nationality and allegiance to their country [...] All pigeon owners had to apply for a licence [...] and to notify all movement of lofts and birds, all birds had to have fitted with an identification ring and use was made of this to record all the coming and goings of all the birds [...] messages were nearly always in code and were enclosed in a small capsule strapped to the pigeon's leg.[3]

The job of NPS representatives was to visit lofts with the police, organise birds to meet the military's needs and enforce the ban on any unauthorised race meetings. These powers were rushed through in August under Regulation 9 of the Emergency Powers (Defence Act) 1939, which regulated virtually everything to do with keeping pigeons. Although the role was unpaid, the NPS representatives received a number of attractive perks, including a telephone, petrol coupons and exemption from Home Guard duties.[4]

Initially the Home Office wrote to each of the NPS representatives asking them to report to their nearest police station so they could be called upon when needed. They had hoped to recruit at least 40,000 fanciers to the service out of a total of over 100,000, but they struggled to generate much interest and by the end of 1939 only 2,000 pigeon owners had become members, many keepers being distrustful of the government. However, in 1940, with Hitler threatening to invade Britain, and the military situation looking increasingly bleak, membership increased rapidly to approximately 7,000 as fanciers responded to the national emergency.

The first service to be supplied with pigeons was the Royal Air Force (RAF), and pigeons were delivered to bases across Britain from November 1939. Each RAF station had its own civilian Pigeon Supply Officer and a deputy who was responsible for providing enough birds to accompany the bomber crews. This was a voluntary role that they took very seriously (two birds were provided to each bomber or reconnaissance aircraft and kept onboard in a specially designed waterproof basket. If the aircraft had to ditch or crash land, the plane's co-ordinates could be sent back with the pigeon so the RAF could launch a search and rescue operation). To reimburse fanciers, a fee of £5 per year was originally proposed by the NPS, but this was deemed too expensive by the government so a price of 4d (or 4 old pence) per flight was agreed.

As well as relying on local fanciers, many RAF bases built their own lofts. Mobile lofts were also constructed so birds could be quickly and easily transported to where they were needed. However, a problem soon arose when returning birds from downed aircraft were shot down, not by the enemy, but by local farmers. The RAF were incensed, particularly RAF Coastal Command who were in charge of protecting Allied convoys. In response, the government issued posters and put out radio broadcasts aimed at educating farmers about the difference between homing pigeons and wood pigeons.

On 24 January 1940 the issue was raised in Parliament by John Morgan, the Labour MP for Doncaster, with the Secretary of State for Air, Sir Kingsley Wood. He asked the Minister what complaints he had received about losses of homing pigeons on service, 'due to their being shot down other than by enemy action' and, in particular, from the

Bircham Newton aerodrome authorities. (RAF Bircham Newton was situated near Docking in Norfolk and, as part of No. 16 Group, played a key role in RAF Coastal Command.)

The Secretary of State for Air (Sir Kingsley Wood)
Two reports, one of which came from the Royal Air Force Station at Bircham Newton in November last, have been received of the shooting of pigeons on Royal Air Force service. The need for care to avoid shooting homing pigeons has already been emphasized in broadcasts and I am arranging for further publicity to be given to this matter.

Mr. Morgan
Will the right hon. Gentleman suggest to his right hon. and gallant Friend the Minister of Agriculture that when his Department is sending out fresh notices about the shooting of wood pigeons they should have a paragraph or two about this particular matter, because it is important at the present time?

Sir K. Wood
Yes, Sir. I will gladly confer with my right hon. and gallant Friend.[5]

The NPS, as well as administering the scheme, also had to police it. On 9 May 1940 the case of Christopher Newbould was brought up in Parliament by his local MP, Alfred Edwards, who represented Middlesbrough East. Newbould had been charged by the NPS with keeping homing pigeons without a permit, and despite pleading guilty, he had received a hefty fine. His MP argued that there was no criminal intent and asked for the fine to be rescinded, but the Secretary of State for the Home Department, Sir John Anderson, remained unmoved.

The success of the RAF scheme, bar the shooting down of pigeons by farmers, soon prompted the army to follow suit. As the British Expeditionary Force was forced to retreat to Dunkirk, the Army Pigeon Service was hastily reformed in May 1940. The service operated along the same lines as the RAF but fanciers were only paid 2d per flight, reflecting the shorter distances flown. The Intelligence Services, including the code breakers at Bletchley Park, were also provided with birds (in total during the war over 1,800 birds served on clandestine operations working for the Special Operations Executive and MI5).

As part of Britain's defence against invasion, pigeons were given to the Civil Defence Services (the police, fire and ambulance), the Home Guard and the Air Raid Precautions organisation. By June 1940, with German forces massing on the French coast, urgent measures were rushed through to guarantee the safety of pigeons on war service work. They included the destruction of all lofts and birds if they should fall into enemy hands, certificates of exemption only being available for those birds already deployed on war work. At the prompting of the NPS, they also included measures to control the pigeons' number-one predator, the peregrine falcon.

The peregrine falcon, the fastest bird of prey in the world in a dive, was at the start of 1940 breeding along much of Britain's coastline where its diet was made up mainly of seabirds and the occasional pigeon. However, the NPS deemed it such a threat to pigeons on war work that it demanded Parliament bring in measures to control its numbers. As a result, in June 1940 Regulation 9 of the Defence Act 1939 was amended, allowing peregrines to be destroyed. The details were recorded in Hansard, the official proceedings of the House of Commons:

ORDER IN COUNCIL AMENDING REGULATION 9 OF THE DEFENCE (GENERAL) REGULATIONS, 1939
S. B. & O., 1940, No. 1016
June 19, 1940
1. After paragraph (4) of Regulation nine of the Defence (General) Regulations, 1939 (hereinafter referred to as "the principal Regulations"), the following paragraph shall be inserted : —
(4a) Notwithstanding anything in the Wild Birds Protection Acts, 1880 to 1939, or the Wild Birds Protection Act (Northern Ireland), 1931, or in any order made under any of those Acts, the Secretary of State may by order provide that, in any area specified in the order, being an area through which, in the opinion of the Secretary of State, homing pigeons carrying messages to or from members of His Majesty's Forces or other persons in His Majesty's service are likely to fly, it shall be lawful for any person authorized by or on behalf of the Secretary of State to take or destroy at any time peregrine falcons or the eggs of peregrine falcons.[6]

Two weeks later the Destruction of Peregrine Falcons Order 1940 was passed in the name of the Secretary of State for Air, Sir Archibald Sinclair (1890–1970). The schedule published in Hansard outlined the areas in which the destruction of the birds and their eggs was to take place, including Cornwall, Devon, Pembroke, Caernarvon, Anglesey, Denigh, Yorkshire and much of the Scottish coast including Orkney and Shetland. Specific areas were also added to the schedule to cover the location of secret military bases, such as the naval base at Scapa Flow in Orkney, where it was thought fifth columnists may be operating.

The shooting of peregrines and the destruction of their nests started almost immediately. A 'Falcon Destruction Unit' was formed which targeted the south coast of England, a peregrine stronghold, this area being prioritised because of the threat of invasion. Unlike in the First World War when a similar campaign was waged against the humble house sparrow – which was accused of eating the nation's precious food supplies – a price was not put on the head of peregrines but instead expert marksmen and gamekeepers were employed to shoot them.

In September 1940, as the Battle of Britain raged in the skies overhead, the schedule was extended again to include Dorset, Sussex and Kent. Here the resident peregrines were persecuted ruthlessly as this area was thought to be the most vulnerable to attack. So, as the RAF battled the Luftwaffe for control of the air, another aerial conflict was being played out over the white cliffs of Dover between the peregrine falcon and a team of marksmen employed by the Air Ministry. Unlike the Battle of Britain, though, it was a totally uneven contest in which the end result was never in any doubt.

One marksman employed by the Air Ministry covered an astonishing 2,400 miles and shot seventeen peregrines in one month. A mobile unit was also set up with five Air Ministry marksmen headed up by a retired Irish colonel. The team toured Britain in an American Packard towing a caravan in which the men slept. During the breeding season the team would scour the cliffs with high-power binoculars looking for eyries or nests. When they found one, a marksman would abseil down the cliffs leaving a gin trap disguised in the nest. The trap contained a sprung 'treadle plate' which snapped shut when stepped on by the falcon, trapping the bird's legs in two interlocking pieces of metal with sharp, serrated edges.[7]

Many peregrines died a slow and agonising death. If the birds were lucky, one of the team would abseil down to kill them, but many were just left to die while the young starved (the gin trap was banned in 1954 by the Pests Act). Due to the precarious and inaccessible location of many eyries, it was dangerous work and one of the team fell 200ft to his death. Outside the breeding season peregrines were trapped or shot at their roosting sites, which ranged from a cliff edge to the side of a tall building such as a church. Soon the magnificent blue-grey peregrine falcon with its distinctive 'kak, kak, kak' call had disappeared from much of the coast of southern England. So important were pigeons to British intelligence that the Destruction of Peregrine Falcons Order 1940 was extended twice during the war, once in 1941 and again in 1943 to cover much of the country.

Peregrine falcons were not the only threat pigeons faced while doing war work. Near the end of 1940 supplies of pigeon food began to run dangerously low and there were urgent meetings between the Ministry of Food, the Air Ministry, the War Office and the NPS to resolve the problem. After much negotiation it was decided that pigeon food needed to be rationed and restricted to those birds doing war work for the NPS. Like food rationing for people, this was done using coupons, the exact mix being specified by the 'Feeding Stuffs National Priority Mixture Order 1941'. The first coupons were issued in the February of that year, the 9,000 members of the NPS receiving 7lb of corn mixture per week for every ten birds they owned.

Amazingly, in 1940 and 1941 much of the pigeon food was still being shipped across the Atlantic from America. As a result of shortages in supply, and the armed services getting their own lofts, restrictions were placed on the number of fanciers who could join the NPS. However, this did not go down well with the majority of fanciers who were not members and they angrily complained to their Members of Parliament.

While the British were arguing over pigeon food, the Germans were busy training pigeons for use in their *Blitzkrieg* on Europe. They had successfully used pigeons as messengers during the First World War after seeing how effective they had been in relieving the siege of Paris in 1870. The army had continued using them after the war and when the Nazis came to power in 1933 they quickly conscripted over 50,000 fanciers and formed the German Pigeon Union. Pigeon owners, like everyone else, needed to be able to prove their ancestry, so members had to have a certificate stating they were Aryan, Jews and foreigners being banned from keeping birds.

Before the war the Nazis had organised two big international pigeon races from Britain to Germany. Over 1,000 birds had flown from Lympne in Kent and Croydon in London (then an international airport) back to Germany. The Germans had used this information to set up their own pigeon network, right under the noses of MI5. Pigeons were especially favoured by Heinrich Himmler, the head of the SS, who was a keen fancier, and at the start of the war both the army and the SS were equipped with them. By 1941 birds were attached to most units and a secret pigeon base was operating out of Spandau in Berlin. This housed over 2,000 birds that were specially bred for clandestine missions behind enemy lines.

When the German *Blitzkrieg* machine swept across the Low Countries and then France in 1940, they captured thousands of pigeon lofts which were quickly put to good use in the service of the German army. The British responded by sending in thousands of their own birds in a secret mission called 'Operation Columba' (the operation got its name from the Latin or scientific name for the pigeon – *Columba livia*). Enclosed in the container on each bird's leg was a questionnaire asking the finder to send back any information they thought may be valuable. This included not just military activity but also what life was like for ordinary people living under the yoke of Nazism.

On 8 April 1941 the first batch of over 16,500 British pigeons were dropped by parachute in special containers behind enemy lines by an RAF Whitney bomber. Over the next four-and-a-half years tens of thousands of birds were dropped by plane from Denmark in the north right down to the south of France. The aim of Operation Columba was to gather intelligence from Nazi-occupied Europe, in particular during the early years to see if the Germans were going to invade Britain.

The questionnaire was similar to the Mass-Observation surveys then being conducted in Britain and tried to find out what everyday life was like for ordinary people living under German occupation. It included questions on subjects like the BBC World Service, the answers being written on a small piece of rice paper which was put back in the canister attached to the bird's leg. As a way of encouraging people to return their questionnaire, the form finished with a rousing patriotic call to arms which read, 'Thank you. Take courage. We will not forget you.' However, when released, many birds were shot, both by the Germans and those living under them, and ended up as pigeon pie.

When the operation had first been mooted, MI5 had voiced serious reservations about its success, but within two days of being dropped the first pigeon had made its way back to Britain. The message came from a small village called Le Biel near the Belgian border and revealed the location of a large German ammunition dump, and to MI5's relief, that 'The Bosches do not mention an invasion of England.'[8] Over the course of the next three-and-a-half years over 1,000 messages were sent back from occupied Europe. They contained a goldmine of information, from secret German bases and the work of the Gestapo to the impact of Allied bombing and the number of civilian casualties it caused.

Despite the success of Operation Columba, MI5 soon realised that pigeons were not just flying back from the continent but were also regularly observed flying the other way. These sightings were investigated by a Flight Lieutenant Richard Walker, who headed up the 'Pigeon Service Special Section' at the intelligence agency. Walker was a fanatical fancier and passionately believed pigeons could help win the war as long as they were working for the right side: 'Out of a hundred birds of the same stock perhaps one will be that bird all breeders hope for,' he wrote in a classified memo to his superior officer, 'a bird of highly individual character, courageous and resourceful. Much depends on the individual bird and especially its character and intelligence.'

Walker was soon alerted to the fact that two German pigeons had been blown across the Channel during a gale and had been found with training messages attached to their legs (they became 'prisoners of war', a government memo noting them 'working hard breeding English pigeons'). In response he produced a map of Nazi-occupied Europe with known pigeon lofts marked on it so they could be targeted by SOE operatives working behind enemy lines. At home, Walker believed birds had been smuggled into Britain using E-boats ('enemy boats') and U-boats and then returned by fifth columnists with top-secret information about Britain's defences. He identified the hot spot for this activity as the Isles of Scilly, so in 1942 he sent in a crack team there to search and destroy any enemy pigeons.

Ironically, the team's preferred method for killing the pigeons was none other than the peregrine falcon. So while one section of the Air Ministry was busy destroying falcons all along the coast of England, in the spring of 1942 another section of MI5 headed to the Isles of Scilly to establish a falconry unit using them. It comprised a head falconer, Ronald Stevens, and two assistants together with three peregrine falcons who were tasked with intercepting and destroying any enemy pigeons seen flying over the islands.[9]

The falconry unit spent five weeks training in Pembrokeshire where the birds were taught to kill practice pigeons. When the unit started work on the Isles of Scilly it was based on a local golf course. The peregrines brought down twenty-three pigeons in total, including some over the course while golfers teed off. The problem was that all the birds were later found to be British: unfortunately, the peregrines were not able to distinguish friend from foe. It was a fiasco made worse by the fact that two of the British pigeons downed were found to be carrying important information in the canisters on their legs. In a final ironic twist, local boys shot dead two of the peregrines, emulating the Air Ministry's example.

In contrast to their use in Britain, pigeons were put to a very different purpose in the United States. Project Pigeon was the brainchild of the psychologist, behaviourist, author, inventor and social philosopher, Burrhus Frederic Skinner (1904–1990). His idea was to use a pigeon's cognitive abilities as a homing device, with the bird pecking at screens to guide a missile on to its target and in the process paying the ultimate price. Skinner's dream was to create a kamikaze bird-guided bomb.[10]

To test his idea, Skinner designed a special harness that would hold the pigeon's body securely in the nose of a bomb while enabling its head and neck to move freely so it could peck the screens. After various modifications, his tests showed the harness worked well. Convinced that he had discovered the ideal bird guidance system, Skinner formally approached the US government for help, but was rejected time after time. However, the attack on Pearl Harbour on 7 December 1941 transformed his prospects and he was awarded a contract in June 1943 worth $25,000 for a 'homing device' with the title Project Pigeon.

Skinner put his pigeons through a series of rigorous tests concluding that hunger was the best way of motivating birds to peck away at the target on the screens. Just when Project Pigeon was looking promising, Skinner got the devastating news that his contract had been cancelled. Despite this he did not give up on his idea, continuing with his pigeon research at home for the next six years. He concluded that, though never tested in battle, if his birds had seen action they would have succeeded in their mission. (One spin-off from his research was the electrical conducting glass developed for Project Pigeon inspired the touchscreens used in our smartphones and tablets today.)

Back in occupied Europe, the bravery of British pigeons serving behind enemy lines had not gone unnoticed. In 1943 Maria Dickin (1870–1951), a social reformer and animal rights activist, approached the RAF Pigeon Section at the Air Ministry with a proposal for an animal medal. Dickin had founded the People's Dispensary for Sick Animals (PDSA) in 1917 in the cellar of her home in Whitechapel, London. The PDSA provided veterinary care to all animals regardless of the owner's ability to pay. The sign on her door read 'Bring your sick animals/Do not let them suffer/ All animals treated/All treatment free'. As a result, in 1929 Dickin was awarded an Order of the British Empire for her services to animals.

Dickin secured a meeting with Wing Commander W.D. Lea Rayner, the officer in charge of the pigeon section, who instantly saw the huge propaganda value in the medal. She proposed the award be given to any animal displaying conspicuous gallantry in the line of duty and so together they designed the medal. It was made of bronze, had a laurel wreath around the edge and was inscribed with the words 'PDSA; For Gallantry; We Also Serve'. The ribbon was composed of three equal vertical stripes of dark green, brown and pale blue. At Rayner's insistence they called it the Dickin medal in her honour. The award soon popularly became known as 'the animals Victoria Cross' and the first animal to win it was a pigeon called Winkie.

In the early afternoon of 23 February 1942 a Bristol Beaufort bomber belonging to No.42 squadron was heading back from a mission over occupied Norway when it crash landed in the North Sea, the result of engine trouble caused by enemy fire. The plane broke up as it hit the water and although the radio operator had been able to get out an SOS before they ditched, the signal had been so faint that RAF Coastal Command couldn't get a fix on it. An air search had been ordered which had covered over 70 square miles but no sign of the plane had been found. Immersed in the icy cold water on impact, the crew soon started to suffer from hypothermia in their dinghy.

Their only chance of survival was a blue chequered hen pigeon, number NEHU.40.NS.1, who, like the crew, had also been plunged into the water before her container had floated back to the surface.

At four o'clock in the afternoon they let the pigeon go, and following a gruelling flight, she had arrived back at her loft in Broughty Ferry, near Dundee, at 8.20 the next morning, bedraggled and covered in oil. Her owner, George Ross, calculated that the pigeon could not possibly have flown from the area being searched during the hours of daylight (pigeons dislike flying in darkness, especially over water, so it was assumed that Winkie had spent the night roosting on an oil tanker or convoy ship). Estimating that the pigeon had flown between 120 and 140 miles, Ross was able to calculate approximately where the plane had ditched, using the difference between the time the faint SOS signal had been received and when the pigeon had returned to her loft. A plane was soon dispatched from RAF Leuchars in Fife and later found the dinghy 129 miles from the base with all the crew still alive.

That evening, after they were rescued, the crew held a dinner in their pigeon's honour, each member drinking a toast to her achievement. During the dinner the exhausted bird appeared to be constantly winking one eye, the result of muscle strain, so the crew gave her the nickname of Winkie. For her bravery Winkie was awarded the first Dickin Medal by Maria Dickin on 2 December 1943. The citation read 'for delivering a message under exceptional difficulties and so contributing to the rescue of an Air Crew while serving with the RAF in February 1942'. (When Winkie died, Ross donated the bird and her Dickin Medal to the McManus Art Gallery and Museum in Dundee where it can still be seen.)[11]

Two other pigeons also got the Dickin medal on the same day. Tyke served with the Middle East Pigeon Service in North Africa. Also known as 'George', Tyke was hatched in Cairo, Egypt, and given the service number MEPS.43.1263. In June 1943 the American bomber on which he was flying was shot down and crash landed in the Mediterranean Sea. In order to get help, the crew released Tyke, but were only able to write a partial message which read 'Crew safe in dinghy 10 west of …'. An air search had previously been launched for the plane but had been abandoned due to bad weather. Undeterred, Tyke flew over 100 miles back to his loft in extremely poor visibility. On arrival, the incomplete message was read and a successful new search was mounted, the crew later crediting Tyke with saving their lives. Tyke's citation read, 'For delivering a message under exceptionally difficult conditions and so contributing to the rescue of an Air Crew, while serving with the RAF in the Mediterranean in June, 1943'. (In July 2000 Tyke's Dickin Medal was auctioned by Spink Auction House in London and sold for £4,830.)[12]

The third bird was White Vision who was stationed with RAF 190 Squadron at Sullom Voe in Shetland. A nearly pure white hen bird, she was given the service number SURP.41.L.3089. On 11 October 1943 at 8.20 in the morning the flying boat with White Vision onboard, a Catalina bomber, was forced by high winds to ditch in the North Sea near the Hebrides, off the west coast of Scotland. A sea rescue search was deemed too risky because of the bad weather and an air search impossible because of thick mist. With the plane's radio out of action, White Vision was released and flew some 60 miles against a strong headwind of 25 mph in visibility of only 100 yards, arriving back at her pigeon loft at five o'clock that afternoon. Attached to her leg was the message, 'Aircraft ditched safely. N.W ... Heavy swell, Taxying S.E. No casualties.' As a result, the search was resumed as soon as conditions allowed and the crew were found safe and well just after midnight the next day. White Vision was credited with saving the lives of all eleven members of the air crew after they had spent eighteen hours in the sea. White Vision's citation read: 'For delivering a message under exceptionally difficult conditions and so contributing to the rescue of an Air Crew while serving with the RAF in October 1943.'[13]

As the war progressed twenty-nine other pigeons received the Dickin medal. They included Royal Blue, a cock bird bred at the royal loft at Sandringham, Norfolk, and owned by King George VI. When war had broken out in 1939 the king had made all his pigeons available to the NPS, Royal Blue being selected because of his speed and stamina and given the service number NURP.40.GVIS.453. He was less than a year old when, on 9 October 1940, the bomber he was travelling in was forced to crash land as a result of heavy enemy fire during a night raid over Holland. Released at 7.20 am the next day, Royal Blue covered the 120 miles to his loft in just over four hours, all the crew later being safely recovered. His citation read: 'For being the first pigeon in this war to deliver a message from a forced landed aircraft on the continent while serving with the RAF in October 1940.' Royal Blue received his Dickin medal from Rear Admiral Roger Bellairs and Wing Commander Rayner in April 1945, a message being sent with the pigeon to Sandringham asking if King George VI would accept the medal on his behalf. The medal resides in the Royal Collection to this day.

The real-life inspiration for the film *Valiant* was a grizzled cock bird called Gustav who had the service number NPS.42.31066. He was the first pigeon to bring back a message following D-Day from the beaches of Normandy. Gustav had already developed a reputation for punctuality and reliability under fire, having successfully relayed back secret messages from the Belgian resistance. As a result he was selected for a top secret mission, being one of six pigeons loaned to the Reuters news correspondent Montague Taylor. He was aboard an Allied warship on D-Day, 6 June 1944, and had been specially selected to send messages back to mainland Britain with the news of the landings.

As the first troops waded ashore under heavy fire, Taylor released Gustav, who flew back the 150 miles to his loft at RAF Thorney Island, near Chichester in West Sussex, in five hours and sixteen minutes while facing into a strong headwind blowing at over 30mph. Attached to his leg was the message, 'We are just 20 miles or so off the beaches. First assault troops landed 0750. Signal says no interference from enemy gunfire on beach ... Steaming steadily in formation. Lightnings, Typhoons, Fortresses crossing since 0545. No enemy aircraft seen.' Due to the fleet maintaining radio silence at the time, Gustav's message was the first word to reach Churchill that the invasion had been a success.

Gustav was presented with his medal on 27 November 1944 by Mrs A.V. Alexander, the wife of the then First Lord of the Admiralty. His citation read, 'For delivering the first message from the Normandy beaches from a ship off the beachhead while serving with the RAF on June 6 1944.' Gustav is judged by the Imperial War Museum to be the greatest animal to have served this country and in 2005, the same year that *Valiant* was released, his medal went on display at the D-Day Museum in Portsmouth, Hampshire. (Sadly, Gustav died in an accident after the war when someone accidentally stepped on him while cleaning out his pigeon loft.)[14]

In contrast to the celebrated success of the pigeon, by 1945 the peregrine falcon had disappeared from large areas of the British countryside. Its relentless persecution made little difference to winning the war, but had deprived the nation of one of its most enigmatic falcons. It was not missed by 'Country diary' columnist 'JHH' who wrote in *The Guardian* newspaper from Penrith in Cumbria on 25 April 1945:

> This handsome raptorial, which is very scarce in the North of England, nests in the crags above the moors and forages over a wide area. Naturalists have for years been rather sore at the destruction of these fine birds; but the chief complaint against them, other than that of the gamekeepers is that they have a habit of intercepting pigeons and making a meal of them. This trait has been particularly objectionable during the war years, when men's lives have often depended on the safe delivery of pigeon-borne messages.[15]

During the six years of the Second World War nearly a quarter of a million pigeons served with the Army, RAF, the Civil Defence forces, the Home Guard and the Intelligence Services. Pigeons in particular served with distinction in Bomber Command and the Special Operations Executive where they flew thousands of clandestine missions from occupied Europe. Their bravery was recognised through the award of thirty-two Dickin medals out of total of fifty-four given out during the war – more than for all the other animals combined.

Pigeons contribution to the war effort was also commemorated in 1951 when a memorial bird garden to the National Pigeon Service was unveiled at Beach House Park in Worthing, Sussex. The only memorial of its kind in Britain, it was commissioned by the actress and ornithologist Nancy Price (1880–1970). A leading actress whose career spanned silent films, talkies and television, she wrote a bird book about nests called *Winged Builders* in 1959 and was awarded a CBE for her services to the theatre. One stone in the rockery reads 'In memory of Warrior Birds who gave their lives on active service 1939-45 and for the pleasure and use of living birds.' The other says 'A bird of the air shall carry the voice and that which hath wings shall tell the matter [Ecclesiastes 10:20].'

In marked contrast to the praise piled on pigeons, by the end of the war over 600 peregrine falcons had been killed and our most evocative bird of prey had disappeared from much of the coast and nearly all grouse moors in England, Wales and Scotland. It was a loss felt by the ornithologist, broadcaster and Colonel in the Scottish Command of the British Army,

Henry Douglas-Home, who wrote 'I am sad to say that my position in the military world at the time made me partially implicated in this measure being undertaken in Scotland. I think it was a mistake because I doubt if their numbers even then warranted it, but in those dark days when the presence of German U-boats ruled out any possibility of radio contact with our ships in the Atlantic, even the chance of losing one message-bearing pigeon for the sake of a bird seemed unacceptable beside the risk to human life.' For many gamekeepers the passing of the Destruction of Peregrine Falcons Order in 1940 was just the excuse they needed to kill them and all other birds of prey considered a threat to their precious grouse. Over seventy-five years after the end of the Second World War, the relentless and now completely illegal persecution of birds of prey on grouse moors continues unabated.

Chapter 6

Birds Behind Barbed Wire

Birds not only fought and died alongside our troops but were also incarcerated with them. In May 1943 a unique bird book was published in extraordinary circumstances. *An Introduction to Malayan Birds* was written by the ornithologist Guy Charles Madoc with illustrations by his friend Dr B. David Molesworth and research by Carl Alexander Gibson-Hill.[1] What made the book so special – apart from the fact that it was limited to a print run of one – was that all three ornithologists were prisoners of war and the book was produced inside the notorious Changi prison in Japanese-occupied Singapore. Put together from memory and using notes smuggled into the prison by Madoc, it was typed on paper stolen from the Japanese commandant's office using a commandeered typewriter. Since its initial publication, the book has been reprinted numerous times and over seventy-five years later remains one of the best introductions to the birds of the region.

The origins of the book can be traced back to the 15 February 1942 when Lieutenant General Arthur Ernest Percival (1887–1966), commander of the Allied forces in Singapore, went down in history for capitulating to the Japanese Imperial Army. It was the largest surrender of forces in the annals of the British Army, Winston Churchill commenting ruefully at the time, 'I speak to you all under the shadow of a heavy and far-reaching military defeat. It is a British and Imperial defeat. Singapore has fallen … This, therefore, is one of those moments when the British race and nation can show their quality and their genius.'

The British race's 'quality and genius' had been in short supply in the preceding weeks in Malaya when the Japanese had successfully invaded the peninsula, Singapore itself falling in just seven days. As the fighting intensified, the city descended into chaos, thousands of people trying to escape by sea before 'the Gibraltar of the East' fell. Among them was the Director of Raffles Museum, Frederick Nutter Chasen (1896–1942), who boarded the coastal steamer HMS *Giang Bee*, on 12 February 1942.

The Chinese-owned ship had been converted to a patrol vessel and was carrying over 300 civilians, mostly women, children, elderly people and VIPs. It left the harbour at 10pm and early the next day came under attack from Japanese aircraft, the vessel later being sunk by a Japanese destroyer. In the encounter two of the four life boats on the ship had been destroyed, so many of those on board, including Chasen, drowned.

Following Chasen's death at sea, the Under Secretary of the Straits Settlements offered the role of Assistant Curator to Carl Alexander Gibson-Hill (1911–1963). He was a doctor who, with his wife, Margaret, had just arrived in Singapore after having spent the preceding three years on the remote Christmas and Cocos-Keeling islands in the Indian Ocean. Gibson-Hill loved wildlife from an early age, painting and photographing nature despite having very poor eyesight. As a teenager he established his own personal natural history museum in his parents' attic, his exhibits, from a fox skull to barn owl pellets, being collected on forays around his Birmingham home. After boarding school at Malvern, where he received the Boldero prize for natural history three times, he went on to study at Pembroke College, Cambridge, where he gained a second in the Natural History tripos (course) in 1933 and edited the university paper, the *Varsity News*. The university's oriental and science departments had strong links with British colonies in Southeast Asia, and it was here that Gibson-Hill's interest in Malaysia was first kindled, many previous graduates having taken up leadership roles in the Far East.[2]

After graduating, Gibson-Hill began work on his first book about his native Warwickshire, and, at his parents' behest, also enrolled in medical college so he could get 'a proper job'. His book on Warwickshire was published in 1936 to critical acclaim, but, rather bizarrely, under the pseudonym of John Lisle, Gibson-Hill perhaps not wanting to further inflame relations with his parents. At medical college he met and married Margaret Halliday, who was still completing her training. Soon after the wedding, Gibson-Hill departed on the adventure of a lifetime, spending two years on Christmas Island as Resident Medical Officer while Margaret completed her studies.

Lying in the Indian Ocean south of Java, Christmas Island was a birdwatchers' tropical paradise comprising 135km^2 of rainforest, reefs, waterfalls and atolls. For Gibson-Hill the posting was a dream come true, and he systematically collected and catalogued all the island's wildlife in his spare time. Before departing for the island he had met Chasen, the Director of Raffles Museum, and, encouraged by him, meticulously recorded all the species he found in his extensive notebooks. The list included over 200 different birds of which six, much to Chasen's delight, were new to science.

In early 1941, Gibson-Hill received another medical posting for ten months to the Cocos-Keeling Islands where he was joined by his newly graduated wife. The Cocos-Keeling Islands, which comprise twenty-seven islands midway between Australia and Sri Lanka, was another dream posting. With only a few hundred people to look after, it was an idyllic existence for the bird-mad doctor and his long-suffering wife. In their ample free time they went about cataloguing the islands' wildlife, their search being complemented by some historic documents which Gibson-Hill had been given by the owner of the islands, J.S. Clunies-Ross. During their time there the Gibson-Hills both successfully applied for permanent jobs on the mainland, after deciding they wanted to make British Malaya their home because of its beauty and its biodiversity.

On 12 December 1941 the couple arrived back in Singapore where Margaret had got a job at the hospital and her husband was due to start a new role as a rural health officer working for the city's health department. Just as the Gibson-Hills were settling down to write up the surveys, their lives were rudely interrupted by the arrival of the invading Japanese Army. Wisely seeing the writing on the wall, Margaret escaped back to England on one of the last boats out of the city. However, Gibson-Hill, buoyed by having been appointed Assistant Curator at Raffles Museum following Chasen's death, decided to stay and tough it out. The move, totally characteristic of the bullish and headstrong Gibson-Hill, was a decision he would have ample opportunity to regret.

As the battle for Singapore raged the British army converted the museum and its library into a field hospital, the library's roof suffering bomb damage during the siege. When the conquering Japanese arrived in Singapore they soon started renaming all the landmarks in honour of their emperor. Raffles was renamed the *Syonan Hakubutsu Ka* (*Syonan-to* means 'Light of the South' and *Hakubutsu Kan* 'museum'). To head up the new institution they appointed the vulcanologist and geologist Professor Hidezo Tanakadate, who arrived from Saigon to take over all the islands' 'scientific matters.' Like all Japanese Army appointments, Tanakadate arrived at the museum immaculately dressed in his military uniform where he found the 'Wildman of Malaya', Gibson-Hill, busy at his desk among the detritus of war, looking as though he had been pulled through the proverbial hedge backwards. When Tanakadate formally announced himself and demanded Gibson-Hill bow, the museum director failed to look up from his work, his 'insolent manner' being further reinforced by a blank refusal to meet Tanakadate for lunch the next day.

Tanakadate left in a volcanic mood, the next day arriving very early at the museum where he again found Gibson-Hill slumped over his desk, this time having just finished breakfast. There he was presented by the sight of Gibson-Hill 'seated barefoot in an old chair, one leg sprawling over an arm of the chair, one hand flourishing a very long cigarette-holder with a lighted cigarette, and in an open necked shirt, displaying a tangled ginger beard. He did not get up.' Incensed by his lack of respect, Tanakadate pulled out his revolver and demanded Gibson-Hill stand up and bow, but he simply laughed at the Japanese professor and carried on looking at his bird books. Three days later Gibson-Hill was escorted from the museum at gunpoint by Japanese guards and interned at the infamous Changi prison on the edge of the city. It was to be the start of over three long years incarcerated behind barbed wire.[3]

Gibson-Hill was interned with hundreds of other civilians captured during the fall of Singapore at Changi prison which had been built by the British in 1936. The prison was designed in a 'T' shape with two cell blocks on either side of a central administrative block, separated by a courtyard. Military prisoners of war were also kept on the site but were housed in the nearby British Army Selarang Barracks. This was the location for the book *King Rat*, written in 1962 by the Australian novelist and screenwriter James Clavell who was interned there (Clavell also wrote the screenplay for *The Great Escape* in 1963).

Gibson-Hill, like the other civilians sent to Changi, found the cells squalid and overcrowded. At its peak the prison held over 3,000 prisoners although it was designed for just 600. For someone who lived for the outdoors and birdwatching it was initially almost unbearable, the only consolation being his Cocos-Keeling notebooks, which he had managed to smuggle into the prison. Allocated a shared cell in the men's block with only a tiny window, he vainly hoped to use his time behind bars to write up his next scientific paper on the birdlife of the archipelago.

Incarcerated with him in the separate women's block was a seventeen-year-old girl by the name of Sheila Allan (1924–) who was imprisoned with her Australian father, a mining engineer, and Thai stepmother. Allan's Malayan mother ran their home in Penang supported by a Chinese *amah* (maid) before she left, her father later remarrying. An only child, she had a happy childhood, going to several covent schools and having two dogs, a cat and a monkey as pets.

Allan and Gibson-Hill couldn't have been more different. Allan was a typical teenager, highly emotional, intensively private, naively idealistic and a romantic dreamer, all of which made her a great people watcher. To her, Changi was a place she found both brutal and fascinating and in trying to make sense of her time there she grew up quickly. Gibson-Hill was in many ways her opposite, a serious and erudite man, old beyond his years (he was only thirty-two when he was interned) to whom human relationships were not nearly as interesting as those of birds. For Gibson-Hill the war was a huge personal inconvenience, something to be endured until he could get back to his research. However, during their time together in the prison the two formed an unlikely friendship, Allan attending Gibson-Hill's lectures and writing to him on many occasions asking for his help (inmates were not allowed to fraternise but could write to each other, the letters being censored by the Japanese).

Allan wrote a secret diary which she recorded on tiny scraps of paper and kept hidden from her Japanese captors. Unlike Gibson-Hill, who recorded little of his personal experiences in the camp, Allan was a great diarist because, like many teenagers, she wrote from the heart.[4] In it she captures the drudgery, boredom, violence and squalor that the inmates endured during their stay. They were, she said, a 'motley crew of humanity [...] with different nationalities, ages, religions and levels of education.' Like so many people imprisoned against their will, the internees tried to hold onto their sanity by organising schools, lectures and concerts. It had, according to Allan, 'a very British air of formality that helped keep our community together'.

Not long after arriving, Allan described the food on offer, commenting, 'Menu stinks! Rice and water – called bubu – tasteless and looks like dishwater.'[5] Despite Allan's poor view of the accommodation and food on offer, Changi was, by Japanese standards, one of the better prisons, but it was still a frightening and ugly place to be incarcerated. The camp commandant was Lieutenant Okasaki who reminded Allan of 'a peacock when he struts up and down on inspection days. However, he seems to like the children a lot – that's something in his favour, I suppose. As for the rest of the sentries – they can be pigs sometimes – no, most times. Often we would be slapped or given a kick in the bottom if we don't bow correctly or get caught whispering!'

During her first few months of imprisonment in 1942, to pass the time Allan and the other women made quilts for the camp hospital. The men, who had to do all the heavy work and the cooking in the prison, were only allowed to see the women if they were ill under armed guard. Unable to see their men, each woman instead stitched a secret coded message or symbol into patchwork squares on the quilt. Four quilts were made, one celebrating the Girl Guides and one for each for the Red Cross organisations of Britain, Australia and Japan, the Japanese one being included so as not to arouse suspicion from the camp guards. Allan for her square did a picture of Australia with a sailing boat, her father telling her about the country which she dreamed of visiting after the war was over (all the quilts survived the war. The Australian War Memorial, a museum in Canberra, now holds the Australian, Japanese and Girl Guide quilts, the other one being owned by the British Red Cross. The Girl Guides quilt was kept by Allan who donated it to the museum).

Like all the prisoners, Gibson-Hill was appalled at the conditions, but was determined to make the best of it, and in particular to use his time to carry on his research. A library was soon opened which, at his request, included a number of bird books taken from the museum including the four volumes of the *The Birds of the Malay Peninsula*. Gibson-Hill made the library his second home, helped out in the prison hospital, and became secretary of the ironically named 'Leisure Hours Committee'. Here to boost morale, he read and put on plays by Shakespeare such as Henry V, a passion he shared with Allan who had inherited a love of the Bard from her father (at the same time, on the other side of the world, the actor Laurence Olivier, 1907–1989, at the behest of the Ministry of Information, was working on the film adaptation of Henry V, which was released in 1944 and patriotically dedicated to the 'Commandos and Airborne Troops of Great Britain, the spirit of whose ancestors it has been humbly attempted to recapture').[6] Gibson-Hill also gave lectures to the internees, frequently talking about some aspect of Malayan life or

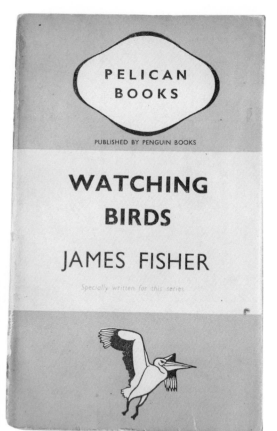

Watching Birds by James Fisher was published in 1940 at the height of the Blitz, people reading it on the bus, in their air raid shelter and even on fire-watching duty. It went on to sell over 3 million copies. (*Author's collection*)

James Fisher said in the introduction 'Some people might consider an apology necessary for the appearance of a book about birds at a time when Britain is fighting for its own and many other lives. I make no such apology. Birds are part of the heritage we are fighting for.' (*BBC*)

'There'll be bluebirds over the white cliffs of Dover' was immortalised by the forces sweetheart Vera Lynn and was written by the lyricist Nat Burton. But what birds was Burton referring to? And was there a hidden meaning in the verse? (*Author's collection*)

'A nightingale sang in Berkeley Square' was written by Eric Maschwitz. He lifted the title, transporting the nightingale from the Mediterranean to Mayfair and substituting the obscure village of Le Lavandou in France for the more glamorous Berkeley Square in London. (*Author's collection*)

The avocet made a remarkable comeback following the flooding of the low lying coast of East Anglia in 1940 to prevent a German invasion. The Royal Society for the Protection of Birds later adopted the bird as their logo. (*Chris Gomersall*)

As the Blitz raged and large parts of London were reduced to rubble or razed to the ground, one of Britain's rarest birds, the black redstart, found an unlikely home among the bombed remnants of the city. (*Chris Gomersall*)

The film *The First of the Few* told the story of the most famous plane in the world, the Spitfire and how its revolutionary inventor, R.J. Mitchell (Mitch), came up with the design based on the shape of a seagull. (*Author's collection*)

The film starred Leslie Howard as Mitch and Rosamund John as his wife, in this promotional shot looking through binoculars at the seagulls circling around the cliffs. Howard turns to John and says 'Look at them! Those curved wings – what a beautiful line! We've got to learn from the birds if we want to fly properly, and faster.' (*RKO Pictures*)

The film *Tawny Pipit* was released in 1944 and tells the story of Jimmy Bancroft, an injured fighter pilot and his nurse, Hazel Court, who rescue a pair of very rare nesting tawny pipits. However, in real life tawny pipits only occurred in Nazi-occupied Europe so instead the film company had to make use of meadow pipits. (*Universal-International*)

In 1939 the RAF Comforts Committee produced 'Knitting for the RAF'. On the back of the booklet, reflecting Berkeley Square's most famous resident, was a picture of a nightingale. Sat on the bough of a darkened tree, it is singing 'knit, knit, knit!' in the moonlight. (*Author's Collection*)

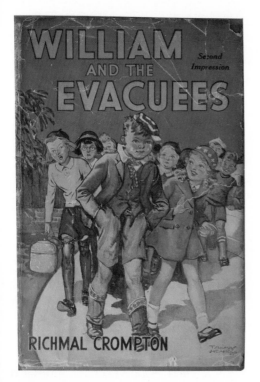

William and the Evacuees by Richmal Crompton was published in 1940, part of the hugely popular Just William series of books. With invasion imminent it included a story called 'William and the Bird Man'. (*Author's collection*)

THE MAN HAD TAKEN UP TWO OR THREE BRICKS FROM THE FLOOR, AND WAS PUTTING THE ENVELOPE INTO THE HOLE.

William follows the Bird Man home and discovers him hiding an envelope underneath the floor. 'From where he stood William could see some of the titles .... Birds of the British Isles, Birds of the Tropics, Birds .... Birds ..... Birds .... Gosh! He must know a jolly lot about birds.' (*Author's collection*)

"I FOUND THIS IN YOUR SISTER'S POSSESSION," SAID THE WING-COMMANDER.

"OH THAT SPARROW'S STOMACH THING," SAID WILLIAM EASILY.

The Wing Commander instantly recognizes the diagram in the envelope for what it really is – not a sparrow's stomach but a detailed map of the aerodrome. So William saves the day by exposing a Nazi spy masquerading as a birdwatcher. In real life a German agent used the cover of being a wildfowler to spy on the British fleet. (*Author's Collection*)

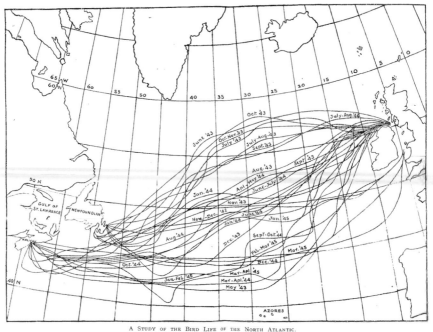

Matthew Rankin, a surgeon on destroyers and Eric Duffey, a pilot with the Royal Naval Volunteer Reserve, collaborated on a unique study of seabirds as the Battle of the Atlantic raged. From May 1943 to April 1945 they spent on average nearly 28 days a month at sea counting birds. (*British Birds*)

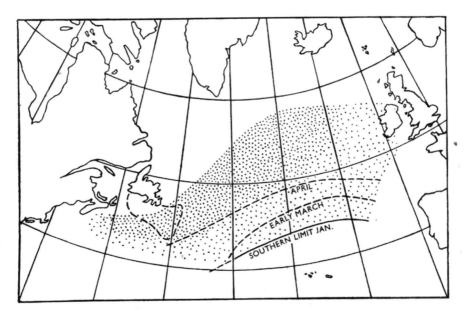

Fig. 14. KITTIWAKE. WINTER DISTRIBUTION AND SOUTHERN LIMIT
Density of dots indicates frequency of birds.

The winter distribution of the kittiwake mapped by Rankin and Duffey. Their paper in *British Birds* magazine was published in 1948 and was based of their war records, their time at sea being spent counting both U-boats and seabirds. (*British Birds*)

After the war Eric Duffey became one of the world's leading authorities on spiders, publishing five books and numerous papers on arachnids. (*Arachnology*)

Charles Madge and Tom Harrisson were the architects of Mass-Observation. Unusually for an ornithologist, Harrisson found watching people as interesting as watching birds. So Mass-Observation became, in his words, the 'study of Briton's rather as if they were birds'. (*National Portrait Gallery*)

Right: Valiant was released in 2005 and tells the story of a group of homing pigeons who were 'featherweight heroes' in the war just before D Day. (*Wikipedia*)

The real-life Valiant was a homing pigeon called Gustav. He made a major contribution to winning the Second World War and was awarded the Dickin Medal, the animal version of the Victoria Cross, by the founder of the People's Dispensary for Sick Animals, Maria Dickin. (*PDSA*)

Carl Alexander Gibson-Hill, a doctor and ornithologist, was made the curator of Raffles Museum in Singapore in 1942 just before the fall of the city to the Japanese. To survive being a Prisoner of War (POW) he helped to form the Changi Ornithological Study Group and carried out studies of the Malayan long-tailed tailorbird and the spotted munia. (*Lee Kong Chian Museum*)

Incarcerated with Carl Alexander Gibson-Hill in Changi was a seventeen-year old girl by the name of Sheila Allan. During their time together in the prison the two formed an unlikely friendship, Allan attending Gibson-Hill's lectures and he treating her ill father. (*Sheila Allan*)

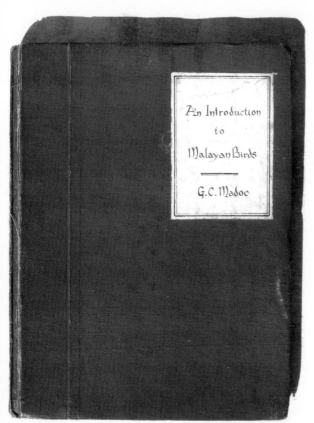

Another member of the Changi Ornithological Study Group was Guy Charles Madoc. He wrote *An Introduction to Malayan Birds* while a POW in Changi prison in Singapore. (*Fenella Madoc-Davis*)

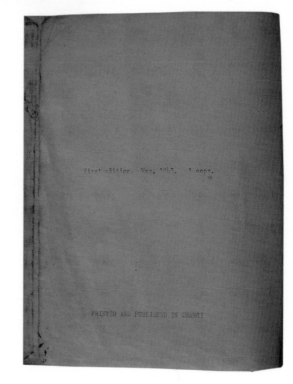

First edition. May, 1943. 1 copy.

PRINTED AND PUBLISHED IN CHANGI

Published in May 1943, the book was limited to a print run of one and was bound in red leatherette by two French prisoners, the cover having been ripped from the seats of a wrecked car. (*Fenella Madoc-Davis*)

Put together from memory and using notes smuggled into the prison by Madoc, *An Introduction to Malayan Birds* was typed on paper stolen from the Japanese commandant's office using a commandeered typewriter.

PREFACE.

Within these four walls so much interest has been displayed in Malayan birds that I have felt encouraged to write this little book. Though I hope that the reader may find some matters of interest in it, a desire to enlighten my fellow-prisoners has not been the sole incentive to authorship. Its composition has enabled me to jot down many facts of which I no longer possess written record, and to crystallize and sift my knowledge. If my readers derive from a perusal of these pages one third of the benefit that I have gleaned during its production, I shall be well content.

The standard work on Malayan avifauna is "The Birds of the Malay Peninsula" by the late Mr. H.C.Robinson and Mr. F.N.Chasen, an official publication of the Federated Malay States Government. The fifth (and final) volume has not yet been published. This exhaustive work describes in detail all the seven hundred odd forms which have been recorded in the Peninsula from the Isthmus of Kra southwards to Singapore. It is quite invaluable to the serious student; but the beginner is likely to be deterred by its bulk, its price (ten guineas), and its detailed technical descriptions which do not readily assist the amateur to identify a bird in the field.

It was largely the lack of "field descriptions" which decided Messrs A.T.Edgar, V.W.Ryves and myself to write a simple, yet comprehensive, book, in one profusely illus- -trated volume, which would be an adequate guide to the birds of British Malaya. Though Mr. Ryves has now retired to Africa, and though recent events have resulted in a cataclysmic loss of material, I adhere to the hope that the projected book will appear within the next ten years. That being so, there is no reason why this

Introduction to Malayan Birds also should be unleashed upon a Malayan public which is likely to find its hands very fully occupied with more essential matters for some time to come. Therefore it will be confined to one (Changi) edition, of which this will be the only copy!

Let me apologise in advance for any errors or omis- -sions in this booklet. Luckier than most of my fellows, I have managed to save a small fraction of my bird notes, and they have proved of considerable value. For the rest, I have had to rely largely on my memory and the memories of the Changi Ornithological Study Group. Last but by no means least, I have borrowed freely from The Birds of the Malay Peninsula, particularly in the composition of field descriptions. No doubt I have infringed the copyright of the F.M.S. Government by referring constantly to the excellent illustrations in their publication - an additional reason why this book should be withheld from circulation in the great outside world!

My acknowledgements are due to Dr. B.D.Molesworth for his excellent illustrations and diagrams, and for most patient assistance and advice; to Dr. C.A.Gibson- -Hill for his help in compiling the definitions in Appendix A; to the binders; and - not least - to the kind gentleman who has lent me his typewriter, and whose identity must remain a secret lest he be overwhelmed by the many machineless typists in Changi.

Changi   G.C.MADOC

                                              May, 1943

When it came out the book proved very popular with the inmates and whenever a prisoner spotted a bird, they would consult with it. (*Fenella Madoc-Davis*)

The Black-necked Tailor-bird.

The illustrations for the book were done by a third POW, B. David Molesworth, who was a medical doctor before the war and ran a leprosarium. (*Fenella Madoc-Davis*)

The Black and Red Broadbill.

The artist materials used by Molesworth to illustrate the book were smuggled into the camp by prisoners sent to clear the wreckage from the war-torn city. (*Fenella Madoc-Davis*)

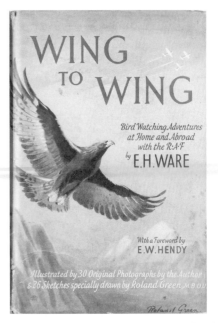

For E.H. Ware, a wireless mechanic in the RAF, birdwatching was a way of surviving service life and whiling away the long hours on duty. He got to 'study birds in two continents and five countries at the Government's expense'. (*Author's collection*)

Ware wrote *Wing to Wing* 'during spells of night duty'. It was published in 1946 with the subtitle *Bird Watching Adventures at Home and Abroad with the RAF*. The book celebrated birds but also the work of the RAF's unsung heroes – its ground crew. (*Author's collection*)

Alan Francis Brooke was the head of the British Army during the Second World War and was the principal military advisor to Winston Churchill (here having his portrait painted by Reginald Eves on 30 April 1940). To forget about Churchill and the immense responsibility, he filmed birds which soon became his war hobby. (*E. G. Malindine*)

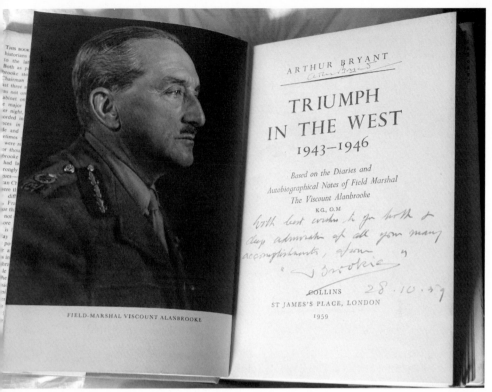

FIELD-MARSHAL VISCOUNT ALANBROOKE

ARTHUR BRYANT

TRIUMPH
IN THE WEST
1943–1946

Based on the Diaries and
Autobiographical Notes of Field Marshal
The Viscount Alanbrooke
K.G., O.M

COLLINS
ST JAMES'S PLACE, LONDON
1959

Alan Brooke found Churchill almost impossible to work with, his love of birds providing him with solace and the will to carry on. He published his diaries in 1957 and 1959 with the journalist Arthur Bryant but they were heavily redacted due to their criticism of Churchill. (*Author's collection*)

Peter Scott was an accomplished artist, fanatical wildfowler and Olympic sportsman. In 1931 he went to hear Adolf Hitler speak at the Bürgerbräukeller in Munich and was 'duly roused'. (*Scott family*)

The author in Scott's library. In 1946 after the war Scott established the Wildfowl and Wetlands Trust at Slimbridge and later helped to found the World Wide Fund for Nature. (*Author's collection*)

Scott's first wife, Elizabeth Jane Howard, was 17 when they met and was 'unsure of herself, of her worth and her intelligence'. With Scott away all the time fighting the war in the navy, she took up writing. (*Howard family*)

Scott's first bird hide was a three-tier pill-box which had been built to deter a German invasion in 1940. (*Author's collection*)

Welcome to Sir Peter Scott's first bird hide

This type 26 pill box was built in WWII as a look-out for enemy invasion on the Severn Estuary.

It has thick walls and open slots for rifles and light machine guns. The sea wall was behind the pill box in those days, so the view of the Severn was really clear. (The sea wall was rebuilt in its current position in 1990).

In 1946 Peter Scott started his Wildfowl Trust at Slimbridge. This little structure with its open slots, made it a great place to watch birds without disturbing them. The three pillboxes along this section of river became the first Slimbridge bird hides. Scott would later modify one to have extra storeys for even better views.

Of the 28,000 pill boxes built in the war fewer than 7,000 remain today.

The plaque on the side of Scott's first bird hide. (*Author's collection*)

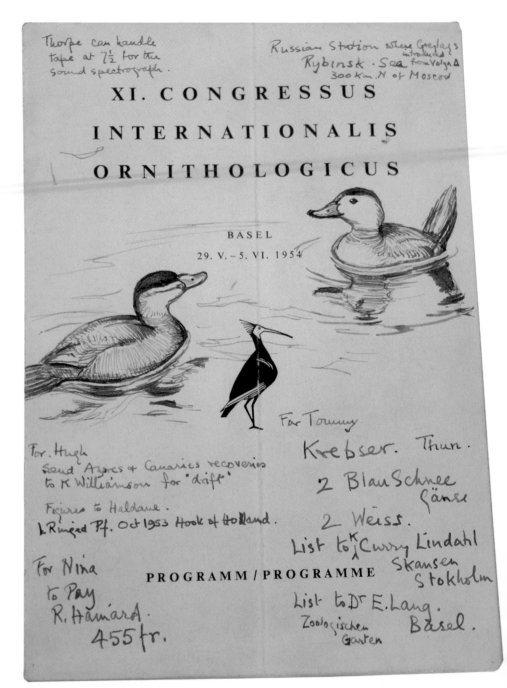

XI. CONGRESSUS

INTERNATIONALIS

ORNITHOLOGICUS

BASEL

29. V. – 5. VI. 1954

Thorpe can handle tape at 7½ for the sound spectrograph.

Russian Station where Greylags introduced Rybinsk · Sea from Volga 300 km. N of Moscow

For Hugh
Send Azores & Canaries recoveries to K Williamson for "drift".

Figures to Haldane.
L Ringed Pf. Oct 1953 Hook of Holland.

For Nina
to Pay
R. Hanard.
455 fr.

PROGRAMM / PROGRAMME

For Tommy.

Krebser. Thun.

2 Blau Schnee Gänse

2 Weiss.

List to Curry Lindahl Skansen Stokholm

List to Dr E. Lang.
Zoologischen Garten
Basel.

In May 1954 Scott joined over 600 other ornithologists from 40 countries around the world at the 11th International Ornithological Congress held in Basel, Switzerland. The biggest delegation came not from Britain but Germany, birds not only serving in the war but also helping to build the peace. (*Wildfowl and Wetlands Trust collection*) natural history. On Wednesday, 11 August 1943 Allan recorded in her diary, 'Our Monday night lectures are a real treat – Mr Gibson-Hill on Evolution and Modern Man.'

Incarcerated for most of the day in his cell, or made to do hard labour, Gibson-Hill, like many prisoners, became severely depressed at his predicament. He tried to write up his paper on the Cocos-Keeling islands but found it an almost impossible task as he was constantly monitored by the guards and liable to be beaten if caught writing. The one part of the day he looked forward to was the roll call and daily exercise in the courtyard. Here he could breathe the air, see the sky, and if he was lucky, spot a bird as it flew over the prison or see a sparrow, munia or tailorbird in the yard. It was here that Gibson-Hill met two other ornithologists who were to transform his time behind bars and become lifelong friends: Guy Charles Madoc and B. David Molesworth.

Madoc (1911–1999) was born on the Isle of Man where his father was Chief Constable and at twenty moved to Malaysia. Following in his father's footsteps, after training in Kuala Lumpur he worked for the Colonial Police Force of Malaya, in the remote rural district of Jelebu. When not upholding the law Madoc was an avid ornithologist and egg collector, submitting all his records to Raffles museum. In 1939 he discovered an unidentified variant of the blue rock thrush. Believing it to be a new subspecies, he submitted a paper to Chasen at the museum. The new record was accepted and so the bird was named Madoc's blue rock thrush, *Monticola solitarius madoci*. (The original male bird that he shot and stuffed for identification is still on display at the Lee Kong Chian Natural History Museum in Singapore.)

Following the fall of the city, Madoc was not immediately interned but was used by the Japanese occupying forces to keep law and order. He and other members of the Colonial Police Force were issued with armbands and for three weeks patrolled the city. They found that the Japanese forces regarded them with surprising deference, often stepping off the pavement to allow them to pass. Only later did they discover that the armbands identified them as members of the *Kempeitai*, the dreaded Japanese secret police. After the real *Kempeitai* arrived in force Madoc was transferred to Changi, also smuggling his bird notes into the prison. The third ornithologist, Molesworth, was a medical doctor who, before he was incarcerated, ran a leprosarium (hospital for people with leprosy) in the city of Sungai Buloh in Selangor. He was also a talented bird illustrator and photographer who shared Madoc's love of ornithology, his work gracing many handbooks and guides on the region.

Gibson-Hill, Madoc and Molesworth together formed the Changi Ornithological Study Group, a unique birdwatching club in the annals of ornithological history because all its members were incarcerated behind bars during wartime. Unable to birdwatch, Madoc instead decided to produce a bird book using the notes he had smuggled into Changi (he had been planning a book before the war with two other colleagues but they had fled when hostilities broke out). The 146-page *An Introduction to Malayan Birds* was written by Madoc, illustrated by Molesworth, with appendices by Gibson-Hill and had a print run of one. The book was started in March 1942 and published in May 1943 on paper stolen from Okasaki's filing cabinet by a prisoner friend who cleaned his office. It was produced on a 'portable typewriter' borrowed from another inmate and bound in red leatherette by two French prisoners, the cover having been ripped from the seats of a wrecked car by Madoc.[7] The art materials used by Molesworth to illustrate the book were smuggled into the camp by prisoners sent to clear the wreckage from the war-torn city (after the war two further editions of the book were produced and it is now a standard text on Malayan birds). In the foreword, Madoc wrote:

> Within these four walls so much interest has been displayed in Malayan birds that I have felt encouragement to write this little book. Though I hope that the reader may find some matters of interest in it, a desire to enlighten my fellow-prisoners has not been the sole incentive to authorship. Its composition has enabled me to jot down many facts of which I no longer possess written record, and to crystallize and sift my knowledge. If my readers derive from a perusal of these pages one third of the benefit that I have gleaned during its production, I shall be well content.

When it came out the book proved very popular with the inmates, and whenever a prisoner spotted a bird they would consult with it, the book doing the rounds in both the men's and women's cell blocks. As a result Madoc was invited to lecture on birds and was even permitted to give a talk to the women's camp. During one presentation he caused considerable consternation when he imitated the song of the helmeted hornbill by doing a series of hoots building to a crescendo. The guard, feeling threatened, leapt to his feet, brandished his bayonet and bellowed at Madoc to stop.

The writing of books in the prison, even innocuous ones such as bird books, was, like the keeping of a diary, strictly prohibited. Despite this, prisoners did both and on 10 October 1943 the *Kempeitai* arrived unannounced at the gaol following a guerilla attack on the city and searched every cell. Allan, who like so many of the inmates was suffering from malaria, recorded their visit the next day in her secret diary which she had hidden between her school books, praying it wouldn't be found. 'Yesterday's episode is now being referred to as the "Double Tenth" – the day the Japanese Kemp-Tai (Secret Military Police) descended on Civilian Internment Camp. They were sure they would find a spy ring, transmitters etc with the idea that we were going to sabotage the Island of Singapore. The result – 28 men were taken away and a couple of women. Even the Bishop of Singapore was included. They were taken away to be questioned and tortured I guess. We don't know what exactly is to become of them.'

By early 1944 conditions in Changi prison had deteriorated markedly with food and medical supplies being in very short supply. As part of the increased security following the attacks on Singapore, Japanese guards now regularly patrolled the women's as well as the men's blocks. Although relations between female prisoners and guards were strictly prohibited, some women still traded sexual favours for cigarettes, food or medicines, and fights often broke out if someone was accused of 'prostituting' herself. Other women, through having so little to wear, attracted the unwanted attention of the guards. For a young girl like Allan, the atmosphere was constantly threatening. She recorded in her diary how one of her fellow inmates tried to use a humorous letter to encourage all the women to cover up.

For whom it may concern (present and future). The following letter has been received from a member of this Camp. It voices the feelings of many – "Long internment seems to have exhausted many people's resources in the clothing department and the Scantiest of Scanties and the Flimsiest of Panties have been evolved to meet the needs of the moment and to stave as long as possible the day when Changi of necessity becomes a Nudist Colony. Until that evil day arrives could it be suggested that now sentries are in the Camp at all hours and we have no privacy, the more frail of undergarments should be discreetly veiled when doing chores such as ironing and only worn without covering when inside one's cell. We have no orders from the Nipponese as to what we should or should not wear 'below the waist' but they did mention 'Suntops as being inadequate'."[8]

The awful conditions at Changi took a deadly toll on the weaker or ill prisoners, Allan recording in her diary the death of many friends. However, in the spring of 1944 rumours began to circulate that they were going to be moved, and on 7 May 1944 all the prisoners at Changi were rounded up and transported to another camp in nearby Sime Road. Allan recorded the event in her diary: 'New Camp! Left Changi Prison about half past 2 this afternoon – in 7 lorries – men helped with luggage – gave hot tea to drink. A lovely, cool ride but not long enough. Fresh air – green, green everywhere – everything looks so normal!'

The camp was the former headquarters of the British Army and the RAF in Singapore and had been holding thousands of POWs, including men who had worked on the infamous Burma or 'Death' Railway. Due to the number of repeated escape attempts the Japanese had decided the POWs should swap places with the civilians in Changi prison as it was deemed a far more secure site for holding troublesome prisoners. For the long-suffering Allied soldiers the move must have come as another severe blow to their morale, but to the civilians, especially Gibson-Hill, the change was a literal breath of fresh air. Unlike Changi, the new camp was outside and although still chronically overcrowded and squalid, it was equipped with two hospitals and a garden for growing vegetables. For Allan the new camp meant a new hut and new sleeping companions. She recorded in her diary on 13 May 1944: 'At last moved (officially) to Hut 1 – it's smaller than the others but it has a verandah and I've claimed a space there. Hope there won't be too much windy, wet weather – I could get a bit wet but at least I won't be disturbed by too many people and I'll be able to write without too many questions being asked. I think I shall sleep well tonight.'

After Changi the new camp must have seemed like paradise for Gibson-Hill – it gave him not only the opportunity to write, but much more importantly, to birdwatch. Surrounded by scrub and jungle, the camp was regularly visited by a variety of birds typical of the surrounding villages and gardens. These included barbets, bulbuls, cuckoos, cuckoo-shrikes, doves, flycatchers, flowerpeckers, hoopoes, kingfishers, magpie robins, munias, orioles, owls, sparrows, starlings, sunbirds, swallows, swifts, tailorbirds and woodpeckers. In the trees there were roosting fruit bats and at night the camp echoed to the haunting sound of them leaving to hunt en masse, as well as the strange 'tok-tok-tok' call of long-tailed nightjars.

As most of his original notes on his visit to the Cocos-Keeling islands had been lost, Gibson-Hill now decided to dedicate himself to making an in-depth study of two of the most common species occurring at the camp – the Malayan long-tailed tailorbird and the spotted munia. Both nested in the camp grounds and allowed close observation, carrying on with their lives seemingly oblivious to much of the chaos going on in the camp around them.

Gibson-Hill spent most of his free time watching the birds, writing down any and every piece of information on them on tiny scraps of paper which he hid in his hut. He also made detailed line drawings of the nest, eggs and chicks. It was a remarkable achievement, particularly as he was frequently watched by the guards, which often prevented close inspection of the nests. After the war in 1950 Gibson-Hill wrote up both monographs in the *Bulletin of Raffles Museum*, each species account stretching to fifteen pages. In his introduction to the long-tailed tailorbird (*Orthotomus sutorius*) he wrote:

> The longtailed tailor-bird occurs widely throughout the lowlands and foothills of the Malay States. Its favourite haunts are areas of scrub vegetation, gardens and orchards. In these and similar habitats it is the commonest of the tailor-birds in the western states at least, and on the islands of Penang and Singapore. It is by no means a shy bird and freely takes up breeding territories in gardens inside the municipal limits of the larger towns. The greater part of the original field data recorded here was obtained in the Sime Road Internment Camp, on Singapore Island, in 1944-45; the remainder has been gathered subsequently in the Tanglin district of the town.[9]

In the case of the spotted munia (*Lonchura punctulata*), Gibson-Hill plotted all the nests throughout the camp, recording ten in total. Each of these he faithfully sketched and reproduced in his paper to show the different shaped nests the bird made. He also discovered that occasionally a male bird enticed two hens to lay in the same nest, commenting, 'one is a nest taken on 4 July 1944 which contained 5 fledglings about 80 mm long and 2 fresh eggs; the other taken on 14 April 1945 contained 4 fledglings about 84 mm long and 3 apparent fresh eggs.' This was the first time that double clutching had been recorded in the species, a new behaviour that it would only have been possible to record with sustained observation.[10]

When not watching birds Gibson-Hill helped out at the men's hospital trying to treat the bewildering and shocking range of diseases which ravaged those in the camp. One of those he treated was Allan's father who had malaria and dysentery, both conditions exasperated by hard labour and a very poor diet. As a result he had grown increasingly frail and depressed at his predicament, and his daughter became very concerned for his mental and physical health. Following the transfer to the Sime Road Camp, Sheila Allan had decided that after the war she wanted to be a nurse to help ill people like her father so she had started volunteering at the women's hospital. On Friday, 26 May 1944 she wrote clandestinely to Gibson-Hill, whom she had given the nickname 'Shakespeare' because of his love of the Bard, asking for his help in treating her ailing father. She recorded in her diary: 'Despatched letter to "Shakespeare" [Gibson-Hill] in Dads letter … Evening received letter from Dad saying he knew of Shakespeare – disapprove of the separation [of the letters] and to be careful of name [the Japanese often being suspicious of nicknames, believing them to be code words associated with escape attempts].

Gibson-Hill wrote back from Hut 40 in the men's camp saying he would do what he could for her father. Allan received the letter on Saturday, 3 June 1944. (It seems likely that Allan had developed a crush on Gibson-Hill, an unlikely teenage heart-throb. She commented in her diary that day: 'wonder if I should secretly try to see him. Aunty Maud teasing me but paying no attention – somehow feel relieved that he is married.')

As the war entered its final phase Allan again wrote to 'Shakespeare', asking if he would continue to keep an eye out for her father. On Sunday, 17 June 1944 she was told that her father had been diagnosed with pellagra (a disease caused by a lack of the vitamin B3; symptoms include inflamed skin, diarrhoea, dementia and sores in the mouth). To help, he was prescribed Marmite and excused from the daily work party in the camp. Like many prisoners, Allan also found herself laid low with malaria, for which she was taking large doses of quinine, recording in her diary that she had temperature of 103–104°F.

By the summer of 1944 Gibson-Hill, Allan and the other inmates were so hungry that they spent long periods trying to find or barter for food, even the less palatable local wildlife being considered fair game. As the birds were hard to catch, and out of bounds because of Gibson-Hill's research, Allan tried eating earthworms but couldn't bring herself to swallow them whole, instead deciding to cook them, commenting on Saturday, 15 July 1944, 'All that was left after the cooking were thin strips of dried-up skins – not appetising – but hunger took over – took a bit of a piece – not that bad – a sprinkle of salt and it tasted like bacon rind – well imagine that's how bacon rind would taste – crackly and salty! Did I tell anyone? – No way! They might think I've gone "cuckoo" – eating worms indeed – what next?'

Allan answered her own question five days later, hunger forcing her to eat something that made her physically sick. 'Did a dreadful thing today – thoroughly disgusted with myself – I swallowed a baby mouse! Found a nest of baby mice in the lalang [grass] – so tiny and pink and helpless – I was so very hungry after working in the garden and food was getting scarce. Without thinking I scooped up one and popped it in my mouth and before I realized what I had done, I swallowed it.'

By the end of the summer it was not just lack of food and disease that was taking its toll on the inmates but also the increasing violence of the Japanese guards as the war turned decisively against them. On 26 July 1944 Hugh Fraser, the British Colonial Secretary of the Straits Settlements (including Singapore), who had been taken by the *Kempeitai* in October 1943, was returned to the camp. However, he was close to death after being tortured for months, and died the next day from his injuries. Fraser's death deeply shocked the camp, including Gibson-Hill who joined the other prisoners in making wreaths out of flowers found around the grounds, twenty-one of them being draped over the coffin.

By the autumn of 1944 American B-29 Superfortress bombers were regularly seen over the camp, bringing hope and fear in equal measure to the inhabitants. Allan's father continued to get weaker, and she worried about his deteriorating health and what would happen if she got caught writing her diary. On Tuesday, 5 September she wrote: 'I must be very, very careful that I don't get caught writing this. In fact I don't know how much longer I can continue to write – am having trouble getting another exercise book and have to resort to writing as small as I can – no more ink so looks like I will have to be writing in pencil again.'

By early 1945 rations had been cut to the bone, Allan recording in her diary on Saturday, 10 February 1945: 'Ration cut down – Children 7 ozs; Non-workers 8 ozs; Camp workers 10 ozs and Nip workers 18 ozs.' Two weeks later a large number of B-29s appeared over Singapore causing much excitement in the camp. Allan commented: 'A large "flock" (between 120–130) of silver plumaged birds dropped enormous "eggs" at five places at least – dark mass of smoke rising in a huge column, higher and higher like a great moving snow-capped mountain – below orange sky – it was a grand sight – action at last! Seems like war has come back to Singapore – maybe the Nips (I hope) are getting what's due to them!'

On 15 April 1945 Allan's father was again admitted to the hospital, this time with a cut on his forehead, a black eye and a sore hand. She later learnt that he had been badly beaten up, not by one of the Japanese guards but by one of his fellow inmates after stealing from him. Just as relations in the camp reached breaking point, the next month finally brought some good news. The internees learned that the war in Europe was finally over. Allan recorded on Monday, 14 May 1945: 'News – y – on 7 May – peace treaty with Germans, country divided into four sections – 2 for Russia, I each for Merican and E-land. Army occupation for 10 years. Java and Suma in Br hands – heavy fight in Mau- "birds" to drop "eggs" over Nippon if resist. Food still bad – "Slush and Ash" as some call it.'

By helping others in the hospital and always being upbeat despite the dreadful conditions, Allan was popular in the camp and counted many of the elder women as her friends. Despite this, having an Australian father and a Malayan mother meant that she still suffered from the casual racism which the British used to denigrate the Japanese. She commented on Monday, 21 May 1945: 'Have been ill all the week – 6th attack [malaria] – nursed in the Hut – everyone very kind – did not go to the meeting [about camp]. Told M [woman in her hut] about Dad and said see what can be done and before she left she said "You will go!" with a look that made my heart leap and I nodded. Am called "That slit-eyed Chink!"'

Just as it looked as though Allan's war was finally coming to an end, tragedy struck. On Saturday, 9 June she was told to rush over to the men's camp because her father had suffered a seizure, but by the time she got there he was dead. In the entry for that day she wrote, 'Dad died today', poignantly adding:

Tried to remember Dad as he was but tears kept clouding my eyes. How I wished I was there before he died and even after death. I would have liked to have been able to touch his face and hold him close to me and to say that I love him and wish him goodbye. Oh, Dad – sorry we were too late to see you. Are you at peace and looking down at us poor mortals? I am going to miss you so oh much – and there is so much I wanted to say but most of all I wanted to say "I love you, Dad. Goodbye – rest in peace, Dad".

Allan's father was taken out to the camp cemetery and promptly buried after a short service, his distraught daughter not even knowing where his grave was located. Gibson-Hill, together with many other members of the camp, sent their condolences, clubbing together to collect food parcels for the teenager and her grieving stepmother. Allan commented remorsefully in her diary, 'Later food parcels were given out – how sad I felt as I opened them and almost choked at the sight of the food, thinking how Dad loved food, always talking about the parcels and so thankful at any extra given. It doesn't matter now as he won't be needing them, again – ever again!'

Despite the food parcels giving temporary respite, hunger was now endemic in the camp and at the end of July 1945 Allan recorded bitterly that the 'Nip workers get Camp workers ration too'. By now both she and Gibson-Hill were severely emaciated, the result of malaria, dysentery and hunger. At last, on Thursday, 16 August, Allan recorded in her diary: 'STOP PRESS The latest – great excitement POWs spoke to Hut 1- "War over on 15th". Our military is taking over on 20th. 4 delegates and Stanley Jones [1888-1962, former Colonial Secretary of Straits Settlements before Hugh Fraser] are on their way to take over on 24th.'

On Monday, 24 August the church bells rang out across Singapore. Allan wrote, 'Heard Church bells. PEACE! Saw our planes – a lovely sight and flying low. Felt both sad and happy. Roll Call – Yamato [Camp Commandant] spoke – said in charge – to behave – keep what we think in our hearts – when he goes can do as we like! Chinese sending in eggs, butter, milk. Chinese living outside killed two pigs and threw them into the Camp to us.'

On Friday, 24 August Allan recorded the end of the war in the Far East in her diary with the chilling words: 'Read circular about Emperor's speech – said he declared war on 14th December 1941 in their interest – millions have died by the new invention of bomb – the Atomic Bombs – needed two to end the war – one completely wiped out one island.'

On Monday, 3 September 1945 the Union Jack was again hoisted over Singapore, and on Wednesday, 12 September 1945 a victory parade was held in the city, the Japanese formally surrendering to Lord Mountbatten (1900–1979, Supreme Allied commander of the Southeast Asia Theatre) on the steps of the municipal offices. That night, Allan, Gibson-Hill, Madoc, Molesworth and all the other prisoners cheered, danced and sang themselves hoarse, Allan stating, 'Time stood still as we let our hair down – for a moment we forgot those 3½ years as we went into a frenzy of dancing singing – we are FREE, FREE, FREE! AT LAST!'

For Allan, the end of the war and her release from the Sime Road camp was both an intensely exciting and daunting time. The camp had been her whole life for the last three-and-a-half years, and during that time she had gone from being an awkward teenager to a confident twenty-one-year-old. She wrote: 'Crying because we are free – crying because soon we'll be saying goodbye to the friends we've made in this "Hell-hole" – tears and more tears – we hugged each other and we gave in to joyous laughter. How does one describe this feeling – something wonderful – touching, sad and yet joyous – oh, it's hard to describe this emotion that we all feel!'

For Gibson-Hill, the end of his time at the Sime Road camp must have seemed like the end of a prolonged nightmare. However, he left having made two lifelong friends in Madoc and Molesworth, and with a bundle of tiny pieces of paper in which he had recorded the most intimate details of two birds occupying the camp, the long-tailed tailorbird and the spotted munia. Despite all the depravations and the cruelty of his Japanese captors, Gibson-Hill had continued with his ornithological research.

After her release from the Sime Road camp, Allan went on to become a nurse, in 1946 starting her training at the Queen Victoria Memorial

Hospital for Women, graduating in 1949. She worked in country hospitals until 1958, afterwards settling down in Sydney and marrying Frank Bruhn, with whom she had a son and daughter. In 1992 she went back to Singapore for the fiftieth anniversary of the fall of the city, where she located her father's grave and marked it with a plaque. Learning that the cemetery was to be developed, she took her father's remains back with her to Australia. Two years later in 1994 she published her story with the title *Diary of a Girl in Changi*, dedicating the book 'To my father's memory and to those internees who shared my life during those three and a half years in Changi Prison and Sime Road Camp'. In 1996 her husband Frank died and she remains in retirement in Sydney where she is a proud grandmother.

For Gibson-Hill release meant the opportunity to travel, and a few months later he set off on a whaling vessel to South Georgia where he photographed the wildlife and collected specimens for the Falkland Island Museum. True to form, Gibson-Hill went on to publish several papers about it and to add books on the region to his extensive personal library. Afterwards he returned to England on an oil tanker where he worked as health officer, finally being reunited with his wife, Margaret, in March 1946. Back at home he published two books on seabirds before returning to Singapore in 1947 where he once again took up the post of Assistant Curator of Zoology at Raffles Museum. Here he dedicated his time to collecting and photographing Malayan culture and expanding the museum's bird and animal collections. He also continued with his bird research, publishing a prolific series of papers and books on Malayan birdlife right up to his retirement and death in 1963. His collaborations included papers with his two fellow internees at Changi and Sime Road, Madoc and Molesworth, who also added their own contributions to the bird collection at Raffles.

After his release, Madoc returned to Britain for four months, but the lure of Southeast Asia and its birds drew him back to Malaysia where he rejoined the police, retiring in 1959. He then came back to Britain and settled in his native Isle of Man where he spent the next forty years birdwatching, motorcycling (including being a marshal at the island's famous TT race) and gardening. He died in 1999 of a stroke. After his death his daughter, Fenella Madoc-Davis, donated much of his notes to the British Natural History Museum but still retains the original copy of

An Introduction to Malayan Birds produced in Changi. Molesworth also returned to his old job at the leprosy hospital and made a significant contribution to ornithology in the region, helping with Madoc to found the Singapore branch of the Malayan Nature Society in 1954.

The story of the creation of the Changi Ornithological Study Group was mirrored in Europe when in 1941 four British soldiers started an ornithological society in a German prisoner-of-war camp near Warburg. 'In the summer of 1940,' wrote the ornithologist and commando John Buxton (1912–1989), 'lying in the sun near a Bavarian river, I saw a family of redstarts, unconcerned in the affairs of our skeletal multitude, going about their ways in cherry and chestnut trees [...] the next spring came, and with it the first returning redstarts, I determined that these birds should be my study for most of the hours I might spend out of doors.'[11] Buxton decided to study the redstarts, and with other POWs, including the future director of the RSPB, Peter Condor (1919–1993), and the ornithologists George Waterson (1911-1980) and John Barrett (1913-1999), would use the research to survive the squalor, brutality and stupefying boredom of the camp.[12] In 1950 Buxton published his seminal work 'The Redstart', the second in the *New Naturalist* series, based largely on his wartime experiences.

Despite the austerity of postwar Britain, the book was published in conditions which couldn't have been more different from those of Changi prison. So it seems unlikely that the remarkable story of how during wartime three prisoners published a bird book under the noses of their brutal captors will ever be emulated.

Chapter 7

Wing to Wing

Writing bird books was not only a way of surviving imprisonment but also whiling away the long hours on duty. *Wing to Wing* by E.H. Ware was published in 1946 with the subtitle *Bird Watching Adventures at Home and Abroad with the RAF*.[1] It is a book celebrating birds but also the work of the RAF's unsung heroes – its ground crews. *Wing to Wing* reveals what life was like for ordinary service personnel during the Second World War, written not by an officer or a pilot but by a wireless mechanic and ornithologist. It tells the story of signing up, the discipline of training, the excitement of a posting overseas, engaging with the enemy, the prospect of dying, the longing for leave and above all the long periods of boredom, all made bearable by a love of birds.

Born in 1907, Ware inherited his love of birdwatching from his father, collecting eggs in his youth and in 1935 buying a camera to photograph birds. At the outset of the conflict he began writing his book, using thirty of his own photographs to illustrate it. Ware believed that his service with the RAF during the Second World War would have been a 'colossal waste of time' had it not been used to 'study birds in two continents and five countries at the Government's expense,' and to write *Wing to Wing* which he did 'during spells of night duty'.

The foreword was written by the author Ernest William Hendry (1872–1950), a man who eschewed scientific ornithology in favour of populist bird books. He wrote, 'It is not just "another bird book" – still less is it a war book – but a book that will appeal not only to those who have learnt the charm of birds, but also to the general readers [...] Nor is this a scientific treatise of interest only to a minority of expert ornithologists, but a very human, and at times humorous account of the author's experiences at home and aboard.' *Wing to Wing* was illustrated by Roland Green (1890–1972), a Norfolk artist who for the jacket painted a picture of a golden eagle rising majestically up to challenge intruding enemy planes, which, according to the cover flap, 'symbolises the title of the book'.

Ware's book starts on 26 August 1940 with him on a train to RAF Cardington in Bedfordshire where he would begin his training as a wireless mechanic. A keen amateur radio ham, he had signed up following a broadcast appeal for people to join the RAF by Air Marshal Philip Joubert de la Ferté (1887–1965), a veteran Great War pilot who was then in charge of RAF Coastal Command. Looking out of the train window as the countryside rushed by, Ware had reflected on the first year of war. He was particularly annoyed that the German breakthrough at Sedan in May 1940, which would lead to the fall of France, had rudely interrupted his plans for a fortnight's holiday on the island of Skomer studying seabirds.

Encapsulating the Blitz spirit, Ware refused to let Hitler or his threatened invasion of Britain get in the way of his holiday plans, commenting, 'So on the very day that the sign-posts came down all over the country [in case of invasion], the trunkful of provisions, and our baggage, and a portable wireless set, and my quarter-plate camera with its accessories, and my hide for bird photography, were all somehow transported to Martinshaven, piled into the waiting boat and safely carried across to that avian paradise, Skomer Island [...] What a haven, – no, heaven – in the midst of war that had been!'

Now Ware was in the RAF and what he feared most was that signing up would mean an end to his beloved hobby of birdwatching. He wrote in his diary, 'Soon this [his holiday], and all my bird-watching, would be but a memory, I thought, for this very night would see me in the RAF. This day the war, for me, had started.' In fact, the RAF and the war would not see the end of Ware's birdwatching but the start of an exciting new adventure with opportunities to birdwatch both at home and abroad. But he did not know that at the time of signing up, or where the fortunes of war would take him. So he resigned himself to his fate and on arrival at RAF Cardington was pleasantly impressed with the RAF's selection procedures. He described the air base as a 'huge sorting-machine' into which came 'dukes and dustmen, earls and engine drivers, courtiers and criminals. I shall never forget the mixture sleeping in my dormitory that first night: from the quiet youth kneeling in prayer by his bedside to the two raw East-Enders who, by their language, must surely have been Billingsgate fish-porters.'

Following a month's hard 'square bashing' at another RAF base in Morecambe, Ware had been posted to his first operational unit, a new RAF signal station at Braintree in Essex. He had been dreading a sprawling concrete base with not a bird in sight, but upon arrival at his new posting was again pleasantly surprised: 'It was built in a rather marshy grass field in a very pleasant situation, being – most unusual for a wireless station – almost surrounded by trees. Between it and the main road was a tumble-down country house, whose overgrown and tree-filled garden proved to be a paradise for birds. Needless to say, it was not long before I had applied for, and received permission to wander there at will.'

Ware arrived at the RAF signal station in September 1940, just after the Battle of Britain but before the Blitz on London and other British cities. There he found himself surrounded by both professional and amateur radio engineers who, like him, had come straight from basic training but knew nothing about soldiering. Not only were there not enough arms to go round, but when they did arrive most of the men didn't know how to fire a rifle. As it was a small station, Ware was allocated a private billet so his wife was able to join him. On the night she arrived, however, the station was bombed: 'Jerry welcomed her by dropping a stick of six bombs less than two hundred yards from the house. Apart from denting a perfectly good tennis court they did little damage, but were a good foretaste of what that bomb-torn winter was to bring.'

Ware's billet backed onto fields and at the bottom of his garden he had a fence supported by stout posts. Over the next two years he collated a garden list which would be the envy of many birders. Some of the more unusual birds to grace his fence included a goshawk and a red-backed shrike which would 'sally forth flycatcher-fashion after winged insects, bumble bees, cockchafers etc returning to the post, or flying off with them to its nest.' (The red-backed shrike went extinct as a British breeding species in 1988, although there have been sporadic records since then. It is interesting to note how common it was in 1940.)

Ware did not confine his birdwatching to his leisure time, but also kept his eyes peeled and ears open when he was at work. He had instant access to his binoculars which were kept inside the station control-room in case German planes appeared. However, Ware turned out to be much better at identifying birds than he did enemy planes: 'We used to see them, squadrons of them, high in the sky making for London by the back door as it were. We had no A.A. [Anti-Aircraft] weapons at that time. Perhaps it was as well, for aircraft recognition was not our strong point. I well remember one afternoon of low cloud and heavy showers. The sound of a nearby plane caused us to rush for the door (strictly against orders). "It's all right, it's only a Hampden," shouted someone. Just then down came a stick of bombs. It was a Dornier!'

In contrast to hostile war birds, the real birds brought nothing but joy to Ware and the station crew. One day, after a thunderstorm which silenced all the birds around the station, a nightingale began to sing: 'On and on it sang, as if its very throat would burst. On and on, unaccompanied, unrivalled: the peerless singer held the stage in the heat of day as surely and as clearly as it does at night. Encore after encore it gave, until, one by one, as if shamed by the fearlessness of their little brown rival, the daylight musicians took up their parts, and once more the full orchestra was in possession of the stage.'

Ware also went birdwatching on his '48s' or 'a 295 for 48 hours' or, put more simply, two days off duty, using the opportunity to go further afield. On one of these sorties in May 1941 he went to the Norfolk Brecks, marvelling at the stone curlew: 'weight on one yellow leg, other leg bent, with head forward and large yellow eye most conspicuous, it was unmistakable. Seeing me it ran off, then took wing, to be joined almost immediately by its mate.' Searching for the nest, Ware nearly trod on the eggs because they were so well camouflaged against the flint-strewn sand. On another occasion he went to Hickling Broad where he visited both a Montagu's harrier and a marsh harrier nest with his RAF group captain, the warden, Jim Vincent (1883–1944, Ware dedicating his book to him), and the erudite editor of *British Birds* journal, Harry Forbes Witherby (1873–1943). Together they tracked down a range of reed bed speciality birds including the bearded tit and the bittern. The only disappointment was that the male bearded tit was looking bedraggled in the rain and was not, in Ware's words, the 'Beau Brummell of the Broads'. Later that evening the renowned bird photographer Eric Hosking stopped by Vincent's home to talk about birds and photography, the session going on into the small hours. Feeling overwhelmed by the esteemed company, the 'tyro' Ware commented, 'I sat at the feet of the masters, metaphorically speaking, and listened and learned a great deal. It was indeed, for me, a memorable evening.'

In June 1942 Ware and his wife visited the Highlands of Scotland, taking advantage of seven days' leave and cheap service travel to go birdwatching and forget the war. Ware's first impressions of Scotland were not good as his hotel served him a very poor breakfast: 'porridge with no milk and dried eggs, plain, for which they charged 4s. 6d. each!' Ware and his wife spent the next week cycling around the Cairngorms and ticking off a range of Highland speciality birds, including the crested tit, golden eagle, dotterel, ptarmigan, black-throated diver and the Slavonian grebe, but not the capercaillie, 'so the capercaillie remains the one bird of the Highlands which I have yet to find.' Yet even in one of the remotest places in Britain Ware could not totally escape the war. As he was trekking through Rothiemurchus his wife, Margaret, came across an adder coiled in the heather, and then, 'a full-strength Indian frontier regiment went by in single file, complete with loaded pack-mules, small guns of all descriptions, medical units etc., with a real bearded Indian warrior every fourth man or so.'

The Indian regiment Ware stumbled upon was known as Force K6 and was recruited from the British Indian Army. It was made up of over 1,800 soldiers and over 2,000 animals, the mules being trained as pack carriers or to tow two-wheeled carts. The soldiers were drawn from a wide variety of faiths including Hindu, Sikh and Christian but the vast majority were Muslim. They had been part of the British Expeditionary Force in May 1940 and were evacuated at Dunkirk, afterwards being trained in mountain warfare. Moving to Inverness-shire from Wales, K6 had a camp at Aviemore and their HQ at nearby Grantown-on-Spey. During the training exercises in the hills, when Ware met them, nine men tragically lost their lives. They were all from animal transport mule companies and came from modern-day Pakistan (then part of India), some dying from accidents on exercise, others from illnesses such as tuberculosis, while two took their own lives (the reason for the death of so many men during training has never been properly explained).[2]

In late 1942, together with 4,500 other army personnel, Ware was packed off on a troopship at Liverpool bound for Algiers (although he didn't know the destination at the time). Algeria, and much of North Africa, had been under the control of Nazi Germany and Vichy France until the Allies had launched the first major offensive of the war – codenamed Operation Torch – on 8 November 1942. Led by the US

General Dwight D. (David) Eisenhower (1890–1969) they launched a three-pronged attack on Casablanca, Oran and Algiers against an army of 60,000 Vichy troops. By 16 November the Allies had recaptured Morocco along with Algeria, establishing a base for the liberation of Northern Africa.

Ware recorded the voyage in his diary: 'Steaming north all night the morning found us off the west coast of Scotland, and here we were joined by our destroyer escort and another group of troopships, the whole making up quite a considerable convoy [...] Later in the afternoon we turned west, and steamed far out into the Atlantic before swinging south having avoided, we hoped, the U-boats that haunted the west coast of Ireland.' For the next nine days Ware steamed south and then west, recording his life on board. He soon found out that being on a crowded troopship bound for an unknown destination was no pleasure cruise. After having been woken at the crack of dawn by a sergeant yelling, 'Show a leg', he had his face trodden on by the soldier in the bunk above him as he scrambled to get dressed. When not working or keeping watch, Ware spent most of his time queuing for everything from wash bowls to the library.

As they approached the coast of Spain there was an air-raid alarm. Dashing outside, Ware found the decks deserted so went back to his warm bunk, being careful not to wake the man above in case he got trodden on again. The next day he learnt that the accompanying ship in the convoy, the *Windsor Castle*, had been torpedoed and sunk by a U-boat. The following morning his troopship finally sailed into Algiers Bay, 'zig-zagging slowly through the minefields'. The voyage had not only been dangerous, it had also been bad for birdwatching, Ware recording only a few seabirds en route. His meagre list was not helped by the fact that he had left his binoculars at the bottom of his kit-bag as he had not been sure how a birdwatcher on board would be received by his fellow crew. 'I, for one, was extremely relieved when it was over,' he wrote in his diary.

Ware's first impressions of Algiers reflected those of a novice traveller and the prejudices of the time. Arriving by sea he saw it as a city of contrasts, but still had to equate it to home, describing it as a 'sort of super-Clovelly, or an eastern Torquay.' However, on closer inspection Ware found Algiers less than appealing: 'Here was a town at first sight clean and white and modern, with many of its buildings almost sky-scrapers by English standards; yet in its very heart the Casbah (the native quarter) was a filthy, overbuilt and overcrowded slum. To call it that is to pay it a compliment.' Exploring the bustling streets he found the contrasts even more pronounced, recording 'ultra-smart French girls with perfect, if artificial, complexions, jostled in the queues with heavily-veiled Arab women draped in the inevitable white sheet (or what looked like a white sheet to me!).'

The one saving grace was that their camp was on a wide sandy beach at Hussein Dey, so after guard duty Ware explored the surrounding coast looking for birds. Here he saw hundreds of gulls including his first little gull, Kentish and ringed plovers, black terns and a bird that was 'a cross between a buzzard and a gannet'. Unable to identify it, Ware rather facetiously recorded it as a 'gazzard' in his notebook. The bird puzzled him for over a year until a fellow ornithologist, Wilfred Backhouse Alexander (1885–1965), finally identified it from his muddled notes as an Egyptian vulture. Inland, the birds were less exciting, though he did see a woodchat shrike, marvelling at its beauty, and found some scarab beetles, busy recycling dung, that were 'near-relatives of the Sacred Scarabs of Egypt and fully occupied with their unsavoury, but very useful, trade.'

After they had set up their base at Hussein Dey, Ware was sent on guard duty to an RAF store 20 miles away over the Atlas Mountains. The trip was a real eye opener, the coastal plain being dominated by vineyards which stretched away 'row upon row for miles', and contrasted with the imposing mountain range. What really excited Ware, though, were the storks nesting on the top of many of the farms, something that thrilled him 'to the core'. On arriving at the stores, which contained wireless parts and instruments, Ware was delighted to find a stork's nest, not on the roof but in an adjacent tree. 'A huge pile of sticks it was, denoting many years of consecutive use. In its massive sides were the untidy, hay-constructed nests of numerous house sparrows, and on it two white storks [...] What a beautiful flight that of the stork is! Incomparably more graceful than that of the similarly-built heron, it soars with the effortless ease of a buzzard or eagle.'

As word spread about Ware's hobby, RAF personnel soon started consulting him on birds they had seen or bringing him injured ones. One of his officers brought an owl from a local Arab and trained it. Ware commented that 'it soon became very tame, and used to sit on his outstretched finger and go to sleep when he stroked it.' Ware was also left an adult scops owl with a broken wing, which appeared to be almost dead. He later discovered that it was feigning a broken wing (this defensive mechanism against predators is used by owls and other birds like lapwings). However, whenever he attempted to feed the owl it put on its most threatening display, which Ware found comical. 'Crouching down so that its fierce little face with those yellow glaring eyes seemed to be right in the middle of its body, it fluffed all its feathers out till it looked twice its normal size, then started to sway rhythmically from side to side, thus making itself look even bigger. At the same time it snapped its beak constantly with loud and threatening "clicks".' All Ware's attempts to feed the bird proved unsuccessful, so in the end he carried it to a nearby bush-covered hillside and released it.

After completing his tour of guard duty at the stores Ware was reassigned 50 miles east to set up a signal station in a village near the town of Bordj Menaiel beneath a 1,000-ft-high hill. The road to their billet was christened 'the street of a thousand smells' owing to a nearby dung heap combined with the 'heavy odour of cactus,' the 'cloying aroma of mimosa [a member of the pea family],' and the 'sweet scent of eucalyptus trees [the locals used a nearby grove as a latrine]'. Ware was billeted in the local school and soon after arriving visited the local market where he found 'blowsy French women or swarthy Arabs, leading their donkeys as they go. And over all the blazing sun, and the composite smell of unwashed humanity, over-ripe fruit, blood and dirt.'

As with his previous posting, Ware was put on a rota and got every third day off, which gave him the chance to explore the local countryside. Here he found the farming methods had changed little since Biblical times with 'an old wooden plough [...] still being dragged slowly and strainingly along by two oxen.' Bird wise he found western black-eared wheatears among the rocks, and a very elusive warbler which he struggled to identify, recording it in his notebook as a 'white-tailed blackcap.' When he got back to his billet he consulted the only available book on the birds of the region, Ramsay's *Birds of Europe and North Africa*, which his wife had sent him. The trouble was, the book 'merely consisted of a museum description of the skin, with no plates, and no notes on signal marks, songs or habits, three pointers which so often help to separate difficult species.' Leafing through all the warblers, Ware concluded it could only be one of two species, the Sardinian or the orphean warbler. Ramsay stated the former had a red eye-rim and brown legs, while the latter's legs were grey. 'Not very helpful distinctions in a small bird', he moaned, 'which insisted on diving into deep bushes every time a watcher produced field-glasses!' After two weeks' patient off-duty birding Ware finally got good views of the warbler in his binoculars and saw the red eye-ring, identifying it as a Sardinian warbler.

To get the community onside, Ware and his colleagues challenged the local children to a game of football but were soundly beaten. When not losing at football or on duty, Ware continued to scour the countryside in search of birds and came across the magnificent hoopoe, a pink- and black-striped bird with a large down-curved beak and a fan-shaped crest on its head. The bird is generally thought of as one of Europe's most beautiful, but Ware was less than impressed, commenting, 'It is a curious bird, bizarre rather than beautiful, and it was a disappointment to find that the lovely fan-shaped crest for which it is famed is raised only momentarily as the bird alights [...] In spite of this bold, even loud, colour-scheme, in the eucalyptus trees, with their brown bark-patches and rapid alternations of light and shade, hoopoes were extremely difficult to see.'

As in his previous posts, Ware's obsession with ornithology soon became well known around the station, where he was known as the 'bird-man'. One night, having turned in early, he was woken by a fellow airman with a 'funny bird'. Ware dragged himself out of his bunk to see it. It was a hoopoe which had been shot by one of the local children with a catapult and had a nasty wound under one wing. Ware noted in his diary: 'It was perky and lively enough, though, and occasionally opened out its crest for our delectation. The owners were trying to sell it, but as I had no wish to encourage them to bring further specimens I would have nothing to do with it. Arabs, I found, were interested in birds, but for one reason only, as "Manager" (food). They had a great idea of their value for this purpose, and while at Bordj I was offered in addition to this hoopoe young bee-eaters and scops owls to say nothing of sparrows and starlings.'

If hoopoes failed to excite Ware, one of Europe's other colourful and exotic species, bee-eaters, more than made up for it. 'They were most beautiful birds,' he recorded, 'their plumage the nearest approach to tropical colouring I saw [...] A mere description of the plumage conveys little, though the colouring, deep red-brown crown shading to golden brown on the back, blue wings, dark green tail, primrose yellow chin and throat, with bright blue-green underparts, is striking enough.' One day

Ware was on duty at a transmitter when, much to his delight, he heard their characteristic chattering call. Looking out, he saw nine bee-eaters sitting in a row on his aerial wires overhead. On another occasion, when he was guarding a crashed plane, he saw a big flock 'flying high for the most part, with a few swooping low to hawk bees over the flowers of the ever-present thistles. There must have been close on a hundred birds [...] they gradually passed overhead, not flying direct, but circling and "drifting" southward; the noise of their calling was tremendous.'

During Ware's birdwatching sorties he mainly recorded in his diary birds that were rare in Britain. He also noted species that were absent at home but had an Arabian equivalent. For example, he recorded that the crested lark replaced the skylark on arable land and in the rough ground associated with the vineyards. 'It is a rather bigger bird,' he noted, 'though similar in build, with a heavy, bat-like flight. It has a very decided pointed crest, much more pronounced than that of the skylark, but its song is greatly inferior, and almost invariably given from some elevated song-post rather than from the air.'

Another bird he found was the barbary falcon, which replaced the peregrine falcon in Britain. On the hottest day of the year, 12 September 1943, during a baseball game in which the temperature climbed to 105°F, he witnessed the southerly migration of twenty falcons, noting in his diary that it was 'a most extraordinary movement of these birds.' However, he was supposed to be following the ball rather than gazing skywards, writing that that his 'attention wandered somewhat from the game, to the other player's pardonable annoyance!' At the end of September the weather finally broke and the next two months proved to be excellent for birdwatching, Ware travelling further afield thanks to a French racing bike he had picked up on the local black market.

During this period there was a striking change in the birds around his station. The summer migrants such as storks, bee-eaters, hoopoes, woodchat shrikes, swifts, swallows, house martins and turtle doves disappeared and were replaced by 'birds so familiar that the sight of them brought a wave of home sickness. They included large flocks of starlings, green plovers (lapwings), meadow pipits, song thrushes, and most nostalgic of all, cheery, red-waistcoated robins.' Ware also came across a bird that had made its home in the bombed-out remains of London. Hearing a familiar 'ticking' noise early one morning, which he could not identify while washing, he ran back to his billet half-naked in search of his binoculars, much to the amusement of his fellow airmen. On his return to the washroom he was delighted to find the bird still there and he watched as it dropped to the sodden grass in search of insects. 'The 'ticking call was kept up almost continuously,' he recorded, 'while from time to time one of them would break into a funny little song from its vantage-point-of-the-moment. I got as near as I dared and raised the glasses, my suspicions were confirmed. They were my first black redstarts.'

Ware's war, like his birds, also reminded him of home. Through the port of Algiers huge convoys and heavily loaded trains moved, harried by enemy aircraft, destined for the desert as Montgomery chased Rommel, the 'Desert Fox', across the baking sands of Tunisia. To cool off, he and his fellow airmen would head to Cap Djinet on the coast where they could swim in the sea. Further along the coast was a quarry where Ware watched 'a noisy dog fight,' not between the RAF and the *Luftwaffe*, but between a pair of ravens and a pair of kestrels. 'It was the battle of Bomber versus Fighter all over again,' he noted rather melodramatically, 'a battle that was age-old before man ever learnt to fly. Flying well over the ravens, the little falcons would stoop steeply at their enemy below [...] the big black birds would take evading action [...] or turn belly up to present their formidable armament of claws to the attacker [...] who would sheer off at the last moment, "zooming" up to gain height for the next onslaught.' Ware watched the action from the bay lying on his back, commenting, 'a queer position for bird-watching but a very pleasant one!'

On his days off Ware also headed to the estuary of the River Isser, where he saw rufous warblers and great grey shrikes 'larger than the red-backed shrike so familiar in Britain, it was a decidedly handsome rascal, and looked very magpie-like in flight.' He also found new species including the black-winged kite, 'which goes to show how misleadingly-named some birds are, for it was neither kite-like nor black-winged!' and two blue-headed wagtails, 'beautiful little creatures they were.' There were also birds that reminded him of home, including a greenshank, Ware commenting, 'the last time that I had seen the wader that was now feeding quietly at the water's edge beyond the reeds was almost exactly a year before, when instead of stalking in the shadeless heat of an African estuary I had been bird-watching beside the snow-fed waters of Loch Morlich in the Highlands of Scotland.' On a subsequent visit, Ware came across another bird that was characteristic of the Highlands, the osprey, which he watched through his binoculars as it caught fish.

As well as birds that reminded him of home Ware also came across some species that were only found in the region. These included the hooded shrike, a bird found only in Morocco, Algeria and Tunisia. 'Unlike the true shrikes,' Ware wrote, 'its beak was not hooked, and I noticed in this and subsequent occasions that it seemed to prefer a song-post on the side of a bush rather than on its top, and from this position it was expert at slipping into cover as soon as it saw that it had been observed.'

In early December 1943, after the Axis powers in North Africa had surrendered, Ware received orders to move. A long convoy of trucks passed through the Djordjura Mountains, the highest in Algeria, in a 'hair-raising climb'. He commented, 'hair-pin bend followed hair-pin bend, and we looked out in turn on walls of cliff or dizzy drops over castellated crags.' They then crossed into Tunisia, passing through the fearsome Messerschmitt Alley: 'a long narrow plain between hills, and the road, which had been the main supply route for the First Army fighting in the final battles to clear North Africa, runs almost dead straight along it for something like twenty miles.' During the height of the fighting in the desert the *Luftwaffe* picked off Allied convoys at will, but now the war had ebbed and the alley was merely a name and a memory. Ware celebrated Christmas dinner here in the open, 'waited on in true Service tradition by the Officers and senior N.C.O.s.' After dinner consisting of tinned-stew pie, peas and potatoes followed by 'plum duff', Ware went for a walk, turning up a marsh harrier and another new species, a crane.

In late December Ware arrived at the harbour of Bizerta where he was greeted by the sight of a giant dump for wrecked aeroplanes. 'All around were ruins; ruins of tiny sea-planes and giant flying boats; speedy fighters and cruel bombers; German, Italian, French, American, British; many types, many nationalities; friend and foe alike, all brought down to one common level in death and destruction.' Ware was posted to guard the dump and was delighted to see among the debris a bird 'with black-and-white upper parts as neat as ever, its almost-crimson breast and tail a grim reminder of the bloodshed represented by the wrecks on which it perched, was my second Moussier's redstart, last seen amidst the natural beauty and utter peace of the Sidi Salem foothills!' Here he spent a week among the shattered desolation of the town, but he found far greater interest in the mudflats surrounding the harbour where he spent many happy hours watching the wading birds, which included dunlin, temminck stint, redshank, curlew, and greenshank. However, Ware was most proud of identifying some rock pipits, which turned out to be a first record for both Algeria and Tunisia: 'a fact which delighted me as I felt that my many hours spent bird-watching had at last brought some tangible result.' It was a high point of his time in North Africa, which had produced so many birds in wartime. Then, his tour of duty over, on 3 January 1944, his boat left the harbour bound for Europe.

Ware left on a landing ship tank (LST), an amphibious tank carrier, in a long British and American convoy bound for Corsica, which had only recently been liberated. He commented: 'Not a convoy reached there [which wasn't] dive-bombed repeatedly, we were told, and to this ever present-danger had recently been added Germany's latest secret weapon, the radio-controlled glider-bomb.' It was a long and rough crossing, Ware finally arriving at the port capital of Ajaccio to find their camp 'swarming with birds,' including stonechats, thrushes and wrynecks 'with beautifully barred breasts, and the peculiar twisted way that they often held their heads, as if listening.'

After a short rest, Ware then made his way in a lorry along a tortuous mountain road to the north-west of the island where he helped set up another signal station at the village of Calenzana with 'snow clad peaks [towering] over us on three sides, and on the fourth, over a six mile downward slope of green, lay the sea.' Here he was treated as a liberator, the locals holding a welcome party for the airmen when 'comely French girls appeared with large flagons of wine and filled our glasses [... and] plates piled high with cakes and buns of many queer flavours.' Ware was delighted to find the surrounding olive groves, cliffs and peaks full of birds including starlings, blackbirds, thrushes, chiff-chaffs, blackcaps, robins, whitethroats, hawfinches, Sardinian warblers, Dartford warblers, dippers, red kites, buzzards and golden eagles, as well as mountain specialists such as rock buntings and alpine accentors. He also heard the familiar 'bell note' of the scops owl, noting in his diary that it 'was a regular feature of the night though the birds were not numerous'. While out walking one day Ware also came across one of the most striking birds of the islands, the blue rock-thrush. He described it as 'a beautiful bird [...] its dark grey-blue plumage gleaming in the sun.' Perhaps the best bird Ware saw was the Corsican nuthatch which is endemic to the island. He recorded in his diary that it was a 'bird so particular as to its habitat that it is found in only one place in the world, the pine forests of Corsica.'

In February 1944, Ware received an unexpected order to pack up as quickly as possible and return to England. He returned via the same mountainous route going back to Ajaccio, the birth place of Napoleon. Here he tried to buy some souvenirs but found there was literally nothing in the shops, comparing it to Britain where people often said, '"There's nothing in the shops these days", but really meant there was nothing they wanted to buy.' However, he soon found that all the shopkeepers 'meagre stocks' were kept 'under the counter' and only available to those who 'paid in kind' (cigarettes, tins of bully beef or cartoons of biscuits). Ware was particularly keen to get his hands on a pair of German Zeiss binoculars, eventually being offered a pair on the black market in exchange for twenty tins of bacon. This he considered extortionate, commenting instead, 'I still use my 8x30 Wray! [a British camera and lens company that was in business until 1971].'

At Ajaccio Ware boarded a Liberty ship (a US cargo ship based on a British design mass produced during the war) and sailed back to Algiers – again a very rough crossing – where to his astonishment the hills were covered in snow, the result of the severe winter that year. He was billeted at a transit camp at Fort de l'Eau, and while on guard duty one night he ran into a genet, 'a relative of the civets, rather rare now in Algeria, and the only un-English animal seen during the whole of my tour abroad.' During his postings Ware's interest in birds had been a source of solace and delight for him, helping to while away the long hours spent on guard duty and doing menial tasks. However, it seems that he was very much in the minority, sadly commenting in his diary, 'during all our stays overseas I had found no one else at all interested in birds.' However, there were curious creatures that all the men at Fort de L'Eau took an interest in as they overwhelmed the camp – processionary pine caterpillars. On warmer days the caterpillars, which were ensconced in silk balls high up in the trees, came down en masse and proceeded to form a procession across the camp floor. Ware counted '259 caterpillars in one line without a single gap, and it was nearly ten yards long.' Although many of them ended up under the wheels of an RAF truck, Ware was able to inform his bemused colleagues that they were merely looking for sandy soil in which to pupate into their adult form, pine moths.

When it finally came time to board their troopship for Liverpool, Ware had to say goodbye to a very special bird that he had adopted as the station's mascot – Basil, the homing pigeon. The unit had acquired it during their first stay in Algiers when a corporal had taken it away from a group of Arab boys who were torturing it. However, there was no room for Basil on the troopship going back to Liverpool. With a heavy heart he let it go in a special ceremony attended by most of the station crew.

Ware's troopship was meant to be part of a large convoy heading for Britain, but following changed orders they slipped out early on their own and joined a small flotilla of four ships, before joining another faster convoy coming up from the port of Alexandria the following day. The same day, they heard on a BBC bulletin broadcast on the ship's loudspeaker system, that their original convoy had been subjected to a very heavy raid by German bombers and many of the ships had been sunk. It was another narrow escape for Ware, who must have reflected on the peripatetic nature of military life and the changing fortunes of war, fate keeping him safe to birdwatch another day. After eight days' sailing he finally saw the mouth of the Mersey with 'the usual Mersey fog shutting out all sight of the England we longed for.' A military band welcomed Ware home with the 1941 George Formby hit 'You'd be far better off in a home!' which includes the lyrics:

When it's over the crowds will shout and bawl
When it's over back to civvies we will crawl
The Sergeant Major can stick his passes on the wall
Then chase himself around the barrack square
Cos you'll be far better off in a home, you'll be far better off in a home
You'll be far better off, far better off, far better off in a home.

Ware's home for the rest of the war was an RAF station near Ottery St. Mary in Devon, from where he continued to build radios, perform guard duty and birdwatch. There, much to his delight, he saw a peregrine falcon over the base one day which 'flicked over in a mock attack on a bird on the ground,' which turned out to be a Montagu's harrier, a bird he had last seen in Norfolk at the beginning of the war. Ware's war had come full circle. So it seemed only appropriate that when his book *Wing to Wing* was first published in 1946 there were two line drawings on the front page: an eagle in flight with its outstretched wings, and the flying badge of the RAF, colloquially referred to as 'wings'.

Chapter 8

Birder Brooke

If Ware was a birdwatcher at one end of the military pecking order, at the other end was Alan Francis Brooke. He was the head of the British Army during the Second World War, a pivotal role which made him the principal military advisor to Winston Churchill and Britain's top soldier. Widely regarded as one of this country's most brilliant military strategists, Brooke had an outstanding army career. His reputation for military efficiency can perhaps best be judged by the nickname given to him by the War Office: 'Colonel Shrapnel'.

Yet equally deserving would have been the nickname 'Birder Brooke'. In 1943, following a long and difficult meeting, Brooke asked his Director of Military Operations, Sir John Kennedy (1893–1970), to stay behind, usually a sign of displeasure or that they needed to discuss something secret. When everyone had gone Brooke reached into his drawer and handed Kennedy a book. 'Have you read this?' he enquired, 'It is most remarkable.' Kennedy looked with amazement at the title: *The Truth about the Cuckoo* (written by Edgar Chance and published to great acclaim in 1940 by *Country Life*, one reviewer wrote that it particularly appealed to the 'avian physiologist').

Born on 23 July 1883 in France, Alan Brooke was one of nine children to Victor and Alice Brooke. His father was a naturalist and big game hunter but died when he was just eight. In 1899 Alan Brooke joined the army and served with distinction during the First World War in the Royal Artillery. Between the wars Brooke held a string of senior appointments before commanding II Corps in the British Expeditionary Force in 1940. A year later he became the head of the British Army when he was appointed the Chief of the Imperial General Staff (CIGS). In 1944 he was promoted to Field Marshal and after the war was created Viscount Alanbrooke in January 1946, a title he has been known by ever since.

At the end of the war, after securing the Allied victory, Alanbrooke found himself broke, the result of some bad investments, a large mortgage and having to support two families. It was a humiliating end to a great military career, and forced him to sell his house, Ferney Close in the village of Harley Wintney in Hampshire, and move into their gardener's cottage. Alanbrooke was also forced to sell his most precious possession – a forty-five-volume set of John Gould's *Birds of Great Britain* which raised over £3,000, twice what he paid for them in 1943. The only other major asset that Alanbooke possessed was his collection of war diaries.

Alanbrooke had kept a diary throughout the war, in direct contradiction of army rules, recording his thoughts in a series of books bought from W.H. Smith in Salisbury (purchased for the bargain price of fifteen shillings, reduced from sixty, they were originally destined for the liner *RMS Queen Mary* which had been converted to a troopship). Alanbrooke's diary was never meant for publication but as a way of corresponding with his beloved second wife, Benita Blanche Brooke (1892–1968, née Pelly), whom he had married in 1929. Alanbrooke was devoted to Benita but spent long periods away from her at work or abroad. So he dedicated his diaries to her, referring to his wife throughout as 'you', the first entry being written on 28 September 1939, just over three weeks after war had been declared. The dedication read:

This book is not intended to be a diary of events, although it may contain references to my daily life. It is intended to be a record of my thoughts and impressions such as I would have discussed them with you had we been together. After living the last ten years with you and never being parted for more than a few weeks at a time, I should feel quite lost without an occasional opportunity of a talk with you although such a talk must necessarily be confined to writing. The thoughts I express may contradict themselves as I wish to give full scope to free expression and do not care if I am forced to change my mind by events. ON NO ACCOUNT MUST THE CONTENTS OF THIS BOOK BE PUBLISHED.[1]

Alanbrooke had first started writing when he joined the army, sending letters to his adored mother, Alice, for nearly twenty years until her death in 1920. By then Alanbrooke was married to his first wife, Jane

Richardson, with whom he had a daughter and a son, but she tragically died in a car crash in 1925, an accident made more devastating by her husband being behind the wheel. His second wife was also to give him a son and daughter, and like her, he was utterly devoted to them. To provide for his family, in the early 1950s he got in touch with the historian and author Arthur Bryant (1899–1985) about publishing his diaries. After protracted negotiations with the War Office, two volumes were eventually published, *The Turn of the Tide*[2] in 1957 and *Triumph in the West*[3] in 1959.

At the time of publication the books caused a sensation because of their criticism of Churchill, whose own memoirs had been published at intervals between 1948 and 1954. Alanbrooke believed these failed to give sufficient credit to his Chiefs of Staff, which angered him greatly. Together with his financial worries, they changed Alanbrooke's mind in favour of publishing his own book. From 1951 to 1956 Alanbrooke added to the diaries, writing a commentary, 'Notes for my memoirs' as an *aide-memoire* to himself and Bryant. Despite the resulting furore, the books had in fact been redacted by Bryant to tone down their criticism of Churchill and prevent any libel case. Bryant had also taken out many of the references to birds, no doubt considering them of little consequence or interest to the reader. It would be over forty years before the full and unabridged version, birds and all, was published in 2001.[4]

When the unedited diaries were released, they showed only too clearly how important birds were in Alanbrooke's life. However, like his friend Sir Peter Scott, Alanbrooke started out not watching wildlife but shooting it. On 7 January 1908 he wrote to his mother from the Royal Artillery Mess in Meerut, India, telling her he had shot wild sheep, mountain goats, swamp deer, antelope, sambur deer, black buck deer, wild pigs, chinkara deer and '17 marmots'. It was, he concluded, 'A rather nice assorted variety for the first year. Unfortunately I missed the Tibetan Gazelle and Red Bear last month, and failed to spear a Hyena; these would have added 3 specimens ... So far the carnivora have defeated me, but I intend to get level with them before I have done.'[5]

By the time of the Second World War Alanbrooke was a changed man, the hunter having turned conservationist, inspired by another great ornithologist, Sir Edward Grey, the Foreign Secretary at the outbreak of the First World War. In 1926 Grey had published *The Fallodon Papers*, a book Alanbrooke cited as being his most important inspiration. In it Grey wrote:

In those dark days I found some support in the steady progress unchanged of the beauty of the seasons. Every year, as spring came back unfailing and unfaltering, the leaves came out with the same tender green, the birds sang, the flowers came up and opened, and I felt that a great power of Nature for beauty was not affected by the War. It was like a great sanctuary into which we could go and find refuge for a time from even the greatest trouble of the world, finding there not enervating ease, but something which gave optimism, confidence and security. The progress of the seasons unchecked, the continuance of the beauty of Nature, was a manifestation of something great and splendid which not all the crimes and follies and misfortunes of mankind can abolish or destroy.[6]

The first reference to birdwatching in Alanbrooke's own war diaries appears on 16 April 1940 as the British waited for a Nazi attack in the west. He recorded: 'Still no move on the part of Germany into either Holland or Belgium! ... In the afternoon I went for a walk in the woods nearby and imagined you were at my side. We discussed the lovely carpet of anemones, and all the nice green young shoots. In the garden M.Rosette [gardener] has found a blackbird's nest that I am watching. I wish I could take photographs of it.' Afterwards, Alanbrooke decided to take up photographing birds as his 'war hobby' at a time when cameras, lens and film were complex, cumbersome and expensive (Alanbrooke made films of birds rather than photographing them but he described his hobby throughout his diaries as 'photography'). This desire to produce films marked a new stage in his relationship with birds and for a man always short of money, a significant outlay. However, all his plans had to be put on hold when the Nazi *Blitzkrieg* swept across Europe.

When Winston Churchill became prime minister in May 1940, Alanbrooke was commanding the II Corps from his HQ at Armentières in northern France. However, he soon found himself managing the retreat of the British Expeditionary Force as they were pushed back towards the sea. On 25 May 1940, fearing his position would be soon overrun, he considered destroying his diary, writing later: 'The prospects were far from bright and I remember the next few days seriously considering destroying my diary as I did not want it to fall into German hands, and this seemed quite a possible eventuality … With catastrophe on all sides, bombarded by rumours of every description, flooded by refugees and a demoralized French army … Had it not been that by then one's senses were numbed with the magnitude of the catastrophe that surrounded one, the situation would have been unbearable.'

After being evacuated at Dunkirk, Alanbrooke arrived back in Britain on 1 June noting in his diary, 'Wonderful feeling of peace after the last 3 weeks.' However, he returned to France ten days later to oversee the final evacuation of British forces before leaving for good on the converted trawler HMS *Cambridgeshire*. 'I thanked God for again allowing us to come home,' he wrote on 19 June 1940, adding, 'I also thanked God that the expedition which I hated from the start was over.'

A month later he was summoned by Churchill and over lunch made Commander in Chief of the Home Forces with the responsibility of defending Britain against the expected German invasion, one of the most important roles in British military history. Asked what he needed, he told Churchill that he wanted light defences along the beaches to 'hamper and delay landings to the maximum,' and in the rear 'highly mobile forces trained to immediate aggressive action intended to concentrate and attack any landings before they had time to become too well established.' Later, contemplating the immense responsibility he wrote, 'I only pray to God that I may be capable of carrying out the job. The idea of failure at this stage of the war is too ghastly to contemplate. I know that you will be with me in praying to God that he may give me the necessary strength and guidance.'

From the beginning Alanbrooke found working with Churchill challenging, admiring his 'marvellous courage, considering the burden he is bearing,' but finding his working methods hard to tolerate, particularly his habit of staying up into the early hours of the morning, which he found 'a very trying procedure'. As the expected invasion neared and the RAF found themselves facing defeat in the Battle of Britain, Alanbrooke came close to utter despair, writing on 8 September: 'Heavy bombing of London throughout the night, the whole sky being lit up by the glow of fires in London docks. Went to the office in the morning where I found further indications of impending invasion. Everything pointing to Kent and E. Anglia as the two main threatened points ... all reports still point to the probability of an invasion starting between the 8th and 10th of this month.'

By the 15 September the pressure had become almost unbearable, 'A responsibility such as that of the defence of the country under the existing conditions is one that weighs on one like a ton of bricks,' he wrote, 'and it is hard at times to retain the hopeful, confident exterior which is so essential.' Yet as the days passed and the impending invasion did not happen, Alanbrooke became more hopeful, recording in his diary on 3 October: 'Still no invasion! I am beginning to think that the Germans may after all not attempt it. And yet! I have the horrid thought that he [Hitler] may still bring off some surprise on us.' But the surprise never came and at the end of the year he reflected, 'I feel, however, that the air battle for England and the German defeat in its attempt at invasion will probably loom as one of the greatest successes of British arms, which will for ever remain famous in terms of the PM's incomparable sentence: "Seldom in the field of human conflict have so many owed so much to so few."'

With the immediate threat of invasion over, in early 1941 Alanbrooke returned to his plans to film birds, investing in a cine camera and a number of lenses. On days off he began to build a housing for his new camera and to construct a hide, writing on 22 February 1941 that he was 'busy carpentering, making combination for cine [camera] and Astro lens.' The next day he stated, 'Church in the morning. In the afternoon experimented with my new Astro lens and the fitting I made to put cine Kodak [film] onto it.'

Over the next few weeks Alanbrooke spent all his spare time putting together his cine equipment and converting his pantry into a makeshift hide for filming birds in his garden. He was keen to get his new equipment up and working before the start of the bird breeding season and laboured away, many diary entries being dedicated to 'carpentering'. At the same time as he was getting to know his cine equipment he was also working on his relationship with Churchill, finding the prime minister even more complicated than his Kodak Special Cine. On 8 March 1941 he spent the afternoon fixing up his new Astro Tele Lens, the next day dining with Churchill at Chequers. The PM was suffering from bronchitis and came down to dinner in his famous 'siren suit', Alanbrooke playfully describing it as 'a one piece garment like a child's "romper suit" of light blue.' Despite his illness, Churchill was on good form. After dinner he sent for his rifle and gave Alanbrooke a demonstration of his fighting skills, showing off his 'long port' bayonet thrust. After the exertion Churchill felt a little worse for wear, so he decided, very unusually, to retire to bed early, giving Alanbrooke the luxury of a good night's sleep. 'I was convulsed watching him give this exhibition of bayonet exercises, dressed up in his romper suit and standing in the ancestral hall of Chequers,' he wrote. 'I remember wondering what Hitler would have made of this demonstration of skill at arms.'

In the spring of 1941 Alanbrooke was putting the final touches to the housing for his Kodak Super Cine camera and Astro Tele Lens, commenting on 6 April, 'a cold, wintry day which I spent mainly making brass fittings for the camera stand.' His relationship with Churchill also continued to develop slowly. Alanbrooke was trying hard to fathom the mind of the prime minister, but still despairing at his working methods, Churchill often working until 3.30am.

In early May he started filming birds in earnest, commenting excitedly to his wife that he had started 'photographing' a blackbird and starling from his pantry. Soon Alanbrooke had filmed many of the more common birds nesting in his garden in both black and white and colour (this was unusual for the time as colour film was particularly expensive) and was keen to go further afield with his cine camera to capture some more interesting species. He put the word out via his gardener that he was on the lookout for nests, and much to his delight the gamekeeper of a friend found him the nests of nightingales and a hedge sparrow with a cuckoo's egg in it. 'These occasional spells of birdwatching did marvels as a means of "re-creation"', he wrote, 'I was able for a short spell to forget about the war [and] all the nightmare of responsibility. For a short spell I was able to step into that Sanctuary of Nature, which Sir Edward Grey describes so well in his Fallodon papers. A sanctuary unaffected by the horrors of war.'[7]

On returning to the hedge sparrow's nest in early June he found to his dismay that the cuckoo chick was dead. However, the keeper told him about a sparrowhawk and a greater spotted woodpecker which he visited the next weekend, writing in his diary, 'Nasty, cloudy day with no sun and unfortunately bad for photography, started by taking a colour spool of grey wagtail in Chadwick Healey garden. After lunch got busy with [greater] spotted woodpecker. As nest was some 30 ft up I had to use large Astro lens. Hope some results may be good in spite of bad light.'

An excited Alanbrooke was filming the sparrowhawk at her nest when Germany launched Operation Barbarossa, the attack on Russia, on 21 June. 'Germany started march into Russia! And with it new phase of war opens up,' he wrote in his diary, adding:

As long as the Germans were engaged in the invasion of Russia there was no possibility of an invasion of these islands. It would now depend on how long Russia could last ... my own opinion at the time ... was that Russia would not last long, possibly 3 or 4 months ... Putting it at 4 months, and as we were then in June, it certainly looked as if Germany would be unable to launch an invasion of England until October, and by then the weather and winter would be against any such enterprise ... This would put me in the position of devoting the whole of my energies towards converting the defence forces of this island into a thoroughly efficient army capable of undertaking overseas operations.

In early July Alanbrooke made a remarkable find when checking the nest boxes in his garden, discovering a wryneck. Overjoyed, he filmed it, commenting, 'This was a great find and I proceeded to set up a hide and take coloured film. It may well be imagined that such an important event as a wryneck nesting in the garden put the war and all its troubles right out of my mind during those happy hours. I returned to my work a new man.' (The wryneck was a very rare breeding bird which was then rapidly disappearing from the countryside. It is now thought to be extinct as a breeding bird in Britain although one or two pairs breed occasionally.)

On 9 July Alanbrooke attended a meeting of the War Cabinet where he briefed Churchill and his colleagues on his plans for a full-scale exercise in London to counteract any parachute attack, the precursor to a German invasion. He got most of the Cabinet onside until Lord Beaverbrook, the new Minister of Supply, started 'pouring vitriol on it,' fearing it would undermine his role, so it was shelved. Alanbrooke was furious, commenting;

The more I see of politicians the less I think of them! They are seldom influenced directly by the true aspects of a problem and are usually guided by some ulterior political reason! They are always terrified of public opinion as long as the enemy is sufficiently far, but when closely threatened by the enemy inclined to lose their heads, and then blame all their previous errors on the heads of the military whose advice they have failed to follow. The more I see of democracy the more I doubt our wisdom of attaching such importance to it! I cannot see how our present system of democracy can produce real qualified leaders of a nation.

The following weekend it poured with rain, which frustrated Alanbrooke's plans to film the wryneck and the sparrowhawk. He only got some good footage after the storm clouds had cleared, writing, 'I took more photos of the sparrowhawk. As usual she came to feed at 6.45 and remained for 30 minutes.' On 20 July Alanbrooke had a week off, proclaiming, 'finally at 7.45pm left for Ferney Close for 7 days' LEAVE!!' On the first day of his leave he reflected on how far he had come since he had been appointed Commander in Chief. 'Have now been C-in-C Home Forces for 1 year and 2 days.' he wrote. 'Have flown just under 14,000 miles during that period and motored some 35,000 miles in my own car. As I have certainly done at least as much in other people's cars when touring round my total road mileage must be somewhere near 70,000 miles in the year. Spent morning photographing bull finches.'

For the remainder of the week Alanbrooke spent time with his family and filmed birds, apart from one day when he drove to meet Churchill who was reviewing army divisions, writing, 'Everywhere he had an astounding reception.' To Alanbrooke's surprise, soldiers lined both sides of the road cheering, 'Good Old Winnie'. He concluded, 'His popularity is quite astonishing.'

At the end of his break as he was preparing to return to work he had a serious crisis of confidence. Depressed at again having to shoulder the responsibility for the defence of the nation, he wrote: 'Have I really taken the proper dispositions for the defence of this country?' Alanbrooke was concerned about whether he had got the balance right between forces in the south and north; whether he had underestimated the air threat; and, if he further denuded the beaches to protect the aerodromes, whether he was 'opening the door to a sea invasion'. If he had indeed miscalculated, 'these are all questions where a wrong answer may mean the end of life as we have known it in this country and the end of the British Empire!'

Reflecting after the war about being overwhelmed by the burden of responsibility, he wrote, 'Such periods of doubt and uncertainty must at times descend on all commanders … they are made all the more difficult to bear since it is essential that these inward doubts must never rise to the surface. Outwardly a commander must inspire confidence in all those serving under him, and equally to his superiors.' Tellingly, he added, 'How often have I seen Winston eyeing me carefully trying to read my innermost thoughts, searching for any doubts that might rest under the surface.'

At the end of August, following a visit to Scotland reviewing defences, Alanbrooke spent a few days game shooting, bagging over 500 grouse. At home he kept himself busy when not dealing with military matters by reviewing and editing the bird films he had shot over the summer. On 8 September he showed his bird films for the first time to B Mess, a contingent of the Home Guard, where it was rapturously received.

At the beginning of October Alanbrooke again found himself at odds with Churchill, this time over his desire to invade Norway. Churchill stated that 'Hitler had unrolled the map of Europe starting with Norway, and he would start rolling it up again from Norway.' The plan had been vetoed by the Chiefs of Staff's Committee due to insufficient air support, but Churchill was insistent, and, much to his annoyance, Alanbrooke was forced to draw up a detailed plan. It was, he concluded, 'going to entail a great deal of wasted work on the part of many busy people,' and it put his relationship with Churchill under further strain.

During a visit to Churchill at Chequers on 16 November, after dinner in the study, he was surprised when the prime minster asked him to become the Chief of the Imperial General Staff (CIGS). This was the highest position in the British Army, in charge of the Chiefs of Staff of each of the services. In his diary Alanbrooke wrote that he was 'torn by many feelings', including loyalty to his predecessor, John Gill (1881– 1944), as well as 'the magnitude of the job', which would mean seeing less of his beloved wife and even less time watching and filming birds. While it was a huge accolade, he also wondered whether he could 'stand the storms of abuse'. After a pause, he graciously accepted. A delighted

Churchill ending the evening by going with Alanbrooke to his bedroom at 2.00am where he held his hand, and 'looking into my eyes with an exceptionally kind look said "I wish you the best of luck".' At the age of fifty-eight, through hard work, steely determination and an unrivalled grasp of military matters, Alanbrooke had become Britain's top soldier.

The military situation he inherited was bleak: Germany was triumphant in Russia and still contemplating an invasion of Britain; Rommel was routing the British in North Africa; the Mediterranean was surrounded by enemy forces and Japan was threatening to enter the war. The only ray of light at the end of a very dark tunnel was the possibility of American assistance, but they remained stubbornly isolationist. 'To pick up the strategic reins at the War Office at such a time,' he wrote, 'was surely sufficient to cause one the deepest of anxiety.' What made matters even more complicated was having to work with Churchill, with his 'impetuous nature, his gambler's spirit and his determination to follow his own selected path at all costs.' Overwhelmed, Alanbrooke, though not a deeply religious man, got out of bed, knelt down and prayed to God for 'guidance and support in the task I had undertaken'.

On 4 December Alanbrooke got into his first serious disagreement with Churchill over military strategy as CIGS with the prime minister wanting to gift tanks and aircraft to Stalin in his struggle with Hitler. Failing to win the support of those present, including Alanbrooke, Churchill completely lost his temper, accusing the Chiefs of Staff of obstructing his ideas but having none of their own. Despairing at the situation, Alanbrooke wrote: 'God knows where we would be without him, but God knows where we shall go with him!'

On 7 December 1941, six days after Alanbrooke had taken over as CIGS, the Japanese launched a surprise attack on the American fleet at Pearl Harbour. Recording the momentous event in his diary, he wrote, 'After dinner listened to wireless to find that Japan had attacked America!! All our work of last 48 hours wasted [Alanbrooke had been trying to stave off the Japanese entry into the war]. The Japs themselves have now ensured that the USA are in the war.' It was the turning point Alanbrooke had been quietly praying for.

In the spring of 1942 Alanbrooke again started filming the birds in his garden, but wanted to take on much more ambitious projects. So he set himself the goal of filming a kingfisher at the nest – a difficult and demanding shoot even for a professional wildlife cameraman. On 26 April he checked out a great potential site at the back of a friend's cottage, but despaired at the amount of time he could devote to filming it, as he had to attend regular Cabinet meetings including ones on a Sunday. After many attempts Alanbrooke finally got some long-range footage of the kingfishers in mid-May, but much to his annoyance,could not find the time to set up a hide at the nest. He also discovered that a vixen was regularly visiting his garden with her cubs, but she also proved very wary, commenting in his diary on 17 May: 'Spent at home photographing blackbirds and trying to get photos of fox cubs without much success.'

Alanbrooke's adventures with wildlife were not all enjoyable. His wife was a keen apiarist and on 31 May, her birthday, they discovered a swarm of bees in their garden which had escaped from one of her hives. After filming the impressive sight of thousands of bees in a black cloud swarming on a pear tree, his wife decided that she would capture the swarm and rehive it somewhere less dangerous. Reading up about it in a bee book, she was 'full of confidence' and she roped in Alanbrooke for the assault, providing him with a face veil and a pair of gardening gloves full of holes. Placing a sheet on the ground, she fetched a stepladder and gingerly climbed up it, Alanbrooke holding on to the steps to steady her. Carefully approaching the swarm, she attempted to shake the branch of the pear tree, but the situation soon got rapidly out of hand, half the swarm going on the sheet but the other half attacking them. Like any attacking army, the guard bees looked for the weak points in the Brooke's defences and soon found them, stinging Benita's neck and his wrists. 'Suddenly she shouted "I can't stand it any longer",' Alanbrooke recorded in his diary, 'and fled into the house. I felt that honour was now satisfied and followed in her wake, shedding bees in all directions.'

On getting back to the safety of their bedroom, Alanbrooke pulled out twenty-two stings from his wife's neck and a dozen from his wrists. Alanbrooke's arm soon began to swell up rapidly and he started to perspire heavily. His wife didn't react as much initially to the stings but after tea began to feel very hot and dizzy, retiring to bed where she soon developed a temperature of 103°F (39.5°C). The next morning her temperature had gone down but Alanbrooke had a very uncomfortable week having to attend several Chiefs of Staff meetings with a very red and swollen arm, much to the amusement of his colleagues. The next weekend he contented himself with filming mistle thrushes, a much less dangerous occupation.

At work the war news continued to be bad. Although the Germans had been stopped the previous winter at the gates of Moscow, by the summer of 1942 they were again on the offensive in Russia. Churchill also continued to agitate for his proposed attack on northern Norway, Alanbrooke stating on 5 June that the prime minister's idea 'appears even more impossible'. To try to forget about the war he took the opportunity to visit the Farne Islands in Northumberland, a place he had long wanted to see. A birdwatcher's mecca because of its seabird colonies, in the summer it hosts hundreds of thousands of birds including puffins, fulmars, kittiwakes, guillemots, shags and razorbills. On 11 June Alanbrooke flew up to Catterick to review his northern command, taking the next day off so he could visit the colony.

Turning up early at Seahouses, the embarkation point, Alanbrooke wrote that it was a 'day I had been looking forward to for months'. However, his trip was over before it had begun when one of his generals stepped out on the dinghy and it capsized, the captain, two sailors and all Alanbrooke's precious filming equipment falling into the sea. 'Luckily Captain rescued camera before it sank,' Alanbrooke wrote in his diary. 'However, he was almost exhausted before he was pulled out [the Kodak Super Cine camera and associated telephoto lens were very heavy] and another sailor fell in in the attempt.' Giving up on the idea of a getting there in a dinghy, a motor vessel was instead commandeered and Alanbrooke and his by now useless filming equipment were loaded onboard. 'Camera, films, lenses and all were swimming in sea water!' he fumed. 'I had an awful job drying out the sea water. Impossible to use camera, opportunity missed, most depressing.' His only consolation was the weather, which was very poor with drizzling rain, making filming almost impossible. It was a day to forget, and Alanbrooke wrote after the war: 'This day was a real tragedy. For 20 years I had been looking forward to the day when I should return to the Farne islands to take photographs there!'

The next Sunday, 14 June 1942, Alanbrooke had hoped to get back to filming birds. However, he had had been summoned by Churchill, who was 'much disturbed at bad turn taken by operations in the Middle East. Rommel certainly seems to be getting the better of Ritchie [General Sir Neil Ritchie 1897–1983] and to be out generalling him.' Three days later they left for Washington, where, in a meeting with President Roosevelt, they received the devastating news that Tobruk had fallen. Alanbrooke also noticed that when it came to military matters Roosevelt had a very different relationship with his military advisors. As the President had little military knowledge he listened to and relied on his general's advice. In contrast, Alanbrooke wrote, 'my position was very different. Winston never had the slightest doubt that he had inherited all the military genius from his great ancestor Marlborough! His military plans and ideas varied from the most brilliant conceptions at one end to the wildest and most dangerous ideas at the other. To wean him away from these wilder plans required superhuman efforts and was never entirely successful in so far as he tended to return to these ideas again and again.'

Following their visit to America on 12 August, and after a whirlwind tour of Iraq, Alanbrooke visited Moscow, flying over the marshes and deltas of the Volga. Making a mental note to visit them after the war to film their birdlife, he wrote, 'I could see white egrets, heron and duck flying about as we skimmed past flying low.' That evening he met Stalin for the first time and was impressed by his 'astuteness' and 'crafty cleverness', concluding that he was 'a realist, with little flattery about him, and not looking for much flattery either.' In Churchill's dealings with the Russian leader, Alanbrooke saw none of the warmth that existed between him and Roosevelt, noting they were 'poles apart as human beings'. The discussions were dominated by the subject of opening up a second front in Europe to relieve the pressure on the Red Army, but the Russians offered little back in return, Alanbrooke reflecting, 'we have bowed and scraped to them […] as a result they despise us and have no use for us except for what they can get out of us.'

Despite Stalin's attitude, by the end of 1942 the war was beginning to turn decisively in the Allies' favour. The first and second battles of El Alamein had seen Montgomery, the Commander of the 8th Army (1887–1976), rout Rommel in the desert. On the Eastern Front at Stalingrad the Germans suffered a catastrophic defeat at the hands of the Red Army. In the Far East the Japanese also suffered their first defeat at Guadalcanal.

On 14 January 1943 Alanbrooke flew to Casablanca for a long trip to discuss the next phase in the Allied offensive in the Mediterranean with the Americans. There, whenever the opportunity arose, he slipped out to go birdwatching along the beach, finding 'a new white heron,

quite distinct from the egret, and a new small owl we could not place.'
He also found 'a black stone-chat on the way home,' and 'located a pair
of spur-winged plover'. Before he left he added 'three new specimens
to our finds in the shape of a wimbrel [sic, whimbrel], sandpiper and
yellow wagtail.'

Next he visited Marrakesh where he explored the gardens of his hotel,
finding several interesting birds. 'It is great fun identifying the European
specimens in the form of some sub-species with minor variations,' he
wrote on 24 January. 'For instance I found the ordinary chaffinch, but
the cock with a blue-grey head instead of the red-brown of the home
specimen. It is also very interesting seeing what a great difference there
is between the bird life at Casablanca and that of Marrakesh, although
the distance between them is only some 130 miles.' His plans for a day's
partridge shooting were curtailed by the prime minister, so Alanbrooke
flew on to Cairo, passing over the Qattara Depression (lying below sea
level, its bottom is covered with salt pans, sand dunes, and salt marshes).
'[A] most interesting sight I would not have missed for a great deal,' he
noted. 'I had hoped to see some bird life of interest, but the resident types
are few, and it is only during the migration that bird life is plentiful. I did
see a white-rumped chat, which I had not seen before, but otherwise only
2 ravens and 1 hooded crow.'

Alanbrooke's shuttle diplomacy continued apace when, at the end of the
month, he flew on to Adana in Turkey to convince the Turks to come in
on the side of the Allies. During a meeting with his Turkish equivalent,
Field Marshal Fevi Cakmak (1876-1950), Alanbrooke's obsession with
birdwatching nearly caused a major diplomatic incident. The meeting
took place across a long table in a railway carriage. While talking to
Cakmak, Alanbrooke suddenly looked out of the window behind him
and saw what he thought was a pallid harrier busy quartering over the
plain. Momentarily lost for words, he began to follow the bird with his
eyes while his host moved uncomfortably in his chair and looked over
his shoulder. 'I had never seen a pallid harrier,' Alanbrooke wrote in his
diary, 'and was not certain whether what I was looking at was one, or a
hen harrier. I was consequently very intent on looking out of that window,
much to Cakmak's discomforture, who kept looking round and possibly
thought that I had spotted someone getting ready to have a shot at him.'
Seeing Cakmak's reaction, Alanbrooke tried in vain to explain through

the interpreter that he was only 'birdwatching'. However, his reason got lost in translation, leaving Cakmak more than a little bewildered.

Pallid harriers apart, the meeting was a great success. Churchill was on good form, leaving his dinner party guests 'convulsed with laughter'. Alanbrooke concluded that the Turks neutrality will 'from now on assume a far more biased nature in favour of the Allies.' (In fact, the Turks remained neutral until almost the end of the war, in February 1945 entering on the side of the Allies.) On the return journey, which took in Cyprus, Cairo, Tripoli and Algiers, Alanbrooke stopped off in Gibraltar to refuel on 6 February. The ambassador met him at the airport and after tea they walked in the gardens looking for birds, spotting a peregrine falcon high up in the sky. The next day Alanbrooke finally returned home, recording that he had flown 10,200 miles over the last month and in the last two years had clocked up just under 55,000 miles.

At home on 9 March on a rare afternoon off Alanbrooke went to Harrods to buy a bookcase for his burgeoning collection of bird books, his wife making sure he chose one that would be in keeping with the decor of Ferney Close (over his lifetime Alanbrooke accumulated approximately 400 books in his library from his family and military career but the majority were bird books).[8] On getting it home, a delighted Alanbrooke began the long process of classifying his precious bird books in ornithological order of preference. In May he attended another White House conference with President Roosevelt, stopping off at Algiers on his return where he again birdwatched on the beach and in the garden of his hotel. There he and Churchill also examined a Mark VI Tiger tank that had been captured from the enemy on 24 April 1943; the first intact Tiger tank taken by British forces. After extensive testing and evaluation, it was displayed around the country as a trophy to help raise funds for the war effort (it now resides at the Tank Museum in Bovington and is the only operating Tiger tank in the world). The seizure of the Germans' most formidable tank marked a symbolic turning point in the war, and meant that Alanbrooke could now spend more time doing what he loved most, photographing birds.

Chapter 9

Birds, War and Winston

With the war going better, Alanbrooke treated himself to another trip the Farne Islands, flying up to Northumberland on 10 June 1943 to inspect his Northern Command where he lunched on gulls eggs and crab sandwiches (during the war a lot of gull eggs were consumed as hen eggs were in such short supply). The next day at 9.00am he left for the port of Seahouses where he met up with an admiral and boarded a ship bound for the islands. Following his disastrous visit to the islands the previous year, in which his dinghy had capsized and he had seen all his precious filming equipment fall into the sea, Alanbrooke was taking no chances. Although he had managed to salvage some of his equipment, the salt water had damaged most of it meaning that it had to be replaced, a costly exercise for a man who was always short of money. This time, however, both the voyage and the weather at the start were much better, a delighted Alanbrooke taking much film of 'eider duck, fulmar, petrel, kittiwakes, guillemots, razorbills, puffins and shags'. The weather held out just long enough for filming, though the trip back was through a heavy storm. The following weekend he went through all his footage from the trip and also began filming a spotted flycatcher which had taken up residence in his garden, its acrobatic sorties in search of insects providing him with some more great bird behaviour to add to his collection.

On 21 June Alanbrooke attended a difficult Cabinet meeting in which the future of Charles de Gaulle (1890–1970), the leader of the Free French Forces, was discussed. Relations with de Gaulle had become strained over a range of issues, including what he perceived to be lack of French recognition for the North African campaign. Alanbrooke commented, 'personally I am convinced that there is only one course to follow, and that is to get rid of him at the earliest possible date.' The next day, to cheer himself up after a haircut and a good lunch, he placed an order for a set of 'Gould's Birds' one of the most expensive and celebrated ornithological works, hoping that they would be a sound investment and that the value of the set would go up in the future.

The Birds of Great Britain by John Gould (1804–1881) was published as a set of 25 supplements between 1863 and 1873 and then as a full set, with the initial print run being just 750. The books contain 367 hand-lithographed plates which Gould collaboratively produced with the German natural history painter Joseph Wolf (1820–1899), and another artist, Henry Constantine Richter (1821–1902).[1] Alanbrooke was delighted with them, commenting after the war, 'My purchase of Gould's Birds was a big venture! There were 45 volumes for which I gave just over £1500, but my forecast was correct and at the end of the war I sold these books for twice their original cost. Meanwhile I had had wonderful value from them as an antidote to the war and to Winston! Whilst looking at Gould's wonderful pictures I was able to forget everything connected with the war.'

At the beginning of July Alanbrooke showed one of his bird films to some guests who had come round for dinner. By this stage in the war he had accumulated a considerable amount of footage of breeding birds both in his garden and in the wider countryside. This mainly comprised of shots at the nest for which he had built a series of elaborate hides, but he had also filmed some shots of birds in their natural environment. He used his films to entertain, but also to gauge the reaction of people whose opinion he valued about the quality of his work.

On 11 July 1943 Alanbrooke spent the day at home playing with his children and rearranging his bookcases to accommodate his new one from Harrods and the volumes comprising Gould's set. The next day he filmed a new bird, the greenfinch, in his garden, capturing perfectly its colourful character including the unmistakable flash of yellow and green as it flew, and its 'twittering, wheezing' song.

A colleague who shared Alanbrooke's passion for birds was his Director of Military Operations at the War Office, John Kennedy (1893–1970, he was promoted to be Assistant Chief of the Imperial General Staff in October 1943). On Wednesday, 21 July 1943 he came to dinner, with the ornithologist David Armitage Bannerman (1886–1979), who was the Curator of the Natural History Museum. Over dinner they discussed Bannerman's new book, *The Birds of the British Isles*, a major series he was producing with the illustrator George Edward Lodge (1860–1954). Afterwards Alanbrooke told his guests how impressed he was with some of the initial illustrations. Two days later he recorded a milestone in his own life, his sixtieth birthday, commenting in his diary, 'when I pass out of the active list of the Army!'

On 5 August Alanbrooke boarded the *RMS Queen Mary* bound for Canada with the prime minister where they were due to discuss the progress of the war with both the Canadians and the Americans. Arriving there five days later, he commented that the countryside reminded him a lot of Scotland: 'The country was lovely. Pine tree covered hills leading down to the lake, whilst bears live in the woods, and beavers had one of their dwellings on the upper of the two lakes that we fished.'

On the trip he received the news that he would not, after all, be offered the position of Supreme Commander of the Allied Forces for the invasion of Europe, a job Churchill had mentioned to him would be his on several occasions. Instead, under pressure, the prime minister had agreed that the job should be given to an American commander, leaving Alanbrooke bitterly disappointed (in the end it went to Einsenhower, Louis Mountbatten being appointed Supreme Commander for Southeast Asia). On 24 August he lamented in his diary: 'if it had not been for the birds and the company they provided, I could almost have sobbed with the loneliness. Tonight the same feelings overwhelm me, and there are no birds!'

At the end of the conference Alanbrooke departed for two days' fishing to unwind, an experience spoilt when Churchill turned up unexpectedly. Compensation came in the form of catching forty trout and also seeing 'an osprey at close quarters as he sat about 50 yards from me. Also a great northern diver, a spruce partridge and a black duck. I also saw a falcon which I thought was a "duck hawk", but am not certain.' Bears were also an ever-present delight, Alanbrooke commenting gleefully that one had 'frightened Louise the cook when she walked out to empty slops behind the camp some time ago!' As he did on most of his trips abroad, Alanbrooke also bought a bird book, recording in his diary on the last day, 'the morning was spent packing [...] and running round to a bookshop to collect a book I had ordered on Canadian birds.' When time allowed, Alanbrooke would always compile a bird list wherever he was in the world and when he returned home on one of his quiet 'bird nights in' would compare his list with his books, hoping to identify any obscure or difficult species (for example the 'duck hawk' is the North American subspecies of the peregrine falcon, its scientific name of *Falco peregrinus anatum* meaning 'duck peregrine falcon').

On 9 September Allied forces landed at Salerno, opening up a second front in the 'soft underbelly' of Europe and beginning the long campaign to liberate Italy. Alanbrooke was initially very sceptical about the success of the exercise, fearing the Allies were under-resourced and they would be pushed back into the sea. When it looked like the tide had turned in the Allies' favour, he began to relax more. On 19 September Alanbrooke invited 'Rusty' (Ralph) Eastwood (1890–1959, in charge of Northern Command) and his wife to tea. Eastwood was also a keen ornithologist and they spent a very pleasant couple of hours going through bird books together.

In early October Alanbrooke treated himself to two weekends shooting on a moor in northern England. Although he was a fanatical ornithologist, like many birdwatchers of his generation, he also enjoyed shooting game birds (at the time this was not seen as a conflict of interest but merely an extension of the hobby, like collecting birds' eggs). Later in the month Alanbrooke left on another long and arduous conference tour of Gibraltar, Malta and Cairo to meet with the Americans, Russians and the leader of the Chinese nationals, Chiang Kai-shek, to discuss military operations against Japan. During the tour Alanbrooke found both Churchill and the American delegation very hard to deal with, but one American he did like was John Gilbert Winant (1889–1947), the ambassador to Great Britain. They met in the library during a stopover in Malta on 19 November 1943 and after hitting it off went for a drive around the island together. Soon the conversation turned to birds, and to Alanbrooke's delight Winant was able to able to add to his extensive book collection. 'We were both discussing the wonderful rehabilitation to be acquired through close contacts with nature, and especially so in time of war,' Alanbrooke wrote in his diary. 'He said no doubt I must have read Earl Grey's views on these matters as contained in the *Fallodon Papers*?[2] I had to confess that I had not!' Following the conversation Winant, ever the diplomat, agreed to send him a copy, which he did immediately on his return to Britain. 'He kept his promise and this book has remained one of my most treasured possessions,' Alanbrooke wrote after the war, adding, 'He later gave me a wonderful folio copy of some 12 volumes of Audubon's *Birds of America*.[3] His friendship I always look upon as one of those great blessings which the war occasionally provided as an antidote to all its horrors.'

The gift from Winant was a very generous one. John James Audubon's (1785–1851) books are considered one of the finest ornithological works ever completed. Printed between 1827 and 1838, they contains 435 life-size watercolours of North American birds, all reproduced from hand-engraved plates. (Despite his undoubted diplomatic skills, Winant led a troubled life. Following career disappointments, a failed marriage – including a doomed affair with Winston's Churchill's second daughter, Sarah – and heavy debts he committed suicide in 1947.)

On 23 November the conference in Cairo started in earnest with the arrival of Chiang Kai-shek, who brought along his alluring American-educated wife, Soong Mei-ling (who went by the name of 'Madame'). With the help of his wife's revealing skirt and 'the most shapely of legs', which distracted Alanbrooke and most of the men in the delegation, Kai-shek managed to dominate the conference. As a result, the more important business of the war in the Mediterranean, support for the Soviet Union on the Eastern Front, and the opening up a Second Front in Europe were delegated to the next stages which were held in Iraq. Here the prime minister's delegation stayed with Alan Charles Trott (1859–1959), the Oriental Secretary at his Majesty's Legation in Tehran. Trott was particularly interested in the flora and fauna of the region, and in his spare time collected specimens which he kept at his house. While staying there, Alanbrooke found out Trott was also interested in birds so they went off birding together whenever time allowed.

By the end of 1943 the war had turned decisively in the Allies' favour. The Germans were being pushed back on the Eastern Front by the Red Army and the successful landings at Salerno began the liberation of Italy. However, the Japanese continued to fight stoically in the Far East, while plans for the Second Front in Europe were still not finalised. The new year of 1944 started well with Alanbrooke hearing on the radio that he had been promoted to Field Marshal. 'It gave me a curious peaceful feeling that I had at last, and unexpectedly, succeeded in reaching the top rung of the ladder!' he wrote in his diary, adding, 'I certainly never set out to reach this position, nor did I ever hope to do so, even in my wildest dreams.' The promotion also helped to ease Alanbrooke's bitter disappointment at not being made Allied Supreme Commander for Operation Overlord, and he celebrated by going shooting.

On 3 January 1944 he proudly picked up his jacket with his new Field Marshal insignia, and following a Chiefs of Staff meeting, discussed with Montgomery ('Monty') his plans for the D-Day invasion. He was due to attend a Cabinet meeting in the evening but had heard that a rare scaup duck had turned up on St James's Park lake opposite Downing Street. The park was the old birdwatching haunt of his great ornithological mentor Earl Grey and of the previous prime minister, Neville Chamberlain, who, like Alanbrooke, shared a lifelong love of birds. Chamberlain had first seen the bird on the lake before the war, on 9 December 1938, alerted to its presence by an ornithological friend who he regularly corresponded with called Gilbert Collett (1887–1964).[4] On hearing that the scaup was again on the lake, Alanbrooke was determined to see it so he slipped out of Downing Street before the Cabinet meeting and scoured the water until he found it. 'Saw that the scaup had returned on the St James's lake,' he wrote triumphantly in his diary. 'The return of the scaup amongst the St James's Park ducks was a great event! It had been there the whole previous winter, but left during the breeding season, only to return again this winter.'[5]

(In his book *London's Natural History*, published in May 1945, the naturalist Richard Fitter (1913–2005) cites the scaup as being a regular on the lake and calls into question its origins, intimating it was an escaped bird. However, the fact that it disappeared over the summer months and only returned in the winter gives veracity to Alanbrooke's belief that it was a wild bird. Most scaup bred in the Arctic tundra, with just a handful breeding in the UK, but they are a much commoner passage and winter migrant, just over 5,200 pairs wintering in the UK.)

Two weeks later, at the king's request, Alanbrooke visited the royal estate at Sandringham to brief him on the war. He stayed for two days, taking part in several shoots, with the sovereign bagging large numbers of pheasants, partridges and woodcocks. 'The one main impression that I have carried away with me is that the King, Queen and their two daughters provide one of the very best examples of English family life,' he wrote on 16 January. 'A thoroughly closely knit and happy family all wrapped up in each other. Secondly I was greatly impressed by the wonderful atmosphere entirely devoid of all pomposity, stiffness or awkwardness. They both have a wonderful gift of making one feel entirely at home.'

In February Alanbrooke again dined with David Bannerman, who was busy writing *The Birds of the British Isles*, and George Lodge, who was doing the illustrations. Lodge had already started on a number of plates for the book and showed them to Alanbrooke, who wrote in his diary: 'Lodge is 82 years old, most attractive old man, found he knew Wolf well and had painted with him [Joseph Wolf, 1820–1899, a German natural history artist who moved to the British museum in 1848, is regarded as the best all-round bird artist who ever lived]. His plates are quite wonderful and should make a historic book.'

At the end of January 1944 the Allies had undertaken a major amphibious landing at Anzio on the Italian coast with the strategic objective of liberating Rome. Although the initial assault was successful the landing had become bogged down after the Germans threw a defensive ring around the beachhead. This caused Alanbrooke serious complications with the planning of Operation Overlord, the invasion of Europe. As a result he was not able to spend the same amount of time filming birds as he had done during the two previous springs. Tired of the very heavy workload and dealing with the continual demands of Churchill, who was increasingly ill with pneumonia, Alanbrooke came close to a breakdown. Aware that he was struggling to cope, he fell back on his love of birds to get himself through. One weekend he decided to film a marsh tit which was nesting in his garden. On 14 May he wrote, 'Spent Sunday quietly at home and photographed Marsh Tit,' adding 'Those 2 hours in a hide close to a Marsh Tit at its nest made Winston and the war disappear in a cloud of smoke. It was like rubbing Aladdin's lamp, I was transplanted to a fairyland and returned infinitely refreshed and recreated.'

On 1 June 1944, mentally and physically exhausted by the scale of the preparations for Operation Overlord, Alanbrooke wrote in his diary, 'I am tired to death of our whole method of running war, it is just futile and heart breaking.' This time not even one of his famous birdwatching dinner parties could take his mind off his troubles. Finally on 6 June, D-Day, the largest amphibious invasion force in history landed on the beaches of Normandy, starting Operation Overlord. Recording the historic event in his diary, Alanbrooke wrote: 'By 07.30 I began to receive first news of the invasion. The airborne landings had been successful, the first waves were reported as going in, opposition not too serious, batteries firing from flanks etc.' Reflecting on the enormity of the event that evening, Alanbrooke added: 'It has been very hard to realize all day that whilst London went on calmly with its job, a fierce conflict was being fought at a close distance on the French coast!'

Six days later, at 8.00am on 12 June, Alanbrooke, the prime minister and a party of senior British commanders left on the destroyer *Kelvin* from Portsmouth bound for the French coast passing an armada of ships and other support vessels on the way. Alanbrooke wrote: 'We continually passed convoys of landing craft, minesweepers, bits of floating breakwater (Phoenix) being towed out, parts of the floating piers (Whales) etc And overhead, a continuous flow of planes going to and coming from France. About 11am we approached the French coast and the scene was beyond description. Everywhere the sea was covered with ships of all sizes and shapes, and a scene of continuous activity.' On landing at the beach they were met by Monty, the whole experience bringing back memories of being evacuated at Dunkirk the last time Alanbrooke had been there in 1940. 'If anybody had told me then that in 4 years' time I should return,' he wrote, 'with Winston [...] I should have found it hard to believe.' In the afternoon they toured the countryside. Alanbrooke used the opportunity to do some birdwatching and was astonished at how little the country had been affected by the German occupation and four hard years of war. He finally got home at 1.00am 'dog tired' but having spent a 'wonderfully interesting day'. The next day, however, the first V1 missiles, or doodlebugs, were launched at London, proving that Nazi Germany was still far from defeated.

In July, Alanbrooke chaired a Chiefs of Staff meeting in which the post-war settlement of Germany was thrashed out, those present agreeing that it should be divided into three zones – Russian, British and American. That evening, 12 July, following a film of the African campaign, he again dined with Kennedy, now his assistant chief, and Bannerman, who was in a very agitated state after a flying bomb had damaged the Natural History Museum. With the start of the V1 flying bomb campaign against London in 1944, the museum had again found itself in the firing line. The day before Alanbrooke's dinner party a flying bomb landed on Cromwell Road and broke all the glass in the west wing, including the museum's prized ornithological displays. Bannerman was working at the museum at the time and narrowly escaped being killed. A sympathetic

Alanbrooke wrote in his diary the next day, 'Poor Bannerman was there, rather shaken after having been bombed twice in 3 days by doodlebugs in the South Kensington Museum! He is now off to Cornwall for some well-earned holiday. Apparently he saved himself from being blown to bits by diving under his oak table.' As a result of the bombing raids during the Blitz, and the later doodlebugs, almost every window and glass display case at the museum was shattered (due to a national shortage of glass, it would take many years for them to be replaced. Even today, some of the older mammal exhibits have to be handled extremely carefully because their fur still contains fine shards of glass).

A week later in the early hours of the morning a flying bomb came perilously close to destroying Alanbrooke's own home. 'A nasty night with about a dozen flying bombs in the vicinity,' he wrote. 'The nearest landed about 150 yards away at about 3am. It displaced the window frame of our sitting room, and blew a lot of glass out of the surrounding houses'. Luckily, Alanbrooke was woken from his slumber and heard the bomb droning overhead so quickly took cover under his bed just in time to avoid the fragments of glass that were showered about the room. Back at his desk early the next morning despite getting very little sleep, he was summoned at 9.30am by Churchill who was in a foul mood as he believed Monty was trying to stop him visiting the front. Alanbrooke flew out at once to Monty's HQ in France near Caen to smooth over the argument.

On 20 July 1944 an attempt was made on Hitler's life, Alanbrooke noting in his diary: 'I was astounded to hear of the attempt on Hitler's life, although this was exactly what I had been expecting for some time. It is hard at present to tell how serious the business may be, and how it will ultimately turn out.' However, Hitler survived and his flying bombs continued to fall on the capital, one coming within a quarter of a mile of Alanbrooke's London flat. The next day Alanbrooke took the Kennedys to see Lodge's studio where they had lunch and watched him at work doing some of the paintings for Bannerman's new book. Back at the office his relationship with Churchill continued to be fraught with difficulties. He wrote on 28 July 1944, 'I remain very fond of him, but by heaven he does try one's patience.' However, the war news at least was much more positive, the Allies making steady progress from their beachhead inland towards Paris.

At the end of July Alanbrooke again hosted one of his bird parties, Kennedy and his wife coming to dinner and examining bird books by Elliot Coues (1842–1899), the founder of the American Ornithologist Union. Two days later, following another trying Chiefs of Staff meeting, he headed to Kew Gardens as it was a lovely evening. Relaxing by one of the ponds, he wrote: 'We sat on a seat and watched some young water hens being instructed by their mother as to how a bath should be taken! She gave a demonstration first, and then those tiny mites followed suit and copied her, a wonderful sight.'

By early August, Alanbrooke's relationship with Churchill had reached a nadir. Ground down by his constant battles with the prime minister over the conduct of the war, a depressed Alanbrooke wrote on 15 August:

I feel that we have now reached the stage that for the good of the nation and for the good of his own reputation it would be a godsend if he could disappear out of public life. He has probably done more for this country than any other human being has ever done, his reputation has reached its climax, it would be a tragedy to blemish such a past by foolish actions during an inevitable decline which has set in during the last year. Personally I have found him almost impossible to work with of late, and I am filled with apprehension as to where he may lead us next.

Three days later on 18 August, at midnight, Alanbrooke left for a tour of Italy where he reviewed the position at Monte Cassino, examined the Anzio bridgehead and did a whistle-stop tour of Rome (it had been liberated on 4–5 June 1944). At the end of the tour he rushed around Rome's few remaining bookshops looking for a book on the birds of Italy but came away empty-handed. Following his arrival back in Britain Alanbrooke attended a thanksgiving service in St. Paul's Cathedral for the liberation of Paris on 28 August (the French capital had been liberated three days earlier, after six days of heavy fighting). Reflecting on the service, he wrote, 'Hearing the Marseillaise boom out gave me a deep thrill which stirred me inwardly. France seemed to wake again after being knocked out for 5 years.'

On 5 September Alanbrooke left on the *Queen Mary* bound for a second conference in Quebec, where the Allies secretly made plans to drop the atomic bomb on Japan. Here, he again clashed with Churchill over his mistrust of the Americans, commenting: 'Never have I admired and despised a man simultaneously to the same extent. Never have such opposite extremes been combined in the same human being.' (Writing after the war, Alanbrooke stated that his criticism of the prime minister was 'unnecessarily harsh' and was written out of exasperation with Churchill's continual badgering and interventions in military plans.) The conference finished with an agreement between the British, Americans and the Canadians over the next stages of the war in Europe and Asia. To recover from the conference, Alanbrooke took a flight from Quebec towards Hudson's Bay, flying over miles of 'virgin forest and masses of lakes'. He alighted at Oriskany Camp where he spent a peaceful couple of days fishing and birdwatching.

On 8 October Alanbrooke departed on yet another foreign tour of the military and political fronts, commenting in his diary: 'It is hard to believe that I dined comfortably in England yesterday, had breakfast in Naples today and may have my dinner in Cairo and possibly breakfast in Crimea tomorrow with lunch in Moscow!' It was a punishing schedule and one that took its toll on him, his diary entries frequently being punctuated with how 'dogged tired' he was. Two days later Churchill, Alanbrooke and their party dined with Stalin. This turned into a three-hour drinking session due to the number of toasts the Russians proposed, Alanbrooke recording: 'It was 5.30 pm when we rose from the table, we had sat for 3 solid hours!! What had we done? Listening to half inebriated politicians and diplomats informing each other of their devotion and affection, and expressing sentiments very far detached from veracity. Are international friendships based on such frothy products of drunken orgies? If so God help the future!'

In early November 1944 Churchill, Alanbrooke, the Foreign Secretary Anthony Eden (1897–1977), Mrs Churchill and other senior civil servants and detectives flew from Northolt aerodrome outside London to Paris where they were met by General de Gaulle, a man many of them despised but who had become a symbol of resistance and hope for many ordinary French people around the world. Alanbrooke was put up in the Continental Hotel in a comfortable suite of rooms where, to his delight, he discovered a surprise waiting for him, writing in his diary on 10 November: 'The hotel is closed. In my room I found a set of the most priceless bird books which had been drawn out of the Natural History Library for me to look at! Juin [Alponse, 1888–1967, French Chief of General Staff,] had asked Archdale of the Mission here if there was anything I might care for in my room to entertain me and he had suggested bird books, knowing me well! They are quite lovely and most of them original drawings.' The next day a grand parade was held to celebrate the liberation of Paris, Churchill and de Gaulle laying a wreath on the Tomb of the Unknown Soldier. Afterwards they marched down the Champs-Élysées, the police soon losing control of the large crowds who 'went quite mad over him, with continuous cries of "Churcheel! Churcheel."' Reflecting on the day's events, that evening Alanbrooke wrote: 'I must say that this morning's parade stirred me up very deeply. It was a wonderful feeling to be standing in Paris watching a review of French troops after the last four years of planning and struggling to get back again to France and to drive the Germans out of it.'

On 16 December Alanbrooke recorded in his diary a surprise German offensive against the Americans in the Ardennes region of Belgium which became known as the Battle of the Bulge: 'Germans are delivering strong counter offensive against Americans, who have no immediate reserves to stem the attack with.' It again showed that the Germans were not finished, but it turned out to be Hitler's last gamble.

Chapter 10

Victory, Hobbies and Hosking

The year 1945 started with Alanbrooke hoping that it would be the last year of war with Germany and complaining how tired he was, writing: 'I have now done 3 years of this job and am very very weary.' As an antidote to the war and feeling old, he again turned to his family and birds. On 20 January he sneaked out of the War Office for a late lunch and spent a relaxing afternoon gumming book plates into his precious bird books. He was also encouraged by the war news, commenting: 'Wonderful news from Russia continues to come in. This may well be the beginning of the beginning of the end! However, I feel that this offensive may still fall short of final victory and necessitate another double offensive, East and West, in the Spring.'

In late January, Alanbrooke chaired a Chiefs of Staff meeting to discuss the war situation followed by yet another War Cabinet, dominated, as usual, by Churchill. 'My God! How I loathe these Cabinet meetings,' Alanbrooke wrote on 22 January, 'The waste of time is appalling.' To recover from it he dined with the charismatic Meinertzhagen, who brought with him the Director of the London Zoo, Julian Huxley (1887–1975), his daughter and niece. Over dinner, much to Alanbrooke's amusement, Huxley told him the story of how on the night of the 27 September 1940 a zebra had escaped from the zoo. Firemen, with the help of war-weary Londoners, had chased it through the ruins of the capital before finally capturing it in Camden Town, cheered on by a huge crowd. The humorous evening, however, was only a temporary respite from Alanbrooke's problems. The next day he again clashed with Churchill at a Chiefs of Staff meeting over the prime minister's refusal to move troops from the Italian to the French front, recording in his diary, 'I don't feel I can stand another day working with Winston, it is quite hopeless, he is finished and gone, incapable of grasping any military situation and unable to give a decision.'

At the beginning of February the war came very close to home when Alanbrooke received the tragic personal news of the death of his *aide de camp* and flatmate Colonel Albany Kennett Charlesworth, known as 'Barney' (1892–1945). He had been killed in an air crash on 2 February while heading for Malta en route to the Yalta conference (as was customary for security reasons having flown out earlier). They had been together since the dark days of 1940, and writing afterwards, Alanbrooke said it was 'one of the worst blows I had during the war'. During his time as CIGS the two of them had often dined together in their London flat and as a consequence he had 'got to know him very well, and he knew me equally well. He was the most excellent companion and it was always a relaxation to be with him.'

The death of Alanbrooke's flatmate had a profound effect on him, the more so as he had no time to mourn or reflect that evening before himself leaving for Yalta where Churchill was meeting with President Roosevelt and Stalin to discuss the final stages of the war. By this time the Allies had liberated all of France and Belgium and were fighting on the western border of Germany. In the east, Soviet forces were only 40 miles from the capital Berlin, having already pushed back the Germans from Poland, Romania and Bulgaria.

In Yalta, following a long morning meeting on 5 February about strategic bombing of the western and eastern fronts, Alanbrooke found himself reflecting on the fickle fate of war which had so tragically killed Charlesworth. To cheer himself up he checked out the birds on the sea in front of his house. Scanning the water with his binoculars for a couple of hours he 'picked up a great northern diver, scoters, cormorants, many gulls and other diving ducks.' He was also delighted to see a pod of dolphins feeding on shoals of fish.

The Yalta conference again finished with lots of Russian toasts, Stalin hosting a special banquet on the evening of 8 February. The next day he wrote, slightly the worse for wear, 'The dinner as usual consisted of a series of toasts which went on continuously, with the result that most of the courses were cold before they reached one, or before one could settle down to try and eat them. Stalin was in the very best form, and was full of fun and good humour apparently thoroughly enjoying himself.' The standard of the speeches was, Alanbrooke thought, 'remarkably low' and he was very glad when the party broke up just before 1.00am and he was able to shake hands with Stalin and retire to bed.

Following Charlesworth's death, the first week of returning to an empty flat was particularly hard and lonely. So on 15 February, after a Chiefs of Staff meeting, he went to visit a local book dealer, Mr Rapheal King, who had a new bird book for him. 'I felt I could have committed almost any extravagance,' he wrote, 'this week trying to get used to Barney's absence has been very very trying. I never realized how much I should miss him and what an awful void he would leave in my life.'

The continuing war gave Alanbrooke little time to grieve. On 23 February at his weekly Chiefs of Staff meeting, they discussed the V2 rocket threat. Alanbrooke concluded that no air action was effective against a rocket that travelled at over 3,000mph; the only way to stop it was to clear 'the area from which they come by ground action, and that for the present is not possible.' The next day, to cheer himself up, he called in at Lodge's house where they discussed his new book, *The Memoirs of an Artist Naturalist*.

At the beginning of March Alanbrooke left with Churchill for the front to visit Monty and inspect the remains of the Siegfried Line, or Westwall, the defensive line built during the 1930s which was Germany's last line of defence. Churchill, who had been wanting to go to the lavatory, relieved himself on the line while the assembled photographers were asked to look the other way. Alanbrooke commented: 'I shall never forget the childish grin of intense satisfaction that spread all over his face as he looked down at the critical moment!'

By now Alanbrooke was looking beyond the war and his army career to consider what he might do when he retired. He had already vowed that he would get more involved in filming birds and conservation, so on 21 March he attended the British Ornithological Union (BOU) dinner, the guest of Jack Whitaker (ornithologist and author) and Bannerman. Founded in 1858, the BOU was one of the oldest and most respected ornithological organisations in the world with an international membership stretching across all continents. The dinner provided him with a good opportunity to network and see what opportunities were available. Meinertzhagen was also in attendance, much to Alanbrooke's pleasure, having recovered from a recent accident in which he had broken his rib.

By the end of March the Allies were massing on the Rhine, the last natural barrier before Berlin, and were preparing to cross it when they came under sustained enemy fire. Churchill, who was visiting the front with Alanbrooke, again left his mark by relieving himself in the river. This amusing episode could not, however, hide the fact that by this stage in the war Alanbrooke and the prime minister were nearly always at loggerheads. 'I feel that I just can't stick another moment with him, and would give almost anything never to see him again!' he wrote. 'The last three years are beginning to tell, and the strain of dealing with him is taking effect.' Relations got worse over the Easter of 1945 when Churchill called a Chiefs of Staff meeting on Easter Sunday. Alanbrooke finally got back to his house at 6.30pm and fumed in his diary, 'the day having been completely spoilt by Winston!' The next day he recovered at home by putting more book plates into his ever growing bird book collection and in the afternoon having Huxley, the curator of London zoo, and some friends to tea.

By the beginning of April the Allies had crossed the Rhine and Alanbrooke was asked to sit with the other Chiefs of Staff for a photograph to be included in the *London Illustrated Post's* victory issue. With the war now in its final stages, on the afternoon of 5 April he sneaked off to Edwards' antiquarian bookshop on Marylebone High Street to browse a copy of Phillip's monograph on ducks (composed of ducks and geese from all over the world, it was compiled by the American zoologist and ornithologist, John Charles Phillips, 1876–1938). Alanbrooke was admiring its beautiful plates when he was called back to an urgent Chiefs of Staff meeting to discuss Stalin, so he asked the assistant to put the copy aside for him. The next day he popped back for it after lunch, recording in his diary, 'to my great joy I collected a copy of Phillip's *A Natural History of the Ducks*. A book I had been looking for for a long time.'

On 2 May 1945 Alanbrooke was listening to the radio when, at midnight, they announced the death of Adolf Hitler. (Hitler had actually died on 30 April, shooting himself in his Führerbunker in Berlin. His wife of one day, Eva Braun, also committed suicide with him by taking cyanide.) Reflecting on the momentous news in his diary, he wrote: 'After longing for this news for the last 6 years, and wondering whether I should ever be privileged to hear it, when finally I listened to it I remained completely unmoved. Why? I do not know. I fully realized that it was the real full stop to the many and long chapters of this war, but I think that I have become so war weary with the continual strain of war that my brain is numbed, and incapable of feeling intensely.'

Alanbrooke celebrated the end of the war by spending a peaceful Sunday at home, in the afternoon visiting Bertie Fisher (1878–1972, retired General Officer Commanding Southern Command) who had located a number of bird nests for him to film. Together they put up hides overlooking nightingale, bullfinch and blackcap nests so that Alanbrooke could capture the parents feeding the young.

On 7 May hostilities with Germany officially ceased. To celebrate the victory Churchill invited Alanbrooke and the other Chiefs of Staff to lunch at Downing Street and afterwards each of them posed for another photograph in the garden. 'So this is at last the end of the war!!' Alanbrooke wrote in his diary. 'It is hard to realize. I can't feel thrilled, my main sensation is one of infinite mental weariness!' The next day was Victory in Europe Day, and huge crowds gathered in London and other cities throughout Britain to celebrate. Alanbrooke described it as a 'day disorganized by victory! A form of disorganization that I can put up with.' He left the War Office at 4.10pm, battling his way down the Mall and through an impenetrable crowd outside Buckingham Palace. After a 'very nice little speech' by the king he left for the Home Office where a balcony had been prepared so the prime minister, Cabinet and Chiefs of Staff could acknowledge the cheering crowds.

On looking out at the crowd Alanbrooke thought how very few in the vast sea of people before him knew what contribution the Chiefs of Staff had made to winning the war, despite them 'working and working incessantly, shouldering vast responsibilities, incurring great risks without the country ever realizing we were at work.' The war was, he concluded, a 'wonderful experience, of never ending interest. At times the work and the difficulties to be faced have been almost beyond powers of endurance. The difficulties with Winston have been almost unbearable proportions, at times I have felt that I could not possibly face a single other day. And yet I would not have missed the last 3½ years of struggle and endeavour for anything on earth.'

The next weekend he spent relaxing with his family, repairing the rabbit hutch and filming birds, writing on 12 May: 'After lunch went to Turgis Green where I met Mussens [Fisher's gamekeeper] and Bertie

Fisher. Mussens had nests of hawfinch, not ready to photograph, and nightingale, bullfinch, blackcap. I spent 1½ hours photographing the bullfinches, light not very good and heat oppressive. Came home for late tea and more work at the rabbit hutch.'

Back at work the next day he attended a thanksgiving victory service at St Paul's Cathedral, the following weekend filming hawfinches and nightingales at the nest. On 24 May Alanbrooke received a paper with scenarios for military action against the Russians, which had created quite a stir in the Foreign Office. Alanbrooke knew Churchill was concerned at seeing 'that Russian bear sprawled over Europe,' but as CIGS he had serious reservations about launching a war on their ally so soon after the ending of hostilities against Germany. That weekend, to put the Russians to the back of his mind, Alanbrooke went fishing and tried to film birds, but it was too wet.

Determined to get away, after inspecting the 43rd (Wessex) Division on 14 June he made another flying visit to the Farne Islands in Northumberland where he filmed the seabirds in lovely weather. It was his second successful trip following the disastrous one in 1943 when he had lost all of his equipment overboard. Very pleased with the results, he had by this stage in the war accumulated a large back catalogue of bird films which he now regularly showed to friends. Looking ahead to the end of his time as CIGS and his army career, Alanbrooke had decided he wanted to dedicate his time and energy to nature conservation but did not know yet what form that would take.

Two days later Winston Churchill called a snap election for 5 July and Parliament was dissolved. The election was the main subject over dinner on 20 June when Alanbrooke dined with Meinertzhagen and Lodge where they reviewed more pictures for Bannerman's book. Also at the dinner was 'Old Trenchard' (1873–1956, Hugh Trenchard, Marshal of the RAF, widely regarded as 'The Father of the RAF'). Alanbrooke commented: 'he gave me a feeling which I have had with a certain type of old soldier; that there is a very definite time in a man's life when it is best for him to go into retirement. I am approaching that age!' After mulling it over, he told Churchill that he wanted to go at the end of the year. However, the prime minister was having none of it, saying that after winning the election he wanted Alanbrooke to reorganise the army to meet the new Russian threat.

Over the next three weeks Churchill and the Conservative party ran a campaign based on the prime minister's popularity as a war leader. In contrast, the Labour party's manifesto, 'Let Us Face the Future', under their leader, Clement Attlee (1883–1967), promised nationalisation of key industries, full employment, a National Health Service and a system of social security. Although the election was held on 5 July, the results were not announced until the 26 July so that the votes from all those serving abroad could be counted.

On Saturday, 14 July, Alanbrooke had a very important meeting that would shape the rest of his life. Sitting quietly at home, he was told that some visitors had arrived unannounced and were putting up a bird hide in the village close to a reservoir and needed his help. Intrigued, Alanbrooke, who normally was very guarded about his private life and family time, went out to meet them. One was Mr Wooton, 'the head of a private school near Sandhurst', and the other was 'Mr Eric Hosking, the great bird photographer'. Eric Hosking was a pioneering bird photographer and filmmaker who had lost an eye earlier in his career while photographing a tawny owl at the nest. Despite his injury, Hosking went back to the nest to finish taking the photographs, the resulting pictures bringing him national publicity. Like Alanbrooke he used heavy and cumbersome equipment which he had to operate manually, but still achieved spectacular results. In 1944 Hosking had published two books – *The Art of Bird Photography*, showcasing some of his best work, and *Birds of the Day* with Cyril Newbury, a book aimed at enthusing people about birds which had sold over 50,000 copies.

Secretly in awe that Hosking should come to see him, Alanbrooke was told they had found a hobby's nest in a young Scots fir tree at a local reservoir, but needed permission to film it. Alanbrooke asked his wife to phone the local water board on his behalf to get permission. In return, Hosking asked Alanbrooke if he would like to make use of the hide. He enthusiastically agreed but explained that he was just about to leave for the Potsdam conference the next day and would be away a fortnight. Hosking assured him that the young would still be in the nest on his return so Alanbrooke took his telephone number and told him he would ring as soon as he got back. Writing after the war, Alanbrooke commented: 'This was the beginning of many happy days photographing with Eric Hosking, to whom I owe a great debt.'

On 15 July 1945, Alanbrooke left for Potsdam to discuss the post-war settlement of Germany. The conference was attended by Churchill, Stalin and the new US president, Harry Truman (1884–1972) who had succeeded Franklin Roosevelt following his death on 12 April 1945. While there, he saw the remains of Hitler's bunker where he had committed suicide, writing in his diary, 'Down below even worse chaos. It is, however, possible to make out one large sitting room probably used for meals, a study for Hitler, a bedroom of Hitler's opening into two separate bath and WC rooms, connecting through to Eva Braun's room. Beyond these an electric engine room, further bunks, gallery and a well equipped surgery.' He also learnt of the first secret test by the Americans of the atomic bomb, which greatly excited Churchill who thought it would 'alter the diplomatic equilibrium' with both the Russians and the Japanese.

On 26 July Alanbrooke recorded the surprising result of the general election in his diary: 'The Conservative Government has had a complete landslide and is out for good and all!!!' The Labour Party under Attlee's leadership had won a resounding victory, gaining a majority of 145 seats. It was the first election in which Labour gained a majority, with Attlee taking over from Churchill at the Potsdam conference. Two days later Alanbrooke got back in touch with Hosking about the hobby nest. Meeting him at 8.30am at the White Lion pub in the village, they then went straight to the nest where Hosking had erected a scaffold tower, viewing platform and a hide. 'A huge erection 26 feet high! but within 12 feet of the nest,' he wrote excitedly in his diary, adding, 'There are 3 young birds. By 9am I was established. At 10.45 the hen came for the first time and was at nest feeding for 10 minutes. At 12.15 she returned and was again there for close on 10 minutes. I took a lot of photographs and only hope that they may be good. It was a wonderful chance, and I believe the first time that a coloured cine picture of a hobby has been taken!'

At the beginning of August Alanbrooke returned to the hobby nest, getting there at 07.30am and starting the long climb to the top: 'By 9.15 I was again up in the hide 22ft above the ground and glad to have the climb up behind me! By 9.45 the hobby was back feeding and I exposed about 100ft of Kodachrome. I felt all was well and I must at least fit in another feed.' However, the female hobby did not return to the nest despite Alanbrooke remaining in the cramped hide for another four hours. 'But no luck,' he wrote, 'I remained until 2pm and she never returned!' The next day he again chaired his usual Chiefs of Staff meeting, which he ensured was 'remarkably short', before hurriedly returning to the Kodak developers where he collected his precious film of the hobby he had taken the previous Saturday. On viewing it he was delighted with the results: 'I am glad to say that it has turned out very good,' he recorded triumphantly in his diary.

At work he was making plans for the invasion of Japan, a military invasion most strategists believed would result in incalculable deaths as the Japanese fanatically defended their homeland. On 1 August he attended his first Labour Cabinet meeting chaired by Clement Attlee, the new prime minister. 'I remember being very impressed by the efficiency with which Attlee ran his cabinet,' he wrote. 'There was not the same touch of genius as with Winston, but there were more businesslike methods.' What particularly impressed him was the speed with which the meeting was conducted: 'We kept to the agenda, and he maintained complete order with a somewhat difficult crowd. Our work was quickly and efficiently completed.'

On 10 August the invasion of Japan was shelved following their surrender after the dropping of two atomic bombs, one on Hiroshima on 6 August and one on Nagaski on 9 August. Alanbrooke recorded the historic date in his diary, 'A memorable day as regards the war with Japan [...] Just before lunch BBC intercepts of Japanese peace offers were received in the shape of an acceptance of the Potsdam offer.' This kept the emperor as sovereign ruler but required the Japanese to surrender unconditionally. They finally signed the Instrument of Surrender in Tokyo Bay onboard the USS *Missouri* on September 2, 1945.

Alanbrooke discussed the Japanese surrender at a long Chiefs of Staff meeting on 13 August, after which he had Eric Hosking and his wife round to dinner when they watched his colour film of the hobby. 'Eric Hosking was delighted with it,' recorded Alanbrooke, 'and very complementary about it.' Two days later Alanbrooke recorded another historic event in his diary, the end of the Second World War, with the words: 'Six very very long years of continuous struggle, nerve wracking anxiety, dashed hopes, hopeless bleak horizons, endless difficulties with Winston etc finished with! When I look back at the blackest moments it becomes almost impossible to believe that we stand where we do. One thing above all others predominates all other thoughts, namely boundless gratitude to God, and to His guiding hand which has brought us where we are. Throughout the war His guiding influence has constantly made itself felt.'

Writing after the war, Alanbrooke sought to qualify his comments about Churchill and to give a more balanced account of his relationship with the prime minister.

From the continued abuse that I find on almost every page of my diary, I feel that I am perhaps conveying a false impression of my relations with him and of my feelings for him. Throughout all these troublesome times I always retained the same unbounded admiration, and gratitude for what he had done in the early years of the war. One could not help also being filled with the deepest admiration for such a genius and super man. And mixed with it all there were always feelings of real affection for the better side of him. In reading these diaries it must be remembered that I had a long and trying time with him and that the writing of the diary presented the only safety valve that I had to pent up feelings of irritation which I could share with no one else.[1]

At the end of 1945, Alanbrooke officially retired from the army and was made a viscount in 1946, later serving on the boards of several banking and oil companies. He also continued supporting the army, becoming Colonel Commandant to the Honourable Artillery Company and the Master Gunner of St James's Park, his birdwatching haunt. However, after retiring he got most pleasure from spending time with his family and pursuing his love of filming birds.

Alanbrooke and Hosking became good friends and together they would regularly visit Hilbre Island, situated on the Wirral at the mouth of the Dee estuary in Cheshire. The islands, which are tidal, are only accessible by foot at low tide and are one of the most important feeding grounds in Europe for wildfowl and waders, particularly as a 'refuelling station' on migration. At low tide Alanbrooke and Hosking would walk out to the islands and there set up a hide to film the birds which were pushed into an ever smaller area by the rising water. 'On our numerous visits to Hilbre Island, in the Cheshire Dee,' Hosking wrote, 'nothing pleased him more than to sit in a hide watching and filming the hordes of waders being pushed nearer to him by the rising tide, until he was sometimes completely surrounded by them.'

In 1946 Alanbrooke became President of the Wildfowl and Wetlands Trust after becoming good friends with its founder, Peter Scott (1909–1989). In 1949, with Hosking's encouragement, he became the Vice-President of the Royal Society for the Protection of Birds, a position he held until his death. A year later, in 1950, he became President of the Zoological Society of London serving for four years. As well as filming birds in his local patch in Hampshire, Alanbrooke also took part in two expeditions to the Coto Doñana in Southern Spain in 1956 and 1957, his films helping to convince the Spanish government to designate it as a nature reserve in 1963. Hosking commented: 'On the two Coto Doñana Expeditions, which were led by Guy Mountfort, Lord Alanbrooke took his full share in the making of the now famous *Wild Spain* film, even climbing the tall pylon hide, when he was almost 74 years of age, to film the very rare Spanish imperial eagle.'

In the bitterly cold winter of 1962 Hosking visited a frail Alanbrooke at home in his garden cottage. On his arrival Alanbrooke asked if he would like to see his hide, Hosking commenting: 'It was so cold I could not imagine anyone wishing to sit in a hide.' Instead, Alanbrooke took him through to his study where he had erected a cine camera focused on a tree stump outside in his garden which he had baited with bird food. There he would sit for hours writing letters, and if a bird landed on the tree he would start the camera rolling. 'There was a twinkle in his eyes,' Hosking recalled, 'as he said to me, "You have never yet built a comfortable hide for me". As we talked a greater spotted woodpecker alighted on the stump – one of his favourite birds.'

On 17 June 1963, Alanbrooke died of a heart attack with his beloved wife, Benita, by his side. For his 80th birthday she had planned to present him with John Gould's *Humming-Birds* so he would once again own a set of his books. The money for them had been contributed by his many colleagues and friends from Winston Churchill to Eric Hosking. Afterwards Benita wrote 'He had known of the plan and the prospect of once again owning such treasures and the affection shown by his friends in obtaining the books gave him much joy...I am happy to feel his memory will live on through his love of nature and in particular of birds.'

In an obituary in *British Birds*, Eric Hosking wrote:

With the death of Field Marshal Viscount Alanbrooke, on the 17th June, within a few weeks of his eightieth birthday, the country mourns the loss of an outstanding soldier to whom the whole free world owes so much. It is not too much to say that without his superb generalship during the Second World War we might all of us be living a very different life today. As Chief of the Imperial General Staff it was he, second only to Sir Winston Churchill, who guided the nation through the difficult years between 1939 and 1945.

Lord Alanbrooke was a man of many parts, obviously most outstanding as a soldier, but with something of the same brilliance as an ornithologist, and the two spheres interacted, for it was ornithology that was his safety valve during the war when the burden he carried seemed nigh intolerable. He knew exactly what to film and what to leave out and he loved to show his films at schools and all kinds of institutions, giving a commentary that was full of enthusiasm and humour. But few people realised that he was among the pioneers of wildlife photography, having taken his first photographs in India during the early days of this century. His exceptional ability to concentrate his whole energies on the task of the moment saved him from cracking up. Whether it was a top level conference of war leaders or the search through his binoculars for some rare wader on the shore, he could give it his whole and entire attention.[2]

Chapter 11

Peter Scott, Hunting and Hitler

Alanbrooke was not the only war hero to find solace in birds. In 1931 a twenty-one-year-old student by the name of Peter Scott was taking a year's study leave at the State Academy School in Munich. He was staying with a distinguished animal painter, Angelo Jank, and his family, hoping to improve both his art and his German. Jank's middle son, Ruli, was the same age as Scott, the two young men studying together and sharing a room in the house at 25 Karl Theodor Strasse in Schwabing, an eastern suburb of Munich. Scott had earlier that year graduated from Cambridge University where he had been studying the history of art, and was already an accomplished artist, a talent he had inherited from his mother who was a sculptor. Scott was also a very keen naturalist and a good shot, spending much of his spare time wildfowling. For entertainment he went to dances, music festivals and tea parties as well as going fishing and attending the World Figure Skating Championships held in Berlin. Then one day Ruli suggested that they go along to listen to an up-and-coming politician speaking at the Bürgerbräukeller by the name of Adolf Hitler.

By this time Hitler was well known on the city's speaker circuit, Munich being the birthplace of his Nationalsozialistische Deutsche Arbeiterpartei (National Socialist German Workers' Party or Nazi Party). Here he had attempted to seize power in November 1923 in the infamous Bürgerbräu-Putsch (Beer Hall Putsch) when 2,000 Nazis had marched on the Feldherrnhalle (Field Marshal's Hall), the headquarters of the Bavarian army, where they were confronted by armed police who shot dead sixteen of them. Hitler had been wounded in the fracas and was arrested, later being found guilty of treason and sentenced to five years in Landsberg prison (instead he only served nine months and used the time to dictate his autobiographical manifesto *Mein Kampf* or *My Struggle*). Seven years later, when Ruli and Scott decided to attend one of Hitler's speeches, the Nazi party was at its zenith and would in a few months become the largest party in the Reichstag (German Parliament) in the federal elections. Reflecting their rise, Hitler had progressed from a prison cell to a luxury nine-bedroom apartment at Prinzregentenplatz 16 and the Nazi Party had established its headquarters, the Braunes Haus (Brown House), just off the grand Königsplatz in the centre of the city. Due to the importance of Munich to the rise of Nazism, the city that Scott had chosen for his study break was known as the *'Hauptstadt der Bewegung'* ('Capital of the Movement').

When asked by Ruli what he thought of going to see Hitler, Scott replied that he did not take him seriously, describing him as an 'indifferent imitator of Mussolini'. Scott was also indifferent to the risk involved, despite Hitler's fiery oration often leading to impromptu attacks on foreigners and running battles with his political opponents. So Ruli and an impervious Scott went along to the Bürgerbräukeller where a large crowd of people were already milling around outside. Opened in 1855, the beer hall was located in the Haidhausen district of Munich on the east side of the Isar River, not far from where they lived. It consisted of a beer garden, restaurant, a number of small rooms that could be hired out for public or private meetings, and its showpiece, the grand hall.

Ruli and Scott went in through the entrance on Rosenheimer Street underneath an ornate archway with the words *'Bürger, bräu und keller'* written in black Gothic script in a semicircle at the top. The walls were plastered with posters advertising the speech, displaying Hitler's name in the centre, in large, prominent letters. At the bottom were written the words *'juden haben keinen zutritt'* (Jews are not allowed). Loitering everywhere were members of Hitler's *Sturmabteilung* (Storm Detachment) or SA, the paramilitary wing of the Nazi party who were colloquially known as *Braunhemden* (Brownshirts) because of the colour of their uniforms. Many were armed with barely concealed knives, clubs and coshes despite a heavy police presence, and they eyed those entering the hall warily, looking for known Communist sympathisers and other enemies of the party. The threat of violence hung heavy in the air as Ruli and Scott joined a long queue of people waiting to enter the hall.

As they waited hawkers walked up and down selling Sturm cigarettes from trays slung over their shoulders, attracting the attention of Scott who was a smoker. The cigarette company sponsored the SA so any member caught smoking another brand was badly beaten (the SA also used intimidation and violence against any shopkeepers stocking alternative brands). After going through a security check in which their clothes and bags were thoroughly searched, they were asked if they were party members while the Brownshirts on the door stared at them aggressively. Ruli explained that they were both here to hear Hitler speak after having heard so much about him. Satisfied, the SA let them pass and they made their way across a packed grand hall to their table. There they took their seats among a noisy and restless crowd of over 3,000 people. So popular was the event that people had crammed in at the back where they stood by the pillars, many craning on tiptoes to get a better view. All around the hall were swastika flags and along the back wall hung two large swastika banners which reached from the ceiling to the floor. Above them sparkling chandeliers concealed the steel beams supporting the ancient timber roof of the beer hall.

After having made their way through the crowd to their allotted table, Ruli and Scott settled down and called over a waitress. They ordered foaming pints of the local Löwenbräu beer, the brewery having purchased the beer hall in 1923. (As the brewery was owned by Joseph Schülein, a Jew, the beer was later boycotted by the Nazis who referred to it as 'Jews' beer', and in 1933, after Hitler came to power, Schülein was forced to stand down.) The grand hall was crowded with Brownshirts, many of whom were already well on their way to being drunk, but there were also respectable middle-class families and city officials in suits at the tables. At this point Ruli produced his sketchbook and discreetly hid it under their table. He was a gifted artist and particularly enjoyed doing caricatures of well-known people, Scott describing him as a 'clever draughtsman and a devastating caricaturist'. Ruli and Scott were both studying at the art academy in the city, but were in different classes and only met in the afternoons when they practised 'life drawings'. Now Ruli was going to try to do a real-life drawing of the city's most famous politician, but he had to do so without attracting the unwanted attention of the menacing Brownshirts all around him. Ruli's clandestine art involved taking a great risk so Scott sensibly decided instead to sit back, drink his beer and listen to the oration.

The tension in the room had been building for some time before Hitler finally made his appearance, over fifteen minutes after his allotted start time. He was met by thunderous applause, most people in the hall jumping up and extending their right arms in the Nazi salute and shouting 'Heil Hitler!' at the top of their voices. At this Ruli got up and Scott quickly followed. Ruli made a halfhearted gesture to join in, but without giving the salute, while leaning over and whispering in Scott's ear, 'How can a man with a moustache like Charlie Chaplin expect to be taken seriously anyway?' When the cheering had finally died down a relieved and grinning Scott took his seat. This dramatic build-up was an important part of Hitler working his audience, and after signalling for them to sit down he then waited another full minute in silence while he looked out across the hall. Behind him on the stage were Nazi flags and a line of SA men who watched the audience like hawks, looking for any sign of trouble. When Hitler finally began to speak his voice was low and almost conversational, Ruli and Scott straining to hear. Almost immediately there were shouts of abuse from a Communist sympathiser in the audience, nearby SA men quickly moving to eject him forcefully from the hall.

Over the next hour Hitler then implored, harangued and seduced Scott, his impassioned speech leaving most of the audience spellbound. As his resonating shouts and histrionics reached a crescendo, Ruli quickly sketched Hitler's enraged face, also capturing his wildly gesticulating arms and hands in his sketchbook. Then Hitler would abruptly stop mid-sentence, turn away and fold his arms to look at his notes, the audience responding by jumping to their feet and 'heiling' in unison. Ruli decided to not only capture Hitler in full flow, his arm slicing through the air as he shouted, *'Deutschland erwache!'* ('Germany awake!') but also the quieter moments as he smoothed his hair down in a steady, unhurried motion. Scott was transfixed, despite not being able to understand all of the speech as his German was not good enough. As Hitler spoke, much to his surprise he found himself being coerced and then slowly but surely being won over. Looking around the hall he saw many people in the audience were overawed or crying tears of joy, especially the women who were among Hitler's most ardent fans. When the speech was finally over, he commented to Ruli, 'One could not fail to be impressed by the oratory, even if I did not understand more than about half of the speech at all, and had little or no conception of the implications. But as a piece of rabble-rousing I, as part of the rabble, was duly roused.' Ruli was less impressed, and according to Scott, 'came out murmuring something about the Fascist shirts at least being black, and why had Hitler chosen dung-colour for his. Next day there were some new and magnificently comical drawings in Ruli's caricature book.'[1]

Five years later Scott returned to Germany for the 1936 Olympics, winning a bronze medal for sailing. Eight years after hearing Hitler speak at the Bürgerbräukeller he served with distinction in the Second World War, fighting against him and everything that Nazism stood for. Scott's long and illustrious career in ornithology would follow a similar path. As a young man he was a 'fanatical wildfowler', but after the war he dedicated his life to conserving the same ducks and geese he had shot in his youth. Asked by a journalist how he could equate killing with his later love of birds Scott replied, 'They were man's traditional quarry and it was part of man's instinct to hunt; it was part of the birds' instinct to be hunted. My delight and admiration for wild geese was based as much upon their supreme capacity to remain watchful and to look after themselves as it was upon their beauty and grace.' When questioned further he said that like most eighteen-year-olds he wasn't sentimental, adding that 'our relations were simple and straightforward, to be carried to the logical conclusion – to the death.' It was a sentiment that would have appalled Hitler, who was a well-known animal lover and hated hunting.

Peter Scott was born on 14 September 1909 and had achieved worldwide fame before he was three years old as the only child of the famous Antarctic explorer Robert Falcon Scott (1868–1912). A few days before he died in his tent in the Antarctic on 29 March 1912, Robert Scott had famously written to his sculptor wife, Kathleen (née Bruce): 'Make the boy interested in Natural History. It is better than games. They encourage it in some schools'. The young Scott lived up to his father's expectation and wrote: 'I was two-and-a-half years old then and I cannot remember a time when I was not interested in Natural History.' Although his father's tragic legacy would always hang over him, his son would, in time, emerge from his shadow to become one of the most famous naturalists in the world.

Although Robert Scott's wife had accompanied him to New Zealand to see the explorer off on his ill-fated expedition, she and her son only learned of his fate almost a year later in February 1913. While most of the tragic consequences of his death would have been shielded from a three-year-old boy, the letters that his father sent and a picture of the three of them together on the sofa would provide the young Scott with cherished childhood memories, although ones very likely embellished by his mother over time. Despite having no father, Scott had a privileged and very happy childhood. He was brought up in a big Victorian house at 174 Buckingham Palace Road, his mother also owning a small coastguard's cottage near Sandwich in Kent. Here Scott played in the sand and would spend hours searching for lizards in the walls.

With the outbreak of the First World War in 1914, the beach where Scott played was fortified against a possible seaborne invasion. Lying on it one day Scott saw overhead a party of German Gotha airships heading towards London to bomb the capital. It was also at Sandwich that Scott, while looking out for airships, saw his first geese, a party of Brent Geese flying low over the sea in a V formation. 'As they passed the afternoon sun shone full upon their bright forms,' he wrote. 'I did not know what they were at the time, but I carried the picture in my mind until long afterwards when I realised without doubt what I had seen – my very first wild geese.'[2]

In 1917 Scott's mother got a job in the British Embassy in Paris and took her young son with her. A few months after arriving, the Germans, who were only 40 miles away, began to pound the French capital with 'Big Bertha', their huge, long-range siege gun, and panic and fear soon spread throughout the population. Scott's mother decided that the besieged city was too dangerous a place to bring up her eight-year-old son and fled back to London. She and her son saw out the rest of the war there trying to avoid the Zeppelin bombers.

After the war Scott was taken to explore St James's Park, which was only a short distance from his home in Buckingham Palace Road. This had been the birdwatching haunt of the Foreign Secretary, Sir Edward Grey, during the First World War (the park would also be the local patch of the future prime minister, Neville Chamberlain, in the run up to the Second World War). With its collection of tame wildfowl and pelicans donated by the Russia Ambassador to King Charles II in 1664, the park was an ideal location for the young Scott to learn about the ducks and geese he would later do so much to conserve. The park also turned up a surprising number of rare wild birds, and Scott liked nothing better than going there with his mother and identifying the different species. Later in life he credited St James's Park with being the catalyst that turned his fledgling interest in birds into a passion. 'Our house was about half-way between St James's Park and Chelsea Gardens,' he wrote. 'Hyde Park and Battersea Park were only a little further, and yet St James's was always the favourite, which must surely have been because of the pelicans and the ducks. This early association with ducks may or may not have had a deep psychological influence and may even have been the true forerunner of my life-long passion for the *Anatidae* [the family of water birds which includes ducks, geese and swans].'

In the autumn of 1919 Scott was sent to board at West Downs, a Preparatory School near Winchester, where he was made to feel very welcome by the headmaster, who admired his father. Here he enthusiastically took up bug hunting, identifying his first poplar hawk moth and keeping the caterpillars in a vivarium. In the school holidays Scott and his mother travelled widely, touring Italy and visiting Tunisia where he revelled in the natural history. It was at West Downs that Scott first got to meet his new stepfather. Edward Hilton Young (1879–1960) was a baronet, politician and businessman as well as a naval hero. He had lost his right arm in the Zeebrugge Raid in 1918 in an unsuccessful attempt to block the Belgian port and prevent German ships and U-boats from leaving. He was also a keen birdwatcher, which endeared him no end to Scott.

After West Downs Scott attended Oundle school in Northamptonshire, spending much of his time fishing and watching wildlife. Here he particularly excelled at making drawings of the birds he saw, recalling 'although they were the animals I enjoyed most, and enjoyed drawing most, I was left in no doubt that this was to be regarded as "play" – it was certainly not biology.' With two friends he published his first bird book, *Adventures Among Birds*, Scott doing the drawings in the margin. The book was privately printed with a limited run of just over 500 copies, but the quality of the drawings clearly illustrated Scott's artistic potential. In the long summer holidays he learned to sail, which like drawing and painting, soon became another passion.

When he was seventeen Scott went on a holiday to a shooting lodge in Scotland where he was first introduced to stalking by his guardian, Lord Knutsford (1855–1931, 2nd Viscount Knutsford), and shot his first stag. 'The shooting of my first stag was steeped in the romantic traditions of the sport,' he wrote, 'and overnight I was an enthusiastic stalker.' Scott finished his time at Oundle in the top half of the biology sixth form but he won no scholastic prizes and only just scraped being a prefect. Despite his distinctly mediocre academic achievements, in the autumn of 1927 he went on to Trinity College in Cambridge to read the Natural Sciences, composed of zoology, botany and physiology, later adding geology.

When not studying, Scott went out three times a week with the local hunt, the Trinity Foot Beagles, and afterwards he joined the Master of the Hunt, Bill Hicks Beach (1907–1975, Tory MP), shooting snipe. Scott soon started shooting on his own, forming the Trinity Duck Hunt and keeping a wildfowling diary of his exploits. One of the locations he visited was Terrington Marsh near Kings Lynn, and here Scott bagged his first goose. In his autobiography he wrote:

> Almost at once the black line of them appeared, a dozen geese full low and passing close behind me. I swung round and fired one shot over my left shoulder, and throwing myself on my back I fired the second. As I watched, one of the geese seemed to be separating from the others. At first, being upside down, I did not realise that it was falling, but as I jumped up I heard a thud on the soft muddy turf. I ran to the spot, and there he was stone-dead on the salting – my very first goose. He turned out to be a bean goose – a considerable rarity. But at the time he was to me a plain wild goose, and that was all that mattered.'[3]

Scott soon started spending much of his spare time wildfowling, first investing in a second-hand punt called 'Penelope' and then commissioning a boatbuilder in Cambridge to make him a bespoke one, which he christened 'Grey Goose'. To shoot he would head to Terrington Marsh (which he gave the codename Sandbanks) in Norfolk, or the Cambridgeshire Fens, where he claimed his first 'right and left' geese, killing two geese with both barrels of his gun in quick succession. 'The feeling of achievement was complete,' he wrote, 'long looked forward to, cleanly executed, utterly satisfying to contemplate. I do not think at the time I experienced any trace of regret at the destruction of these beautiful creatures, such as I should feel were I to do the same thing today [Scott was writing in 1956].' The most exciting form of wildfowling was 'moonlit flighting'. On a moonlit night Scott would wait until the tide had filled the creeks in the lower marsh. Hiding behind a high bank, he could shoot the geese at close range as they flew over low, silhouetted against the moon. On particularly well-lit nights he would carry on until dawn, getting back to Trinity in time for breakfast and his first lectures where he often struggled to stay awake.

Soon Scott had shot each of the seven species of geese found in the wild in Britain. As well as shooting wildfowl, he also began to draw his quarry and 'found a new delight in painting the birds that I spent so much time pursuing.' In particular he used his art to recreate the excitement of being out shooting on the marsh as the ducks and geese came in to roost; man versus nature with just a gun against a silvery moonlight sky. As a result Scott was asked to put on a small exhibition of his work at a local Cambridge booksellers, Messrs Bowes and Bowes. To his surprise he sold most of his paintings and put the money towards future expeditions.

While wildfowling took up Scott's winter nights, in summer he scoured the fens with the Cambridge Bird Club looking for breeding ducks, finding the nests of the pintail and the garganey, both very rare species. When not birding he greatly enjoyed sailing, becoming a member of the Cambridge University Cruising Club. He soon became an expert yachtsman, and in December 1929, to test out his ability at sea, he purchased a 24-ft-long double punt which he called 'Kazarka' after the Russian red-breasted goose. On his maiden voyage Scott saw an unusual goose among a large flock of pinkfeet, later identifying it as a blue goose, a first record for Europe. His adventures wildfowling with Kazarka were what he lived for, eulogising after one trip, 'So ended our three days in the magic world of the wildfowl – to me, at that time, the only world of reality. The University of Cambridge might have been another planet.'

Scott's increasing absenteeism and his lack of interest in his academic work did not go unnoticed. His stepfather was contacted by the university and wrote to him urging him to concentrate on his studies. While Scott's academic record let him down, what stood out was his innate skill at drawing and painting. So, after consultation with the university and his stepfather, he decided to change course. 'As my academic career in Natural Science held no great promise I decided to change horses in midstream, and to complete my time at Cambridge by studying "History of Art and Architecture". At the same time my primary objective in life changed. Instead of a scientist I would be an artist.' In order to complete his new degree he stayed on an extra year and by his own admission worked harder than he had done in the previous three.

In August 1929 Scott had his first pictures of wildfowl published in *Country Life* magazine. They were simple watercolours accompanied by a 'bloodthirsty little article, of which I am not very proud, describing my wildfowling adventures.' However, the magazine was so impressed by Scott's pictures that they regularly graced its pages for years afterwards. The success of the article convinced Scott he could become a professional painter, although he remained under no illusions that he could make a living at it. He graduated in 1930, by which time he had also taken up skating, describing himself as 'moderately proficient on the ice'. In 1931 he went on a year's study leave to Munich where, as well as acquainting himself with Adolf Hitler, he went to his first opera, *Die Meistersinger von Nurnberg*. Like the Führer, he soon became a devotee of Wagner, using his student card to go two or three times a week, and it was not long before he had seen all of Wagner's operas, including *The Ring*. Then one day his quiet existence in Munich was shattered and the reality of living in Hitler's Germany came home to him with a vengeance.

At dinner one evening the Jank family, with whom Scott was staying, received 'some shocking and disastrous' news: the son of a close friend had married a Jew. Frau Jank, who Scott considered a 'kind and tolerant soul, friendly and charitable', was incredulous. Her voice nearly breaking, she proclaimed, '*eine Judin. Ja, wie ist dass möglich?*' ('a Jew. Yes, how is this possible?'), before the whole family joined in. Scott remembered them saying, 'how was it possible that this nice young man could have been so foolish and so unkind to his parents as to marry a Jewess?' The same topic of conversation came up regularly at meal times until one day Scott summoned up the courage to speak out, rebuking his hosts for being anti-semitic. 'It was the first time I had met racial prejudice,' Scott wrote, 'and it was as frightening to me as the social instinct of a swarm of wasps.'

Despite their difference of opinion Scott soon forgave his adopted family because 'they were my friends, these people, and I knew and loved them well. Whatever their views might be, violence was not in their thoughts. This may have been the soil in which to grow pogroms and Auschwitz and a second world war, but in 1931 the seeds had not yet been sown at No. 25 Karl Theodor Strasse.' Yet he had heard Hitler plant exactly those seeds at his speech in the Bürgerbräukeller and seen the reaction. The next time he visited Munich in 1938 his friend Ruli was in the *Wehrmacht* (German army) preparing for war, although Scott still believed he was an 'unwilling Nazi'.

Following his return to England in the autumn of 1931, Scott became a pupil at the Royal Academy which he described as 'two happy years of drawing and painting'. There he perfected his drawing style, learning to skillfully portray birds in different mediums. Soon Scott found himself being lauded as an artist.

When people asked how he could produce such beautiful pictures of birds and at the same time shoot them, Scott would reply that it was man's 'primitive instinct to hunt'. It was an unconvincing argument, and by the spring of 1932 he was beginning to have doubts himself. With a friend he had shot twenty-three greylag geese, among them two wounded birds that, strangely, he hoped would not die. They survived and Scott kept them for many years afterwards as he began to wonder why he had ever taken such delight in killing them. 'Here was something of the awful paradox which faces man in war who is called upon to kill his fellow men,' he wrote. Despite a softening of his heart, Scott could not give up wildfowling, commenting, 'So many things went with the actual shooting – the beauty, the natural history, the exercise, the memories, and particularly the technical skills which in the course of years I had acquired. Especially was this so of punting; the seamanship, the boat handling, the knowledge of weather and tide – all these appealed to me as much as ever.'

Scott now decided that as well as shooting birds he would like to catch them, so he experimented with decoys and nets, finally catching his first pinkfoot. His diary entry read: 'These two days have been two of the most enjoyable I ever spent in pursuit of geese; and the total bag has been one goose ... but alive.' In 1933 he moved into The Lighthouse on Terrington Marsh in Norfolk, where he had enjoyed so many days' shooting, and turned it into his new studio. From here he began to paint prolifically, holding very successful exhibitions at Ackermann's Galleries on Bond Street every year from 1933 up to the start of the Second World War in 1939. Among those buying a painting was Her Majesty Queen Elizabeth, who purchased 'a fiery picture of pinkfeet coming out from inland to the mudflats of the Wash at dusk'.

Prints of Scott's paintings also began to sell well and when he was not painting or drawing he was busy sailing. Soon, thanks to his exhibitions, he could afford his own boat, a 14-ft dinghy, and in 1934 he entered a new transatlantic team race between Canada, the United States and Britain as part of the crew of a boat called *Eastlight* which won several races. He also entered the Prince of Wales Cup, and though he only finished sixteenth he entered again the following year in a new boat called *Whisper* with high hopes of winning. However, during the race the mast snapped, leaving Scott feeling very angry. 'I found it especially hard to be a "good loser",' he commented, 'even though I knew I would lose more by being a bad one. Our misfortune in the Prince of Wales Cup of 1935 was doubtless very good for the character.'

The same year Scott brought out a new book, *Morning Flight*,[4] which was published by *Country Life*. The first edition sold out quickly and a cheaper version soon followed which remained in print for the next ten years. The last chapter of the book juxtaposes Scott's love of birds with his love of music: 'The nightingale and the blackcap and the curlew are nature's soloists but the geese are her chorus, as rousing, over the high sand, as the "sanctus" of Bach's b minor Mass. As they flight at dawn one can imagine that each successive skein brings in the fugue, *Pleni sunt coeli* (full are the heavens).'[5]

The next year in the summer of 1936, Scott entered the infamous Olympic Games held in Germany. The sailing events took place in the port of Kiel where he came third, winning a bronze medal in the O-Jolle category, the dinghy class, taking part in seven races and competing against twenty-four other nations. Scott narrowly missed out on getting the silver when he was forced to retire from the last race after clipping Germany's Werner Krogmann. Over 50,000 citizens attended the closing ceremony, which saw the Germans top the medal table. Scott's bronze medal was a notable personal achievement and a great accolade for the British team, although he felt he should have done better. While racing took up more of his time, Scott continued to paint and draw, doing a series of illustrations for his stepfather's poetry book, *A Bird in the Bush*.[6] However, being a perfectionist he was not pleased with his work: 'A few of the designs were fine and bold but too many of the small birds I was groping for a likeness. For so exquisite a book the illustrations should have been perfect and I was sad that they were not.' The next year, after his fourth attempt, he finally won the Princes of Wales Cup at Lowestoft in a boat appropriately enough called *Thunder*.

In the summer of 1938 Scott again entered the Prince of Wales Cup in a new boat called *Thunder and Lightning*. This time he romped home, winning by over four minutes, but was later disqualified for using a new invention called the trapeze which allowed the crew to lean much further out over the water when steering the dinghy. Much later the trapeze would be allowed by the yachting authorities, but at the time it was deemed a breach of the rules, leading Scott to disdainfully conclude, 'It is tremendously exhilarating to stand out, comfortably supported by the trapeze, almost horizontal and skimming low over the waves. It is sad that a handful of people who did not have the vision to see this should have outlawed the trapeze for so long.'

At home Scott had been building up a wildfowl collection at The Lighthouse, which now occupied about seven acres of salt marsh enclosed by the sea wall and a fox-proof fence. He was also becoming attached to some of the geese, particularly a pinkfoot which he christened 'Annabel'. In March 1937 he watched as Annabel left for Iceland and was over the moon when she returned again in the October. 'I called to her and she walked straight up to me. Any doubt I might have had that this really was Annabel immediately vanished. There she stood, a plump little round person, with her queer angular forehead, her unusually pink bill pattern, and the few white feathers at its base. To me she was as recognisable as a stray sheep to a shepherd or a stray hound to a huntsman.' However, Scott's peaceful life was about to come to an abrupt end as the government tried in vain to appease Hitler.

In the autumn of 1938, as prime minister Neville Chamberlain was taking the last of his three historic flights to Germany, Scott was in Canada as the captain of a 14-foot dinghy team and also planning the launch of his next book, *Wild Chorus*,[7] the successor to *Morning Flight*. He was preparing for an exhibition of his paintings in New York, and about to embark on a shooting and painting tour of America, but due to the threat of war decided to come home in December 1938, sailing on the German liner *Bremen*. On his home-coming he wrote, '"Peace in our time" was the slogan to which I had returned, but it seemed wise to get my name on a Reserve list.' Scott enrolled with the Royal Naval Volunteer (Supplementary) Reserve (RNVR), and as Chamberlain's hopes for peace began to crumble, Scott prepared for war. 'The prospect of war and change was exciting and unsettling. For the adventurous there was no particular merit in the comfortable security of my present existence, but I bitterly resented the prospect of its interruption.'

Chapter 12

Broke, Birds and Camouflage

In the summer of 1939 Scott and his mother went on holiday to stay with the Russian pianist George Chavchavadze (1904–1952) in Venice. One evening, as he was playing for them, they sat on his balcony and watched the moonlight shimmer on the Grand Canal. Seeing the light reflected on the palaces, Scott commented to his mother 'So much beauty'. However, they both knew that the storm clouds of war were gathering, for which he blamed a handful of wicked men. 'European politics hung like a great cumulo-nimbus cloud over the summer,' he wrote. At the end of the piano recital he turned to his mother and said, '"Peace in our time" my foot!'

As a result of the increasing signs of war in Europe, Scott had left the Lighthouse, making arrangements for his birds to be housed with friends. Waiting to see what would happen, he went sailing, entering *Thunder and Lightning* into several regattas. But even the highly competitive Scott could see that racing was now no longer important, commenting, 'all the significance and excitement of it seemed to drain away as we sailed round in a kind of trance.' When Chamberlain finally declared war on Germany on 3 September 1939 Scott was staying with a friend and impatient to serve. He fired off a letter to the Admiralty volunteering his services for the Royal Naval Volunteer (Supplementary) Reserve. It had been set up to attract skilled civilians with naval experience so Scott imagined he would get a speedy reply from the Admiralty. But he heard nothing back and in the meantime kicked his heels, designing a cryptic camouflage scheme for a wheel grinding factory in Stafford.

Frustrated at not being called up, Scott instead decided to improve the morale of the nation by making a special broadcast on the BBC about badgers, having recently watched some near his home. A producer at the corporation had been impressed by Scott's book *Wild Chorus* and asked him to record a piece for a new programme called the BBC Home Service (it was created at the start of the war by merging the BBC National and

Regional Programmes, the latter being closed down so the Germans could not use the transmitters as navigational beacons). Scott started off mundanely enough, telling the listeners that he had an 'adventure the other night' watching badgers in a wood in Wiltshire. However, he turned the piece into an amusing story by telling an anecdote: 'Up until last week my only experience of badgers was that I once caught one in an umbrella. Mind you, I don't suppose many people have caught a wild badger in an umbrella; I'd even hazard a guess that I was the only person who ever had caught a badger in an umbrella.'[1] The listeners were intrigued – and hooked.

'It was up in the Bavarian Alps,' Scott told his BBC audience, 'that I saw a baby badger sitting right out in the open.' Scott was returning home at teatime after a wonderful day trout fishing, wild strawberry collecting and swimming in the river. Over one shoulder was his fishing rod and over the other was his bathing towel, his trusty umbrella hanging from his arm in case of sudden thunderstorms, 'a speciality of the Alps'. Scott saw the baby badger by a wooden hut used to store hay, 'of course, as soon as he saw me he started to run back to his hole which was actually under the hut, and thinking it might be rather fun to have a closer look at him I jumped to head him off. We both had about ten yards to go, but as I went, I had a brainwave – I half-opened my umbrella and blocked the hole with it. The badger finished close second and he ran straight into the umbrella and got caught.' Wrapping his bathing towel around his hand, Scott reached into the umbrella, the badger immediately biting him but allowing Scott to have a good look at the animal. Afterwards he showed the badger to a friend and they decided he was too old to be tamed. Scott informed the audience that they made the 'most wonderful pets, [although] you must start with them when they're very tiny.' When the baby badger was returned to his hole Scott was amused to hear 'the most tremendous sound of grunts and squeaks. Evidently the poor little fellow was getting roundly scolded for being out so long.'

The BBC were so impressed with the piece that they asked Scott to produce another one and so he recorded 'September in the Country' three weeks after war had been declared in 1939.[2] September was, he told the audience, '[of] particular and special significance because it's the month when the wild geese first arrive in Great Britain from their breeding grounds in the far north.' Scott sought to reassure those listening that 'war or no war, they'll come just the same,' and the passing of the seasons would be marked by the arrival of tens of thousands of geese, just like it had for millennia. Nature provided continuity and light, while all around him society descended into chaos and darkness. 'Well, we may think our country is a very different place from what it was last April when the geese went off to breed,' he said, 'and, indeed, for human beings there could scarcely be a bigger difference cast over the face of the world but for wild geese on migration there will only be one real difference that they can detect at once – the black out.' On 1 September 1939 blackout regulations had been imposed across Britain two days before the declaration of war. These required that all windows and doors should be 'blacked out' at night to prevent the escape of any glimmer of light that could be seen by enemy aircraft. Street lights were switched off, while essential lights such as traffic lights and vehicle headlights were fitted with slotted covers to deflect their beams downwards to the ground. For migrating birds, though, Scott reminded his listeners that they had been 'flying to these islands long before even a cave man's fire twinkled below them.'

Despite Scott's upbeat commentary on the immutability of nature, the war was already beginning to impact on his life and those of his beloved geese. For the first time he did not travel up to Scotland to watch the first geese arrive, instead waiting in vain to be called up. The geese on their long journeys now migrated over a world at war as the German *Blitzkrieg* overran Poland. Scott told his listeners: 'During the last few weeks many thousands of wild geese have been migrating over battlefields because one of the biggest autumn migration lines of waterfowl comes through the Polish marshes leading on south through Hungary to the Mediterranean.' He predicted that 'The V's of geese and the V's of bombers must have passed each other in mid-air.'

Scott took great solace from knowing that nature would always prevail but still found it almost impossible to contemplate that the country was at war. He told his audience that his first thought on that bright September morning was that 'it's perfectly impossible that there can be such a thing as a war when the world is so beautiful.' Reflecting on this, he considered 'that for some reason the world, the fields, and the trees and the rivers are so much more beautiful because there is a war.'

Yet nature wasn't just an escape from war, Scott believed that it held secrets that the Allies could learn from to give them victory. Searching for a poplar hawk moth caterpillar one day, he had almost given up hope when he spotted 'the great fat green fellow masquerading as a young leaf right under my nose.' Camouflage was a subject that fascinated Scott and he was already working on radical 'natural designs' that he would perfect later in the war. 'Caterpillars are masters of camouflage,' he told his audience, 'and if it were possible to conceal a munitions factory half so well as the caterpillar conceals his portly person we shouldn't have much to fear from fast bombers.'

He ended his talk by saying that at least the wildfowl and geese would have a more peaceful time than usual that winter as 'there will be fewer humans who have time to pursue them.' The rarer hawks would also benefit too and 'get an extra lease of life when the preservation of game birds ceases to receive so much attention [many wildfowlers like Scott and gamekeepers were being called up].' The arrival of autumn may, he concluded, 'seem to symbolise sad things – things that are coming to an end, but I always like to think of it as ushering in new beauties, and bringing with it new magic, on the wings of wild geese.' The broadcasts helped Scott make sense of a society where there was still beauty and magic but also ugliness and war. 'However irrelevant natural history might seem,' he deduced, 'I was more than ever convinced of its deep-rooted importance to mankind in general and to me in particular. It was in the nature of an escape, but with an urgency which I was to recognise increasingly as the war dragged on.'

When the Admiralty did finally reply to Scott's letter, they said his application was still pending, but a week later he was called up and was given the rank of Temporary Acting Sub-Lieutenant. After ten days' training on HMS *King Alfred*, a 'stone frigate', at Hove, he and an odd assortment of professional men who liked to spend their holidays 'messing about in boats' were passed out as naval officers. In his diary the excited Scott wrote: 'This is all exactly like school again and makes one feel delightfully young. It is fun too … It was the first term of a new adventure and inevitably the greatest for all of us. We were preoccupied with the dreadful possibility that the war might end before we got to sea.'

Scott decided that the vessel which best suited his talents would be a destroyer and to his surprise – and delight – the navy agreed. 'I've just been earmarked for destroyers, which is an absolutely plum job,' he excitedly wrote to a friend, 'It's the thing which every Wavy Navy man dreams of getting into and I'm so terribly cock-a-hoop about it', (the 'Wavy Navy' was so called because the gold braids on the RNVR officers uniforms were serpentine instead of straight).

After a course on destroyers Scott attended one on anti-submarines, which included a torpedo control course. During it he was assigned to an 'A'-class destroyer called *Acasta*, but towards the end of the course he became ill and was confined to bed. The officer in charge came to see him and said that as he had not finished the course he could not serve with *Acasta* and instead after completing it he would be assigned to HMS *Broke*. A few weeks later in the disastrous Norway campaign *Acasta* and another destroyer, *Ardent*, were protecting the aircraft carrier HMS *Glorious* when they were attacked by the German heavy cruisers *Scharnhorst* and *Hipper*. They were both blown out of the water, the German ships going on to sink *Glorious*. From the three ships there were only a handful of survivors.

By the time Scott joined HMS *Broke* she was already showing her age, having been launched in 1920, the second of the so called 'Thornycroft' destroyers. However, he was delighted to serve on her as the ship had a very special connection to his father. HMS *Broke* was the second vessel to bear the name, the first having been commanded by Edward 'Teddy' Evans (1880–1957). Evans had been Robert Scott's second in command during his ill-fated trip to the Antarctic and was the captain of the expedition ship *Terra Nova*. He had accompanied Robert Scott to within 150 miles of the pole but had been sent back with the last support party, only narrowly surviving the return journey. Teddy had then spent the First World War as the captain of the first HMS *Broke*, becoming famous as 'Evans of the Broke' after the battle of the Dover strait in 1917. Now Scott would serve in the second HMS *Broke* to bear the name, continuing the tradition.

The ship was to be Scott's home for the next two years and he initially kept a diary of his time on board. However, this was frowned upon by the Admiralty in case it fell into enemy hands if he was captured so he soon stopped writing it. While Scott had initially embraced his call-up as a great adventure, the reality turned out to be quite different as he felt both lonely and seasick. He had suffered from bad seasickness early on in his life but thought that with all his yachting experience he had developed good 'sea legs'. However, the size of the ship, the rough weather and the swell combined to bring it back with a vengeance. Scott was so seasick that he was sent on shore leave before rejoining the ship again at Scapa Flow. Here, after thirty-six hours onboard, he finally found that he could master the condition if he lay down or was out in the fresh air looking at the horizon. It was a far from auspicious start.

While on board Scott had promised to provide line drawings for a new book called *Grey Goose* by his friend Michael Bratby, but found it hard to concentrate on anything apart from trying not to be sick. Instead he wrote to Bratby, who worked in army intelligence, saying 'life is excessively exciting … [but, talking about the captain of HMS *Broke*, Brian Scurfield] it's a lonely life being a captain. He's had very bad luck as we've been aground, not really through any fault of his, but it has been very nerve-wracking for him. However, I think all will be well. The trouble about a destroyer is that there are so few officers that the chances are small of finding a shipmate with common interests. I suppose you're isolated nearly if not quite as much'. Despite being seasick and being run aground, Scott still found the time to do the illustrations, and the book about their adventures together 'punt-gunning' on the east coast appeared in 1939.

The 'phoney war' saw Scott doing anti-submarine patrols in the Channel but the war soon started to become real when the German *Blitzkrieg* swept through the Low Countries and France and the British Expeditionary Force found themselves surrounded at Dunkirk. When the Admiralty called for an armada of little ships to rescue the stranded soldiers from the beaches, *Broke* was being refitted at Devonport Dockyard. A frustrated Scott again kicked his heels in port but used the opportunity to write an article on greater snow geese for *Country Life* magazine. 'You wouldn't know how hard it is to make oneself think of something else these days – so my job must be quite absorbing really.' he wrote. 'Destroyers are now, to me, a subject by themselves, just like dinghies or geese, and I'm "keen on them", which it isn't difficult to be when they are doing such terrific work. I'm determined to be a pukka "No.1" instead of just a temporary one in a derelict ship in harbour, maybe one day.' While Scott may have been frustrated at being confined to base during the 'miracle of Dunkirk', the war would soon ensure he was in the thick of the action.

On Sunday 9 June 1940, while doing anti-submarine duties off Plymouth, HMS *Broke* received orders to proceed with all haste to the

French port of Le Havre which was being mercilessly bombed by the *Luftwaffe* as the last remaining British troops there held out. As the ship approached the town on a mirror-calm sea Scott saw a 'strange and beautiful sight. Ahead was what looked like a terrific storm. The sky was black as ink, and already the dark cloud covered the sky overhead.' At 3.30am the next morning action stations sounded and *Broke* entered the harbour at first light, expecting to pick up troops, but was met only by men operating barrage balloons. Unbeknown to Scott and the crew of *Broke*, the Admiralty had postponed the planned evacuation.

As they emerged from the protection of the great cloud of billowing black smoke into a sunny blue sky the ship came under instant attack from Junkers 88 aircraft, Scott recalling, 'I heard bullets whizzing by, all round the bridge, so it seemed. We all ducked down and grabbed our tin hats. As I was putting mine on I glanced up and saw a twin-engined machine just flattening out.' As the German bombers pressed home their attack Scott watched in horror as four bombs headed straight towards them. Seconds later one exploded just behind him, lifting the stern of the ship out of the water, while the others exploded to the side sending a huge column of water up into the air, covering the deck. Miraculously, they were not hit, Scott recalling: 'The whole attack was over in fifteen seconds and we had not been able to fire a single shot at them. We had escaped very much more lightly than we deserved. It was a grave and salubrious warning.'

On board, Scott was told the depressing news that Italy had now also declared war on Britain and that France was close to surrendering. As HMS *Broke* retreated back into the Channel she received orders to rescue the 51st Highland Division which had become entrapped at St Valery. They approached the wrecked town that night, Scott bravely going in ahead of the ship in a motorboat to assess the situation. Arriving two hours after the appointed rendezvous time, he went ashore on his own, revolver in hand, to see if the village had fallen into enemy hands. Luckily it had not, and after finding a friendly sentry he was then escorted to the officer in charge of the wounded. 'I could not resist the phrase made famous by the Cossack when rescuing the prisoners from the Altmark [the supply ship to the *Graf Spee*],' Scott wrote. So on entering the makeshift hospital he proclaimed 'the Navy's here!'

Scott then supervised the evacuation of the walking wounded, those unable to walk being put on stretchers and transferred to the ship. However, it was by now beginning to get light, and fearing another air attack, Scott decided to leave, the Highland Divisional Commander telling him in no uncertain terms that the soldiers defending the besieged town could hold out until that night, but no longer. Scott recorded that the wounded were in a 'pitiful' state, but promised the commander solemnly that the navy would come back to rescue them. However, the Admiralty decided that St Valery was a lost cause, and much to Scott's anger HMS *Broke* and the other ships were told to set off for Portsmouth with just the walking wounded onboard, passing the smouldering wrecks of several ships sunk by the *Luftwaffe* on the way.

On arrival back in Britain they sat in the harbour wondering what had become of the men they had left behind. The next day, 12 June, Scott heard on the radio that the 7th Panzer Division under its daring commander, Erwin Rommel, had taken the town and with it over 8,000 British prisoners. 'It was explained that fog had delayed the evacuation and that there were no extensive beaches as at Dunkirk,' Scott heard on the BBC. 'Though many had been embarked, many more had not. We felt very bitter about it. Our little operation had succeeded in its small-scale object, but failed miserably on the major issue.' For Scott the 'greatest adventure of his life' had become a harsh lesson about the futility of war.

After St Valery fell to Rommel on 12 June 1940 General Alan Brooke went to France with the only two fully formed divisions left to the British Army to create a new British Expeditionary Force (BEF). But he assessed the situation as hopeless and two days later he withdrew just as Paris became an open city, France falling days later. None of this was known to Scott as he headed through the night on HMS *Broke* towards Brest to support the new BEF. As they arrived they were attacked by three Heinkel He-111 bombers and *Broke* opened fire with her 3-inch guns. Luckily the planes were flying high at 15,000ft, and the bombs landed wide of their target. While the battle was raging Scott was ordered to take charge of the evacuation of the town and headed for the shore in a motor boat. There he picked up the town's British Naval Liaison Officer, Commander MacKay, and then visited eleven merchant ships in the harbour to see if any of them were able to carry off troops. When he got back to *Broke*, he found the Duke of Westminster's 'yacht', which had been converted into a destroyer, moored next to them. Reporting back about the dire situation on the shore, the ship's captain decided to go in anyway, but he was immediately attacked by another group of Heinkel bombers, this time the bombs landing much closer to their ship.

As *Broke* headed into the harbour under heavy fire they saw the French battleship *Richelieu*, six destroyers and an old cruiser, all abandoned in haste as the French retreated. Passing the ships, Scott heard a massive explosion a few hundred yards away as another vessel detonated a magnetic mine floating in the water. Embarking quickly at the quay, what he witnessed shocked him deeply – strewn all along the shore was the wreckage of hundreds of vehicles, many still smouldering. 'All these vehicles were British,' he remarked. 'They belonged to the soldiers who had brought them a few days before and had now been evacuated leaving all their gear behind them.'

With the Germans expected at any minute and the British ships offshore pounding the town, Scott supervised the transfer of weapons and 200 Polish troops onto *Broke*. Scott was then told that the Germans were expected in Brest at 7.00pm. Looking at his watch, he saw with alarm that it was already 7.30pm, and so rushed ashore again to tell the demolition team that they must blow up the harbour as soon as possible. He returned to HMS *Broke*, and minutes later witnessed 'a number of loud explosions and a big oil fire began to the eastward.'

By this point Scott had been helping with the evacuation for over seventy-two hours without a break. Traumatised, distraught and dishevelled, he suddenly saw a small bird flitting from a gorse bush close to him. 'It was barely light but there was no doubt about its identity – a Dartford warbler,' he recorded in his notes, clearly delighted. 'We could hear a drone of aero-engines. High in the blue some German aircraft – probably Heinkel's – were circling, though it was too dark to see them.' In the midst of the noise and chaos of war it was the rasping contact call of the Dartford warbler that gave Scott the strength to carry on. As he retreated back down the hill a lorry packed with explosive blew up before he boarded his boat and then motored back to rejoin *Broke*.

It was 5.50am as they set off back to Portsmouth, towing two French submarines to prevent them falling into enemy hands. At 5.00pm 'there arose from Brest a most enormous smoke cloud. The smoke from oil fires, still streaming out to sea on the easterly breeze, was plainly visible, but this cloud, white at the top, rose thousands of feet higher.' Scott was about 80 miles away at the time and later learnt that this was the ammunition arsenal at Brest blowing up. On 20 June at 9.20am they arrived back safely in Plymouth Sound, a hospital boat coming alongside to take off the wounded. Scott's great adventure to Brest and back was finally over.

After France had fallen Scott was sent on convoy escort duty. During the dark days of 1940 German U-boats preyed mercilessly on British convoys, sending millions of tonnes of shipping to the bottom of the sea. By the time Scott reached his first convoy seven of the thirty-six ships had already been sunk by dive bombers and four more destroyed in the night by German E-boats. As the convoy headed out into the unforgiving Atlantic a Sunderland flying boat signalled to Scott that she would lead them to a submarine that was in their path. By the time Scott arrived the Sunderland had already attacked it, resulting in a great streak of oil on the surface of the water. Scott attacked three times with depth charges, recording that the 'submarine was almost certainly destroyed.' It was his first kill, and like the first pinkfoot goose he had shot, it brought out the thrill of the hunter in him. They accompanied the convoy, leaving it at dusk in order to meet an important incoming one from Halifax, Canada. Much to his delight, he recorded dolphins 'squeaking and bubbling on the Asdics and jumping all around.'

That night he woke with a start to a deafening noise, thinking the convoy was being attacked, but to his surprise found his own boat had been rammed by a friendly gunboat that had collided with the destroyer in the night. To prevent a repeat of the accident, Scott came up with a unique camouflage scheme for *Broke* based on his knowledge of camouflage in nature. 'It was designed to make her as pale as possible at night because ships nearly always appear as dark blobs on the horizon against the sky,' he wrote. 'Only down moon on a very bright night would she look too pale. Otherwise she could hardly be white enough.' As a result he made one side what he called 'a compromise dazzle scheme' in black and white to achieve the highest contrast. 'The best dazzle schemes,' recorded Scott, 'for deception, deceiving the enemy about the class of the ship, the speed and angle of approach or inclination, are those which have contrasting patches indicating edges and surfaces which do not exist.' He juxtaposed this with bright colours on the other side, suggesting pale pastel shades of blue, green, 'buffish' pink and white, which in bright sunlight would also produce the desired dazzle effect. After having assessed it, the Admiralty decided to use Scott's dazzle schemes on other destroyers, and much to his pleasure, early reports about the scheme from their sister destroyer, *Vansittart,* were very favourable.

Scott was not the only person to see the military potential of learning from camouflage in nature. The artist Raymond Sheppard (1913–1958), whose book *How To Draw Birds* was published at the height of the Battle of Britain in July 1940, wrote 'Just think of all the varieties of plumage, in what lovely patterns this is arranged, on some birds so indescribably delicate. But did you know that this pattern, so lovely in itself, is there to serve the bird a very useful purpose? It is really a sort of camouflage, about which we we have heard such a lot recently, a "protective coloration" which merges itself into the bird's natural background of rushes, grass or stones, and as long as the bird is motionless it is invisible to its enemies. I expect our camouflage experts have learnt a lot from the study of these protective patterns and colors of birds.'

While he was on leave suffering from jaundice Scott started seeing a girl called Elizabeth Jane Howard (known as 'Jane'), who he had known before the war. She wanted to be an actress and to seduce Jane, Scott asked if he could draw her. Howard was seventeen and very shy so the attention of 'this older, glamorous man' from such an accomplished and famous family made a big impression on her. By contrast, Howard came from an unknown upper-middle-class family who were 'austere but close', her father being a timber merchant and her mother a ballet dancer. Jane grew up in a large house with servants in Notting Hill, and was privately educated at home by a governess while her two young brothers were sent away to boarding school. By her own admission she was 'unsure of herself, of her worth and her intelligence.'[3] For his part, Scott was clearly attracted to Jane, but at thirty-one was also feeling the pressure to get married. So, in the summer of 1940, with the Battle of Britain raging over their heads, the couple tried to ignore the dogfights and instead talked about music, painting, acting and writing. 'We laughed inordinately,' recalled Scott later. What Jane didn't know at the time was that Scott was harbouring a secret – he had recently broken up with someone who was very special to him and was on the rebound.

In September 1940 Scott went to Stratford upon Avon where Jane, like so many aspiring actresses, was treading the boards. In bed that evening he told her that someone he'd loved for a long time had decided to get married and that he was bereft. Jane assumed it was one of his old girlfriends, but Scott dropped a bombshell – it wasn't the bride he had loved but the bridegroom. 'He had loved him, more, probably than anyone else in his life, and now it was at an end,'[14] Jane wrote. That night Scott poured out his heart to her about his former love and asked if she understood. Jane was taken aback but tried to be sympathetic. (If more than platonic love, it was a brave admission as homosexuality was then illegal and 'gross indecency' a crime. Scott makes no mention of the episode in any of his books, Jane alleging it after his death in her biography.)

To make matters worse, the war soon inevitably came between them. The nightly patrols from Plymouth to escort the convoys carried on through the late summer and as invasion threatened they were given a new urgency. Scott was away a lot of the time and although he could not keep a diary, he started to write down his impressions of the lonely evenings he spent keeping vigil. Inevitably, on those dark and cold nights Scott's thoughts turned to watching geese. He imagined himself to be a boy again standing on the edge of the saltmarsh on the Wash. There he stood entranced, watching as a skein of geese swept inland, 'caught up in their magic as the glorious chorus of their calling rang out across the marsh.'

With the onset of winter and the threat of invasion over for that year, HMS *Broke* sailed from Plymouth to Londonderry, which was to be her new home. Here she would join the Battle of the Atlantic by guarding the Northwestern Approaches. While it put even more distance between him and Jane, Scott did at least have some good news on rejoining his ship, finding out that he had been promoted. This meant that Scott was now the Captain's 'Number One'. It was also the first time a member of the naval reserve had been appointed to the post over a Royal Navy officer.

Scott found the Battle of the Atlantic both physically and emotionally exhausting. He recalled: 'We fought the elements as much as the enemy. Some of us used to talk of it as "the Battle with the Atlantic". During that first winter the U-boat wolf-packs had it more or less their own way until new methods of defence began to even up the balance. It was a pattern of burning ships, floating bodies, crowded lifeboats and a dreadful feeling of helplessness.' What made the attacks worse was that they were made at night and there was little that Scott could do about them. During the day the U-boats were replaced by Condor aircraft which sent many more ships to the bottom.

The winter at sea proved a particularly testing time, the unforgiving waters of the Atlantic sometimes being an even greater adversary than the U-boat packs that lurked beneath. Respite came in January 1941 when *Broke* was refitted at Belfast and Scott got in some much-needed wildfowling. He headed to Morecambe Bay and there heard again the whistle of the wigeon and the haunting call of greylag geese, recording in his diary that these were 'the right kind of adventures even if they are less terrific than the war ones.'

By now Scott harboured high hopes of his own command, writing to a friend: 'I think there is a chance of getting a destroyer within the next twelve months, with a lot of luck.' In between supervising the refit he escaped to Strangford Lough where he saw a dozen brent geese fly past, and visited another Lough, Swilly, where he saw about twenty whitefronts and a dozen whooper swans. He also managed to fit in some shooting with friends who lived just over the border in Eire where he learnt to track snipe, the shooting providing a 'glorious unforgettable contrast to the life at sea'. On one occasion he took the captain of HMS *Broke* and some crew members with him, commenting, 'as we returned in the darkness it had made the whole thing just bearable again, and we could face another gruelling ten days at sea.'

On 6 April 1941 *Broke* met a homeward-bound Gibraltar convoy and was signalled to rescue the crew of HMS *Comorin* which had caught fire in heavy seas. The captain, Brian Scurfield, and Scott coordinated the rescue. They managed to navigate alongside the stricken vessel and save many of the crew despite the ship being in imminent danger of blowing up. As result they received a message of commendation from the Admiralty, the captain being awarded the Order of the British Empire and Scott being mentioned in dispatches. Scurfield was then given a new command and *Broke* received a new captain, Commander Walter Couchman. Unfortunately, not long after, *Broke* collided with another destroyer, *Verity*, on Scott's watch while the latter was zig-zagging across the stern of the convoy at dawn on anti U-boat manoeuvres. A subsequent inquiry found that there had been fault on both sides and Scott was cautioned. While the episode damaged his reputation, he learnt from it and never again let another ship come within half a mile of his own.

Scott's reputation as a painter also helped him go on some 'exciting adventures' with other services. In 1941 he had shown a number of paintings at the prestigious Royal Academy's summer exhibition where he met Air Commodore Sir Victor Goddard (1897–1987). Goddard was admiring a painting Scott had done of a German bomber attacking *Broke* when Scott mentioned in passing how much he would like to fly with the RAF. So Goddard pulled some strings and Scott found himself in a Stirling aircraft with his drawing pad. He was the observer in a crew of eight on a bombing raid to the German port of Kiel, the base for the U-boats Scott knew so well from his Battle of the Atlantic.

After crossing into enemy territory Scott's plane soon found itself under fire. He commented: 'There was a thin haze or cloud and the gun flashes were below it. Just above the cloud but far far below us were the sparkling pin-points of the shell bursts. It was rather beautiful.' After avoiding the searchlights and night fighters the Stirling released its bombs. Scott was fascinated and fatalistic in equal measure, recording, 'During all this time I had looked on very much as a spectator at the films, with a curious detachment. Everything seemed so remote. The flak was so far below, the whole episode was so very improbable. Since the take-off the nervousness had completely left me and a complete fatalism had taken its place. We should get home or we should not. No action or decision of mine could possibly affect the issue.' However, just as they were approaching the coast on the way home the Stirling's engines failed and they went into a steep dive. Scott grabbed his parachute and was about to bail out just as the engines spluttered back into life. He finally got back home after forty-six hours with no sleep. Exhausted, he left for a week's leave at Fritton in Norfolk where his parents had a cottage.

Relaxing at Fritton, he painted Jane and enjoyed walks along the River Waveney where he chased butterflies. He then visited London, where he lobbied the Admiralty about commanding his own destroyer on the pretext of talking about the collision. Scott was told that he would have to wait another eight months to a year. He recorded in his diary that this was 'rather slow but probably worth waiting for.'

His paintings again helped open doors for him when he popped in to see Sir Archibald Jamieson (1884–1959), the chairman of the armaments and aircraft manufacturer, Vickers. Jamieson had bought one of Scott's swan pictures for his boardroom, telling him that the Russian resistance had been a big shock to Hitler and if they could hold out this winter the tide would turn. 'So much seems to have changed in that year that maybe in another year we shall see our way clear to victory, in time to watch the pinkfeet arrive in the Solway,' Scott mused.

The next day, 31 August 1941, Scott took off on a second RAF 'Op', again in a Stirling, heading for the German city of Cologne. This time on the flight Scott's plane got caught in the beams of several converging searchlights and was lit up by a brilliant white light. Amazingly no flak or fighters descended on them and they were able to bomb Cologne after finding a small hole in the cloud cover and recognising a big bend in the river Rhine which signified they were south of the city. Down below Scott saw the continuous 'flickering flashes of bombs and gunfire and shell-bursts and flares [...] through it shone the red flush of the fire.'

When they got back to base the crew were interrogated by an intelligence officer about their mission, each one turning to Scott as the observer and saying, 'You saw that, didn't you? Well, you describe it.' The intelligence officer was, in Scott's opinion, not very clever, and was trying to 'pin them down to exact things which could only be guesses, and then write the guesses down as exact things.'[5] Afterwards they all had bacon and eggs and Scott talked with the crew until he finally fell asleep at 4.00am. The next day he heard that seven planes had not returned and that most of their bombs had missed their target due to the low cloud. Reflecting on his trips, he wrote: 'I had learned a good deal about "how the other half the world lives",' adding, 'I returned to the Navy with a new and profound respect for the RAF's Bomber Command.'

Scott rejoined *Broke* in September 1941 and steeled himself for 'sea again and in front of us [was] another miserable North Atlantic winter.' To his great joy he found out that his new captain enjoyed wildfowling, but he also found him highly critical of people, commenting, 'I used to think I didn't suffer fools very gladly myself, but I am a paragon of patience by comparison.' Jane continued to act at Stratford and had landed a minor role in *The Doctor's Dilemma*, a play by George Bernard Shaw. Despite the previous collision, Scott's career was going from strength to strength. His camouflage scheme for *Broke* was going down well with the Admiralty and as a result he was commissioned by the Commander-in-Chief of the Western Approaches, Admiral Sir Martin Eric Dunbar-Nasmith (1883–1965), to design the camouflage schemes for fifty obsolete American destroyers which the British had received as part of a lend-lease agreement with the United States. Under his direction they had been painted in a very pale tone, Scott reflecting that at night 'no paint could ever make a ship whiter than the sky behind it.'

At Nasmith's request he wrote down ten points about camouflage to which he thought all ships should adhere: 'the first-all important principle is its operational object. In this case it is to avoid being seen by a U-boat on the surface at night.' Following the sinking of a number of vessels, Nasmith wrote to his commanders operating out of Londonderry, Greenock and Liverpool, stating: 'Four corvettes having been torpedoed up to date every endeavour is to be made to hasten camouflaging of corvettes in accordance with Peter Scott scheme.' It was a significant accolade, and one that made the captaincy of his own vessel much more likely. However, it didn't make Scott popular with some captains, who felt it increased the risk of collisions at night, or with some crews, because the light colours were prone to showing dirt and rust so the ships had to be cleaned more often.

Scott continued doing escort work throughout the winter, often feeling that the weather was a greater threat than the enemy, but slowly seeing the tide of the battle turn in the favour of the Allies. By January 1942 he felt 'the Escort Groups were definitely on top of the U-boats,' and that the majority of convoys were getting through. At the end of 1941 *Broke* was ordered into Portsmouth for a long refit where she was prepared for the North Africa campaign. Scott found himself needing a new job and was offered command of a steam gunboat, the Admiralty telling him there were no vacancies for destroyer captains. Steam gunboats were a 'brand-new type of vessel, attached to the Coastal Forces,' and although he was privately bitterly disappointed, he felt it would be a 'useful stop-gap' and could only enhance the possibilities of getting his own command of a destroyer one day. He wrote, 'one chapter of my naval career was ending and a new one was about to begin. In between was a respite – a chance to get married.'

Chapter 13

Grey Goose, Surrender and Slimbridge

By late 1941 Scott and Jane had been seeing each other for over six months so he had proposed, leaving her feeling 'stunned, flattered, dazzled'. Two days later the telephone rang and Jane answered it in a jokey voice assuming it was one of her girlfriends. 'This is *The Times*,' a stern voice said on the other end. 'Is it true that you're to marry Peter Scott, the son of the famous explorer?' It was an early indication of the role that Jane was now to play, wife to the acclaimed painter Peter Scott, who was son to the celebrated explorer Robert Scott. While outwardly delighted, inwardly she had nagging doubts, but put these down to wedding nerves. 'Something inside me said, "Do you really want to do this?"' she recalled, 'but I stifled it.' Jane told herself she was 'unbelievably lucky to be marrying a brave and famous man. I'd be Mrs Peter Scott [...] one day the war would be over and I'd be married to a painter and he wouldn't talk about guns any longer, and I'd encourage him to paint and draw people more than birds.'

Scott and Jane married on 28 April 1942 at St Mary's Church in Lancaster Gate in London, the reception at Claridge's hotel afterwards being attended by over 100 people. She was just nineteen and had been a virgin when she met Scott who, she soon found out, liked sex but lacked intimacy. Scott's family organised the wedding apart from the music, which was chosen by Jane, and outside the church the photographer from *The Times* snapped the happy couple, she smiling nervously, he looking serious and distant.

For their honeymoon they went to Scott's family cottage at Lacket, near Lockerbridge in Wiltshire. It was early spring and the primroses and catkins were in flower. Blessed with fine weather, Scott showed his new wife 'the countryside in which I had spent so much of my boyhood – our own beautiful dene, the West Woods, the downs, the "valley of dry bones" where the sarsen stones are in great profusion, the Kennet running clear after a spring drought, the great stone circles of Avebury. They were romantic places exactly fitting the pattern of our mood. It was, I believed, for these that we fought our war, for those we faced the winter gales in the North Atlantic, the U-boats, the bombing. For these we'd fight on till they were free and safe for our people.' In contrast Jane, who admirably at the age of nineteen showed an interest in stone circles, 'basked in his indulgence' and recalled that 'he talked about his ship, and his ambition to have a good war, and I tried to be interested in the differences between a Rolls-Royce engine and an Oelikon gun.'

As newlyweds, Scott wanted to get Jane pregnant as quickly as possible, telling her how much he enjoyed sex and what a 'wonderful girl' she was for indulging him. Scott's idea of foreplay, according to Jane, consisted of a soppy comment such as 'I'm just a sentimental old thing,' or a rude remark such as 'I'm just a painter with a vulgar facility.' Jane played up to what was expected of her and was just glad that the sex no longer hurt as much, telling herself that 'this was marriage, and I was now grown-up.' However, reflecting on her big day, Jane presciently wrote, 'He never said, "Actually I have to have courage. I have to live up to my father, and sometimes I'm afraid I won't be able to manage it."'[1] For his part he knew that Jane was naïve when it came to sex, and life in general, but that suited him. Jane admitted she never fully appreciated what a 'serious and informed naturalist' he was, but also how little he really knew about women's feelings. 'He never realized I'd no idea about my own sexuality,' she wrote, 'and that my continuing ignorance of it might prove a danger to us both.'

After the honeymoon Scott returned to see his new steam gunboat in Cowes being constructed, following the building of the boat closely. He was delighted when in her sea trials S.G.B. 9 attained a speed of 36 knots. Visiting Jane at her parents one weekend, he found some puss moth caterpillars which he asked her to look after. Just like with his new steam gunboat, Scott kept a careful eye on their development, writing to Jane's mother to see how they were faring. 'I listed the different species and the precise numbers of each,' wrote Scott, who was rather surprised a couple of days later to get a visit from an investigating officer with the censor. The officer suspected that the list of moths and their numbers was really a secret code identifying the number of ships in the Solent and that Scott was a spy. The Allies were then busy planning a raid on the French port of Dieppe but the first attack had to be postponed after details leaked out. An embarrassed and amused Scott explained about his moth collection, each caterpillar being checked out by the officer. 'As he was also an amateur entomologist it all ended happily,' a relieved Scott recorded in his diary.

Scott and Jane then went to stay with friends while the steam gunboat was finished, and after a few weeks she began to feel sick. When she told him, a delighted Scott said, 'You know what this means don't you?' But Jane didn't. 'It means our son is on the way.' Scott sent her to live with her parents so Jane could get the rest she needed, with his caterpillars for company. A benevolent Jane duly took them back on the train, but during the journey didn't notice that they had escaped from their muslin cage. 'They were soon rollicking all over the furry upholstery which provided them with excellent camouflage,' she recalled. Jane spent a frantic twenty minutes looking for them but only managed to collect half by the end of her journey. The others were left to their fate, with Jane worrying: 'Pete, I thought desperately, would have collected all of them, or better still, would have noticed earlier that they'd found a tear in the sleeve.'

When the Dieppe raid finally got the go-ahead on 19 August 1942, Scott found himself in the middle of the action, his steam gunboat narrowly avoiding being bombed after the raiding party ran into an enemy patrol. Scott was lucky to survive the Dieppe raid unscathed, only keeping awake thanks to taking a Benzedrine tablet, and finally made it back to Portsmouth harbour at 3.00am. The raid was a disaster – the attacking force, of which Scott was a part, put ashore over 6,000 infantry, mainly Canadians, over half of whom were killed, wounded or captured. In the ensuing debacle the Royal Navy lost thirty-three landing craft and one destroyer while the RAF lost over 100 planes against fewer than fifty on the German side. Scott tried to take a rosy view of the fiasco, writing: 'History has delivered a number of rather conflicting verdicts on the Dieppe Raid ... we supposed also that useful experience of the techniques of frontal assault had been gained, and we knew that the naval losses had been much lighter than had been expected.'

At the end of 1942 Scott and Jane moved to London, renting a house in St John's Wood that had once been home to Jane's grandfather. There Scott heard he had been promoted again to Lieutenant Commander and became Senior Officer to the First Steam Gun Boat Flotilla, a significant step towards his goal of getting his own destroyer. More happy news followed when during an air raid on 2 February 1943 Jane gave birth to their baby but it was not the son Scott was hoping for. They named their daughter Nicola, and Scott first drew her when she was just eleven days old. What he didn't know was that after giving birth Jane struggled to come to terms with motherhood and was suffering from severe post-natal depression.

During the summer of 1943 Scott's flotilla was involved in another collision while engaging the enemy, which resulted in a motor gunboat nearly sinking. On seeing it he took charge of the rescue and valiantly managed to get the stricken vessel back to shore under fire. It was potentially another black mark against Scott's record, but again the resulting Board of Inquiry exonerated him of any blame. Later he was awarded the Distinguished Service Cross, a military decoration given to officers for gallantry during active operations against the enemy at sea. Scott's new steam gunboat grew on him, but he found it increasingly hard to live with its official Admiralty designation, S.G.B. 9, as a name. Ever since he had been appointed as senior officer in charge of the flotilla he had been trying in vain to get the boats given names rather than numbers. He approached the Admiralty, and after many weeks of wrangling they finally allowed Scott to come up with some suggested names, which had to be agreed by a 'Naming Committee'.

As a result an excited Scott soon started filling up his notebooks with names for the six boats in his flotilla. Unsurprisingly, bird names immediately came to the fore: 'I particularly wanted my own boat to be called Grey Goose, after the first boat I had ever owned, the duck punt built to my own design in Cambridge.' The others, he decided, also needed to be geese and he came up with the names snow goose, brent goose, blue goose, bean goose and kelp goose, with black goose as a spare. His own crew, who were well used to Scott's ornithological bent, agreed to grey goose, but the other captains were less impressed. He then tried on them a variety of other bird names including sanderling, dotterel, whimbrel and turnstone, but these also didn't go down well either. Thinking on his feet, Scott put forward finches as an alternative and proposed chaffinch, bullfinch and goldfinch, together with some ducks such as goldeneye, garganey, merganser and harlequin. When these also failed to excite his captains, the ever-persistent Scott, who was determined to get his way on the issue, turned to butterflies, proposing swallowtail, fritillary, grayling, tortoiseshell, brimstone, and then moths including hawk moth, tiger moth, ghost moth, dagger moth and fox moth. 'We put all these to the vote in the flotillas, but only at the last moment did we hit on the suggestion which was finally selected,' he wrote. 'If I wanted my boat to be Grey Goose, why did we not use the word "Grey" as the link?'[2] So Scott got his way, and although the Admiralty insisted on them retaining the initials S.G.B. in the names, the other boats became No.3 Grey Seal, No.4 Grey Fox, No.5 Grey Owl, No.6 Grey Shark and No.8 Grey Wolf.

Reflecting the changing fortunes of the war, German E-boats (fast attack craft, usually an armed motorboat or a large torpedo boat), which patrolled the area from their bases in the north of France, now came under strict orders to limit their engagement to firing torpedoes from a distance and laying mines. 'If they were disturbed in their business they were to make a smoke-screen and run for it,' recalled Scott. The result was that the Allies soon started to get the upper hand in the psychological war at sea, Scott boasting proudly that the British Navy operated according to the famous directive of Admiral Lord Nelson: 'Engage the enemy more closely.' As a result, in nearly every naval encounter Scott attacked the enemy while the Germans cut and ran. 'We were the hounds and they were the hare,' recalled Scott, who believed that this gave the Allies 'an incontestable moral ascendancy in all our battles and must, I believe, have played a significant part in the eventual outcome.'

While Scott was engaging with the enemy, at home Jane was struggling to bond with their baby daughter Nicola. Lonely and isolated, she had no-one to turn to while Scott was away for long periods at sea. So to help with the war effort she became an Air Raid Precautions warden, helping to get people into the shelters when the siren went. But her sense of isolation only grew and one day she poured her heart out to Scott's half-brother, Wayland Hilton Young (1923–2009). He became an increasingly regular visitor to the house, especially after losing his job at the Admiralty. Soon Jane started having an affair with him: 'our feelings for each other were – nearly always – counterbalanced by guilt.' So the next time Scott came home on leave they told him about the affair. 'He was at first incredulous, then appalled, and then very angry,' recalled Jane. Scott complained bitterly that it was 'pretty difficult to fight a war with that sort of thing going on behind his back,' and took his wife off to

Holyhead in Anglesey where *Grey Goose* was now based, forbidding her to ever talk to Wayland again.

From the summer of 1943 Scott was in charge of enough steam gunboats that he was able to undertake offensive operations against the enemy for the first time. His flotilla would go on patrol two or three times a week but only had minor skirmishes until 27 July when he was involved in a major fire fight with German R-boats (small vessels built as minesweepers for the German Navy, *Räumboote* in German). During the battle his flotilla came off worst, but again he emerged from the encounter with his reputation enhanced after he got a stricken vessel back to shore. 'A lot learnt – some good experience, a few Germans killed, a few holes in some R-boats,' Scott wrote, 'and four S.G.B.s out of action for periods varying between seven days and six weeks, with seven of their gallant men gone for good.'

In his report of the incident the Commander in Chief at Portsmouth said, 'the action of the Senior Officer [Scott] in laying a smoke-screen between the concentrating enemy and the tow, and drawing the fire on himself, was a well-judged and gallant action which met with the success it deserves.' Yet Scott was haunted by the death of seven of his men. Despite this, soon after the battle he was awarded a bar to go with his Distinguished Service Cross (Scott was one of only 434 people awarded the D.S.C. and bar during the Second World War).

Scott's war at sea in his steam gunboat *Grey Goose* continued to be a mix of highs and lows. Not long after the fire fight with the R-boats, on 4 September, *Grey Goose* was damaged in another action with the enemy, Scott making the situation worse by colliding with a Norwegian minelayer as he brought his boat back into harbour at Dover. Complaining about the sheer amount of paperwork involved in writing up all these incidents, Scott sarcastically commented that it was 'obviously getting out of hand when the Senior Officer was too deeply involved in writing up the last action to go out and fight the next one.' (Coming from Scott, a prolific writer who liked nothing better than going into great detail about every aspect of his life, this was damning criticism indeed of an Admiralty obsessed with paper work.) On other patrols, though, he had better luck, sinking a trawler with one of his torpedoes. To Scott the war remained a great adventure, even if it was one that involved staying up late into the night typing copious notes.

When he was not at sea Scott had an office on HMS *Aggressive* which was commanded by Captain G.W. Heaton. He considered Scott and his flotilla 'his blue eyed boys' as they 'could do no wrong – a very agreeable state of affairs'. HMS *Aggressive* was in fact a luxury office building housed in the London and Paris Hotel on the platform of the Southern Railways terminal in Newhaven. Here, after a night patrol, Scott would relax, taking a bath and then having a good breakfast the next morning. There he wrote: 'Often the night's activities were discussed over the partitions in the bathroom which accentuated the impression that it was all an outsized schoolboy's game.' However, even Scott, who loved adventure, wearied of engaging with the Germans along the Normandy coast and began to show signs of operational fatigue so he was given a new assignment. It was not the longed-for captaincy of his own destroyer, but instead he was sent to teach at HMS *Bee*, another land boat using for training officers based in the backwater of Holyhead in Wales.

The one consolation of being land-based in Holyhead and 'back at school again' was the opportunity to be reunited with Jane. But this was also to prove a bitter pill. According to Scott, 'our baby was staying with her grandparents, and Jane freed from maternal chores, undertook the production of *The Importance of Being Earnest*, in which she also played Gwendolen.' In fact, Jane had not bonded with their daughter, Nicola, and the move simply reinforced how unhappy she was with her life and their marriage. Lonely, bored and missing romance, she took another lover in the guise of Philip Lee who was playing the part of Algernon in the play. He told her, 'the first two things I noticed about you was that you didn't wear a bra, and that you weren't happy.' This time, however, she kept her romance a secret and if Scott suspected anything he didn't let on. 'The temperature between us had lowered to a kind of affability,' she wrote, 'wary on my part, breezy on his. I found it much easier now to play my part.'[3]

By the spring of 1944 Scott was ready 'for the fray again' and longed to have his own destroyer as he saw the war was moving into its decisive stage. However, he was again disappointed as the Admiralty instead appointed him as the senior officer of a flotilla of Motor Torpedo Boats under the Captain of the Coastal Forces (Channel) based at Portsmouth. He had been charged with 'planning for the big show', D-Day, the Allied amphibious assault on Hitler's fortress Europe. For this Scott was given full details of the operation as early as March 1944. He recalled, 'at no time did I ever enjoy knowing important secrets and I can remember the conflict in my mind between curiosity to learn where the invading forces would land and my general distaste for the responsibility of possessing such knowledge.' Scott's job on D-Day was to protect 'The Spout', the wide sea lane from which the initial landings would be supported. At the same time he was responsible for nightly operations in the Channel defending convoys and offensive patrols against the enemy off the French coast.

During this period the German E-boats generally avoided direct confrontation, but on the night of 28 April 1944 four of them sneaked into Lyme Bay and opened fire on a convoy of eight US ships, killing 800 soldiers and sinking two ships. (What the Germans didn't know was that they had come across an exercise for D-Day codenamed Exercise Tiger, the ships and landing craft practising landing at Slapton Ley which doubled for Omaha beach. The Allies considered the incident such a serious threat to D-Day that they imposed a complete news blackout, covering up the scale of the fatalities for decades after the war.) This raid apart, Scott felt he had 'the measure of them, because, near to our coasts, they were detected by radar and their movements were recorded on "the Plot" [a huge billiard table used by the Admiralty to plot the movements of boats in the Channel]'.

On the night of D-Day minus-one, 5 June 1944, Scott's Coastal Forces were out in full strength, in spite of strong winds and heavy seas, to support the invasion. Scott recorded, 'The assault had already been postponed for twenty-four hours because of the weather. General Eisenhower had taken a bold decision to accept no further postponement, a decision which alone may have preserved the vital surprise element. On such a night the German defender had been assured by their meteorologists no invasion could take place. But it did!' Scott's flotilla had been charged with creating a decoy many miles away from the landing beaches, setting off 'fireworks, smoke, gramophone records and balloons to make ship-sized radar echoes.' After returning, he watched the invasion from the Naval Plotting Room in Portsmouth, seeing 'the curtain go up on one of the decisive dramas in human history.' Scott was particularly gratified that the largest armada ever had achieved almost total surprise, the few German naval forces daring to come out of harbour soon turning round when they saw the overwhelming Allied firepower.

Scott crossed the Channel on 15 June, D-Day plus-nine. He spent the next two months as a Coastal Forces Staff Officer on land based at Courseulles, supporting the invasion and reporting back to the Admiralty on the war on land. There he toured the battlefields by car, recording 'overhead the larks were singing, loud above the noise of battle.' When he entered Caen, he was amazed to see that despite the devastation the cathedral had remained miraculously untouched. He came away with 'increased respect for the soldiers who were fighting there', and in August was posted to Cherbourg where he was put in charge of operations against shipping in the Channel Islands. Here he resumed nightly patrols and by September he had cleared the Channel of all enemy shipping with the exception of a few vessels which remained on the Channel Islands (the strategic decision was taken to bypass the islands as they were too heavily fortified so they were not liberated until May 1945).

Finding himself back at Portsmouth with nothing but reports to write, Scott started flying lessons in a Tiger Moth. During one lesson in the first week of September, much to his delight, he saw a single goose while flying along at 2,000ft. 'As he came closer I saw to my amazement that it was a brent goose in the light-bellied form,' Scott later wrote, adding, 'it was incredibly early in the year for such a record. This same day was extremely bumpy and turbulent, and I remember hoping that these conditions were not too common, else maybe I should not take kindly to flying in light aircraft.'

The next month he was moved to Great Yarmouth to join the staff of the Captain of Coastal Forces where, due to his experience, he was asked to interrogate a Kapitän-Leutnant Karl Müller, senior officer of the Tenth Schnellboot Flotilla. Scott was told that he could be 'as frank as you like with him', as the prisoner was in 'for the duration'. Müller had been captured earlier that month and despite being the enemy, Scott took to him instantly, noting that he was known to his friends as 'Charlie'. He told Scott that he knew the war was lost and that 'the quicker it was brought to a conclusion the better for all concerned, particularly the Germans.'

Scott was impressed by Charlie's honesty and his bravery – he had the Ritterkreuz (Knight's Cross of the Iron Cross, the highest award for bravery in Nazi Germany) and had been on 165 patrols; a figure Scott stated was 'far in excess of the most experienced officers in our own

Coastal Forces'. Scott had fought with him while commanding his steam gunboat and found it fascinating to discuss the action. Charlie also told him about a close colleague's visit to see Hitler in Berchtesgaden in March 1944 to talk about E-boat development. Scott had last seen Hitler in 1931 when he went to hear him talk in Munich and was very interested in what the Führer knew about motor torpedo boats. To Scott's amazement Charlie told him that 'Hitler knew intimate details of the boats, asking whether the new four centimetre guns had been a success and discussing technical features of the new guns.'[4]

For the last couple of years Scott had been working hard on the draft of a new book on the coastal forces. He had asked the Admiralty for permission to produce it, which had been granted, and had spent much of his spare time writing it (the fact that Scott could find the time to produce a book as well as write all the reports required by the Admiralty says a lot about his output as an author). The book was originally envisaged to be a companion to the pamphlets on the war produced by the author Hilary Saint George Saunders (1898–1951). He had written a whole series of technical pamphlets including *The Battle of Britain*, *Bomber Command* and *Coastal Command* which had been well received by the public. However, while Saunders had produced the pamphlets with the official permission of the War Office, he had written them anonymously for the government and had received no credit for their subsequent success.

Scott was not interested in writing a book anonymously and therefore approached the Admiralty with the proposal of producing a longer, more historical book, to which they agreed. In order to get the 'greatest historical accuracy' Scott was keen to get the view from the other side so he asked their permission to show the draft to Müller. Amazingly, despite the draft having not yet been passed by the censor, they agreed and a proud Scott presented Müller with a copy. According to Scott, he enjoyed reading the book and soon afterwards received a 'eulogistic letter' from the German officer.

What Scott didn't fully appreciate was that Müller, like all prisoners, still harboured hopes of escaping. He told Scott that he had taken some notes while reading the book, adding, 'if you are not in agreement with this please ring up here, and I shall destroy them.' Scott, who thought there was no chance of Charlie escaping, took no action. In fact, what Müller had written down was a guide to Allied tactics, in particular the vulnerability of the British convoys to a mass attack by E-boats, something the German *Kreigsmarine* (Navy) had previously considered too risky. Not long afterwards Müller was transferred to a prisoner of war camp in the United States where he was selected for a prisoner exchange without crosschecking with the British. Unbeknown to Scott, Müller soon found himself back in the fray. Following his release there was a simultaneous attack by a large number of E-boats on a convoy off the east coast, with so many being involved that it confused the British radar. When Scott heard of the attack he smiled ruefully, and after submitting his book to the Admiralty censor he reminded them of the 'proverb about stable doors'. Scott's book was eventually published in early 1945 under his own name with the title *The Battle of the Narrow Seas* (referring to the Channel and North Sea). He did not send Müller a complimentary copy.

In the spring of 1945, just as the war with Germany was coming to an end, Scott finally got his much longed-for command. However, it was not a destroyer but a new frigate called *Cardigan Bay* which was being built in Leith. A disappointed Scott recorded in his diary that 'the war in Europe would be over before she was commissioned'. Then, after Hitler – who had roused him fourteen years earlier – committed suicide on 30 April 1945 the war in Europe was finally over. Reflecting on the momentous day, Scott wrote: 'Then with mounting acceleration Germany was overrun and the European war was suddenly at an end. The principal aim of five long years had been won.'

Scott went to see the surrender of the E-boats, which he had fought so long against, in the Thames estuary, and due to his smattering of German was asked to be an interpreter. Seeing them for the first time close up made a big impression on the war-weary Scott.

Here they were – long and low and menacing – our opposite numbers, our special opponents in all these years. One had a black panther painted on its side, and both flew the white flags which had been stipulated before they left Rotterdam. This was for most of us the first view of an E-boat in daylight, a dream view, for taking an E-boat in prize had been a universal dream in Coastal Forces, yet it had never been done. No E-boat had yet been brought into a British harbour. That would be done by us today, but the occasion was more interesting than triumphant.

Afterwards Scott selected one German officer to collect any personal effects, making him swear that in the process he would not try to scuttle the boats. In the course of the inspection the officer asked Scott if he would like to take anything so he ended up taking home a large calendar of German pin-up girls as a souvenir of the war.

Not long after the German surrender Scott was sitting at home when he heard a knock at the door. It was the Chairman of the Conservative Association in Rugby. Impressed by Scott's career as a painter, and his war record, he asked Scott if he would like to apply to become their prospective parliamentary candidate for the forthcoming general election, then only three weeks away. Scott was flattered but had only recently taken command of *Cardigan Bay*. 'There was still my ship, my beautiful new Frigate, the command for which I had waited so long,' he mused. 'Was this to be denied me at the last moment?' However, aware that with the war now all but over (the Japanese were still holding out) Scott knew there would be no more adventures at sea under fire. He was also a big fan of prime minister Winston Churchill and believed that his heroic leadership during the war would almost certainly mean a grateful nation would re-elect him. Then there was the vexed subject of his marriage.

Scott's wife, Jane, who out of loneliness and depression had taken lovers while he had been away at sea, was on holiday on the Isles of Scilly. Here she was recovering after having had her tonsils taken out and had started writing. So Scott was faced with a dilemma: the command of a boat he had so long dreamed about versus an exciting new career in politics with the forlorn hope of repairing his broken marriage. 'Here it was then,' he wrote, trying to put a brave face on it, 'the decision which had been at the back of my mind for so long. Not the Navy versus politics, but the war versus my family. And for some time I had been worried about the family.'

Deep down Scott knew his marriage was over, writing honestly, 'I had subjected it to greater strains than it could withstand.' However, he needed Jane to present to the electorate the image of a happy family man; no self-respecting politician at that time being elected without one. Scott had only a night to think it over so he rang Jane. She recalled: 'I said I thought he should opt for Parliament – I felt it was what he wanted me to say,' and recorded that he replied, 'I expect you're right,' with evident relief. The next day Scott was on his way to Rugby, but to his great disappointment, after being interviewed he was not selected to fight the seat. Undeterred, he went back to Conservative Central Office. They were so impressed with Scott that they parachuted him into the newly created safe seat of Wembley North, which he thought 'should produce a Tory majority of between 1,000 and 2,000 votes.'[5]

Scott had just two weeks to win over the electorate in the suburban seat. Jane, recalling the election in her biography years later, wrote: 'I knew nothing whatever about politics, party or otherwise. I don't think Pete did either, but he was a war hero, a natural leader and very good at making speeches and subsequently skating over thin ice if he was asked awkward questions.' Scott found the campaign stressful, his knowledge of economics being 'non-existent', but he 'knew exactly what kind of an England I had been fighting for, and it was not in order to be able to turn the whole thing upside down and start again.' But that is exactly what the electorate voted for, turning its back on the war and its heroes, instead wanting politicians who could provide jobs, healthcare and homes. So Scott was narrowly beaten by the Labour candidate, losing by 435 votes. Writing in his diary, he said he had lost to 'the Labour landslide which had so unexpectedly swept the country'.

Not being interested in 'marking time' by nursing the seat until the next election, Scott wanted to 'get on with my peace, so I plunged back into ornithology and conservation and began painting hard.' He provided the illustrations to a best-selling book called *The Snow Goose* by the American author Paul Gallico (1897–1976).[6] It was about a disabled artist living in an abandoned lighthouse in the marshlands of Essex and his friendship with a young local girl who finds an injured snow goose. Scott had been in contact with Gallico before the war and believed his early life was the inspiration for the book. Although annoyed not to be acknowledged, he thought it a fitting compromise to do the illustrations. He also had an exhibition of his own paintings in New York. Jane accompanied him and while there she started to write a novel. She also met a new man, Robert Haas, vice-president of the publishing company Random House, at a party and the two began an intense correspondence.

In the autumn of 1945 Scott received two letters from ornithologist friends which were to change his life. One was from a farmer near Bristol who invited him down to see the large flock of white-fronted geese that wintered on the Severn Estuary. The other was from another farmer friend who had taken some of Scott's wildfowl collection before the war, including a pair of lesser white-fronted geese. They were, according to Scott, 'perhaps the most beautiful of all the world's grey geese,' and the rarest, as they 'had been recorded only once, and on my list you cannot have a rarer bird than that.' In his letter the farmer told Scott about 'an extraordinary occurrence,' telling him that 'in 1943 a lesser white-fronted goose had come down one day out of the sky and landed beside his tame pair and had stayed there for several days.' This intrigued Scott because the lesser white-fronted goose was very difficult to identify from the much commoner whitefronts, its key distinguishing feature being a golden yellow eyelid. What, he surmised, if the lesser white-front goose actually came regularly to the British Isles but had been overlooked? He then asked himself where you would find them and came to the conclusion that they would be mixed in with the much more common white-fronted geese which migrate to Britain in the autumn from their breeding grounds in Russia.

A few weeks later Scott went down to the Severn Estuary to test out his theory. 'If I was correct,' he wrote, 'I might expect to find a stray lesser whitefront among the larger geese if I could only get close enough to see their eyelids.' There he met the farmer, who led him to a type 26 wartime pill box with a commanding view over the salt marsh. The pill box was one of a line which stretched out along the estuary following the river. During the war they had formed part of the Western Command chain of defence known as the 'Stop Line No 27'. The soldiers based there had often found them lonely and desolate places, but for Scott they provided the ideal base from which to test his theory and the pill box became his first birdwatching hide.

On the first day he saw a great flock of 2,000 geese, mostly Russian-bred whitefronts, but also mixed in were a few bean, barnacle, brent, greylag and some pinkfeet geese, but no lesser white-front. However, the next day Scott was back and after half an hour his binoculars alighted on a lesser white-front. 'My spine tingled delightfully as it does in the slow movement of Sibelius's Violin Concerto,' he recorded. 'Here almost too easily was a vindication of my far-fetched theory. It was, no doubt, a small recondite discovery, a minor ornithological technicality, yet for me it was a moment of unforgettable exultation – a major triumph, an epoch making occurrence, a turning point; or is it only in looking back on it that I have invested it with so much significance because, in the event, it changed the course of my life?'

To his even greater delight, later that afternoon in another large flock he found a second lesser white-fronted goose. A very excited Scott got back and instantly phoned his ornithological friend Bernard Tucker (1901–1950), a lecturer in zoology at Oxford University, the first secretary of the British Trust for Ornithology and the long-time editor of the journal *British Birds*. 'The meticulous and ever-sceptical Bernard Tucker after much cross-questioning professed himself convinced,' declared a triumphant Scott, 'but I was privately glad that he saw them for himself a week later.'

So on that cold and sunny day in December 1945, as Scott walked back from a three-tier pill-box that had been built to deter a German invasion in 1940, he came to the 'inescapable conclusion that this was the place in which anyone who loved wild geese must live.' However, when Jane later visited the site she was less impressed, writing, 'Peter had found the place where he wanted to have his wildfowl, at Slimbridge on the Severn Marshes ... It was a bare and virtually treeless place except for a small clump in which was an old duck decoy. The only time I went there I was ill and the prospect didn't hearten me. I'd not learned to appreciate wild geese.' To Scott, however, he had found his mission in life. 'Here were two empty cottages which might become the headquarters of the research organisation which had been taking shape in my mind over the war years,' he wrote. 'The headquarters of a new collection of waterfowl, of the scientific and educational effort which I believed was so badly needed for the conservation of wildfowl.' As he trudged back through the mud, Scott the painter, wildfowler and war hero looked at his surroundings 'with a new eye, an eye to the future, for this was the beginning of the Wildfowl Trust.'[7]

Scott went on to make an outstanding contribution to nature conservation, establishing the Wildfowl and Wetlands Trust at Slimbridge in 1946 (he originally called it the Severn Wildfowl Trust) and later helping to found the World Wide Fund for Nature. A prolific painter and author, he won numerous awards and was knighted for his contribution to conservation in 1973. He and Jane separated in the summer of 1946, she leaving him and their daughter, Nicola, for Robert Haas. In 1951 Scott married his assistant, Philippa Talbot-Ponsonby, and they had two children together: a daughter Dafila, born in the same year, and a son, Falcon, who was born three years later. Jane continued with her writing and in her seventies wrote five novels called the *Cazalet Chronicles*, about the life and times of a family during the war, which were turned into an acclaimed BBC series. In later life she was reconciled with her daughter and died in 2014. Scott died in 1989, just two weeks short of his eightieth birthday. Philippa kept the trust going until her own death in 2010. Their contribution to natural history was summed up by Sir David Attenborough (1926–) who said Scott was the man who most inspired his career and that 'the Scotts put conservation on the map, at a time when it was not a word that most people understood.'[8]

Postscript

Following the end of the war many of the ornithologists featured in this book crossed paths and in the process established a conservation movement which today boasts over five million members. During the war they probably only knew each other by repute, but afterwards they became friends, colleagues and rivals, simultaneously working together in publishing and broadcasting as well as in natural history and conservation. Pivotal to the relationships which grew up was Peter Scott. In 1946 Phyllis Barclay-Smith, the editor of the *Avicultural Magazine* at the start of the war, and Max Nicholson, a founding member of the British Trust for Ornithology who helped plan D-Day, both became Council Members of the Wildfowl and Wetlands Trust, and Viscount Alanbrooke, Britain's former top soldier, became its first President.

Not long after setting up the trust, Scott started working with Desmond Hawkins (1908–1999) who was employed in radio broadcasting at the BBC in Bristol. Before the war Hawkins lived in London writing novels and editing literary journals. 'The incendiaries and explosives raining down on London, which destroyed my novels, deflected me into the new medium of radio documentaries,' he wrote. 'The world I had grown up in was lost, but a new world lay ahead.' Together they collaborated on the first radio broadcasts from Bristol on natural history. In 1946 *The Naturalist* was broadcast, followed by *Bird Song of the Month* a year later, with Hawkins producing the programmes and Scott presenting them. In 1955 they moved into television and produced a ground-breaking natural history programme called *Look* which ran for fourteen years until 1969. *Look* used footage from a wide range of professional and amateur film makers, including the wildlife photographer Eric Hosking and his protegé Viscount Alanbrooke.

Scott also worked closely with James Fisher, the author of the bestselling war-time penguin book on birdwatching. In 1942 Fisher told the publisher Billy Collins, 'What this country needs is a good series of books on natural history to take its mind off the carnage.' Collins agreed and in 1945 produced the first in the acclaimed *New Naturalist* series, with Fisher sitting on the editorial board. In 1952 Scott and Fisher produced a radio programme called *Nature Parliament* which was broadcast as part of *Children's Hour*. Two years later they wrote a book, *A Thousand Geese*, about a joint expedition to the highlands of Iceland in pursuit of pinkfooted geese.[1]

In the same year the Conservative MP for Lewes, Tufton Beamish (1917–1989), introduced into Parliament a bill that became the Protection of Birds Act 1954. Beamish, a British Army officer, fought in Europe, North Africa and the Far East and was awarded the Military Cross and mentioned in dispatches. After the war he championed the conservation movement and following a long campaign secured Parliamentary time for the bill. Scott was keen to serve on the advisory committee but was not selected until Viscount Alanbrooke intervened on his behalf, writing personally to the Home Secretary. It was at the time the longest private member's bill to go before the House of Commons. The Act was a significant milestone in the development of legislation to protect wild birds and their habitats. Part of the Protection of Birds Act remains in force today, making it illegal to:

- kill, injure or take, or attempt to kill, injure or take, any wild bird; or
- take, damage or destroy the nest of any wild bird while that nest is in use; or
- take or destroy an egg of any wild bird.

In May 1954 Scott joined Fisher, Barclay-Smith and over 600 other ornithologists from forty countries around the world at the 11th International Ornithological Congress held in Basel, Switzerland. Convened every four years by the International Ornithologists' Union since 1884, the congress was one of the most prestigious events in the ornithological calendar. Also in attendance was Richard Meinetzhagen, who had contributed to the black redstart study during the Blitz, and Carl Alexander Gibson-Hill, who had helped research the book on Malayan birds in a Japanese prisoner of war camp. Yet, despite Britain being represented by some of the greatest ornithologists of their generation, the largest delegation to the conference came not from Britain but Germany. Birds not only served in the war, they also helped to build the peace.

References

Chapter 1
1. Barclay-Smith, Phyllis, *The Avicultural Magazine*, October 1939, Vol. IV no.10, pp.311–312.
2. Care of Birds in War-Time, *The Avicultural Magazine*, October 1939, Vol. IV no 10, p.313.
3. Teschemaker, W. E., The Influence of German Aviculture, *The Avicultural Magazine*, February 1917, pp.98-106
4. Douglas-Home, H., 1978 *The Birdman Memories of birds by Henry Douglas-Home*, Readers Union p.149.
5. Fisher, James, 1940, *Watching Birds*, Penguin, p.11.
6. Ibid p.13.
7. Tan, Bonny, 2008, *An orientalist's treasure trove of Malaya and beyond: Catalogue of the Gibson-Hill Collection*, National Library, Singapore, p.9.
8. Royal Air Force Comforts Committee, 1939, *Knitting for the RAF*, Official Book of Instructions.
9. Hayes, Andrew, 2019, *A Nightingale Sang ... Where?* https://andrews birdingstuff.wordpress.com/2016/12/27/a-nightingale-sang-where
10. *The Wren Farthing* (1937–1956), 2005, Brushwood Coins https://brushwood.mt7.uk/coinfactnote2wren.pdf
11. Fitter, Richard, Black Redstarts in England in the Summer of 1943, *British Birds*, Vol XXXVII no 10, pp.191–194.
12. Nicholson, Max, 1995, BBC *Desert Island Discs* https://www.bbc.co.uk/programmes/p0093pbh
13. Garfield, Brian, 2007, *The Meinertzhagen Mystery: The Life and Legend of a Colossal Fraud*, Potomac Books.
14. Fitter, Richard, 1945, *London's Natural History*, Collins.

Chapter 2
1. Colvin, Ian, 1957, *Flight 777 The Mystery of Leslie Howard* Evan Brothers.
2. http://www.south-central-media.co.uk/spitfire/spitfire.htm
3. *Picture Show and Film Pictorial*, 12 September 1942, First of the Few.
4. C. Harvey, V. B. Baliga, P. Lavoie and D. L. Altshuler, 2019, 'Wing morphing allows gulls to modulate static pitch stability during gliding,' *Journal of The Royal Society Interface* https://doi.org/10.1098/rsif.2018.0641
5. Mitchell, Gordon, 1986, *R.J.Mitchell, Schooldays to Spitfire*, The History Press.

6. Ibid.
7. Howard, Ronald, 1984, *In Search of My Father: A Portrait of Leslie Howard*, St Martin's Press.
8. *Tawny Pipit*, 1944, Prestige Productions.
9. Parkinson, David, Tawny Pipit *Radio Times*, Comedy/Drama, 1944 https://www.radiotimes.com/movie-guide/b-mkq5ye/tawny-pipit/
10. Hosking, Eric, 1970, *An Eye for a Bird*, Hutchinson.
11. Crompton, Richmal, 1940, *William and the Evacuees*, William and the Bird Man, George Newnes Ltd.
12. Douglas-Home, H., 1978, *The Birdman Memories of birds by Henry Douglas-Home*, Readers Union pp. 41–42.

Chapter 3
1. Rankin, M. Neal and Duffey, Eric A.G, A Study of the Bird Life of the North Atlantic, *British Birds*, Vol. XLI, July 1948.
2. Eric Arthur Gerald Duffey, 1922–2019, *Arachnology*, 2019, 18 (1), pp.47–52.

Chapter 4
1. Harrisson, T. & Hollom, P.A.D, The Great Crested Grebe Enquiry, Part 1–5, *British Birds* 26 January 1932.
2. Harrisson, Tom, 1937, *Savage Civilization*, Alfred A. Knopf, New York.
3. Moran, Joe, 2007, The Science of Ourselves, *New Statesman*, https://www.newstatesman.com/uncategorized/2007/01/mass-observation-public
4. Mass Observations of Social Problems, *Nature*, 140, 13 November 1937, pp.843–844.
5. Marcus, Laura, Mass Observation as Poetry and Science: Charles Madge and his Contexts, 12 May 2000, *New Formations*.
6. Madge, Charles and Harrisson, Tom, 1939, *Britain by Mass-Observation A Penguin Special*, 1 January 1939.
7. Heimann, Judith M., 2002, *The Most Offending Soul Alive: Tom Harrisson and his Remarkable Life*, Aurum Press, p.154.
8. Harrisson, Tom and Madge, Charles, 1940, *War Begins at Home*, Chatto and Windus.
9. *War Factory A Report by Mass-Observation*, 1943.
10. *Mass-Observation Archive*, University of Sussex, Part 7: Topic Collections – Air Raids, Morale and the Blitz www.ampltd.co.uk/collections_az/Mass-Ob-07/description.aspx
11. *Mass-Observation Clothes Rationing Survey: An Interim Report Prepared by Mass-Observation for the Advertising Service Guild*, 1941.
12. BBC, *Desert Island Discs*, Tom Harrisson Broadcast, 2 October 1943 https://www.bbc.co.uk/programmes/p009y0b3
13. Heimann, Judith M., 2002, *The Most Offending Soul Alive: Tom Harrisson and his Remarkable Life*, Aurum Press, pp.184–185.
14. Ibid pp.211–213.

Chapter 5

1. Wikipedia, *Valiant* (film), 2005.
2. Royal Pigeon Racing Association, *Pigeons in War* https://www.rpra.org/pigeon-history/pigeons-in-war
3. Harding, John Poole, *The Pigeon Message Service*, BBC WW2 People's War, 2003 https://www.bbc.co.uk/history/ww2peopleswar/stories/29/a1151029.shtml
4. Royal Pigeon Racing Association, *Pigeons in War* https://www.rpra.org/pigeon-history/pigeons-in-war
5. *Hansard Pigeon Service*, 24 January 1940, Vol. 356 https://hansard.parliament.uk/Commons/1940-01-24/debates/2aa8231d-a947-4279-b2e5-8ae6f8eb11ed/PigeonService
6. *Hansard Order in Council Amending Regulation 9 of the Defence (General) Regulations* 1939, 1:843.
7. Corera, Gordon, 2018, *Operation Columba: The Secret Pigeon Service*, Harper Collins, pp.91–92.
8. Ibid pp.37–38.
9. *Scilly Now & Then Magazine*, MI5 'tried to catch German pigeons over Scilly in WW2', 1 June 2018.
10. Military History Matters, *Pigeon-Guided Missiles*, 10 November 2010, https://www.military-history.org/articles/pigeon-guided-missiles.htm
11. Sleight, Christopher, *The Pigeon that Saved a World War II Bomber Crew*, BBC News, 23 February 2012.
12. Wikipedia, *Dickin Medal*.
13. Ibid.
14. Herbert, Ian, The hero of the latest British war movie is a pigeon called Valiant. A flight of fancy? No, it's based on real life, *Independent*, 23 March 2005.
15. JHH, A Country Diary, *The Guardian*, Penrith, 25 April 1945.

Chapter 6

1. Madoc, G.C., 1947, *An introduction to Malayan Birds*, The Malayan Nature Society, Caxton Press.
2. Tan, Bonny, *Carl Alexander Gibson-Hill*, Singapore Infopedia, 2016.
3. Tan, Bonny, *An Orientalist's Treasure Trove of Malaya and Beyond: Catalogue of the Gibson-Hill Collection*, National Library, Singapore, 2008, pp.15–16.
4. Allan, Shelia, *Diary of a Girl in Changi 1941–45*, 1994, Kangaroo Press.
5. Ibid, pp.37–38.
6. Wikipedia, *Henry V* (1944 film).
7. Madoc, G.C., 1947, *An introduction to Malayan Birds*, The Malayan Nature Society, Caxton Press Preface.
8. Allan, Shelia, 1994, *Diary of a Girl in Changi 1941–45*, Kangaroo Press.
9. Gibson-Hill, Carl Alexander, *Ornithological Notes from the Raffles Museum*, No.11, 'Nesting notes on the Malayan Long-tailed Tailor-Bird, Orthotomus sutonicus Maculicollis', Bulletin, Raffles Museum (23), pp.82–97.

10. Ibid, pp.98–113.
11. Buxton, John, 1950, *The Redstart*, New Naturalist, Collins.
12. Niemann, Derek, 2012, *Birds in a Cage*, Warburg POW camp, 1941. Four POW Birdwatchers. The Unlikely Beginning of British Wildlife Conservation, Short Books.

Chapter 7

1. Ware E.H., 1946, *Wing to Wing Bird-Watching Adventures at Home and Abroad*, Paternoster Press.
2. Johnston, Hamish, *A Corner of Pakistan in Scotland, 2012*, Highland Family History Society.

Chapter 8

1. Danchev, Alex and Todman, Daniel (Eds), 2001, *War Diaries 1939–1945 Field Marshal Lord Alanbrooke*, Weidenfeld & Nicolson, p.xi.
2. Bryant, Arthur, 1957, *The Turn of the Tide Based on the War Diaries of Field Marshal Viscount Alanbrooke*, Collins.
3. Bryant, Arthur, 1959, *Triumph in the West Completing the War Diaries of Field Marshal Viscount Alanbrooke*, Collins.
4. Danchev, Alex and Todman, Daniel (Eds), 2001, *War Diaries 1939–1945 Field Marshal Lord Alanbrooke*, 2001, Weidenfeld & Nicolson.
5. Ibid, p.xiii.
6. Grey, Edward, 1926, *The Fallodon Papers*, Constable & Co. Ltd, pp.82–83.
7. Ibid, p.160.
8. West Coast Rare Books, 2018, *Alanbrooke A Life in Books*, www.westcoast rarebooks.com

Chapter 9

1. Gould, John, 1873, *The Birds of Great Britain*, London Taylor & Francis for the Author.
2. Ibid p.474.
3. Audubon, John James, *The Birds of America*, 1827–1838, London.
4. Milton, Nicholas, 2019, *Neville Chamberlain's Legacy*, Pen and Sword Books.
5. Ibid p.509.

Chapter 10

1. Ibid p.712.
2. Hosking, Eric, *Field Marshal Viscount Alanbrooke An Appreciation*, Bird Notes, Vol. 30, No.8 Autumn, 1963, pp.247–248.

Chapter 11

1. Scott, Peter, 1961, *The Eye of the Wind*, Hodder and Stoughton, p.136.
2. Ibid p.13.
3. Ibid p.77
4. Scott, Peter, 1935, *Morning Flight*, Country Life.

5. Scott, Peter, 1961, *The Eye of the Wind*, Hodder and Stoughton, pp.167–68.
6. Young, E. Hilton, 1936, *A Bird in the Bush*, Country Life.
7. Scott, Peter, 1939, *Wild Chorus*, Country Life.

Chapter 12
1. Scott, Peter, 1967, *Happy the Man Episodes in an Exciting Life*, Sphere Books.
2. Scott, Peter, 1961, *The Eye of the Wind*, Hodder and Stoughton, p.211.
3. Howard, Elizabeth Jane, 2002, *Slipstream*, A Memoir, MacMillan.
4. Ibid p.105.
5. Scott, Peter, 1961, *The Eye of the Wind*, Hodder and Stoughton, p.389.

Chapter 13
1. Howard, Elizabeth Jane, 2002, *Slipstream*, A Memoir MacMillan, pp.121–122.
2. Scott, Peter, 1961, *The Eye of the Wind*, Hodder and Stoughton, pp.447–448.
3. Howard, Elizabeth Jane, 2002, *Slipstream*, A Memoir MacMillan, p.158.
4. Scott, Peter, 1961, *The Eye of the Wind*, Hodder and Stoughton, p.530.
5. Ibid p.541.
6. Gallico, Paul, 1946, *The Snow Goose*, Michael Joseph.
7. Scott, Peter, 1961, *The Eye of the Wind*, Hodder and Stoughton, p.548.
8. Moss, Stephen, Philippa Scott obituary, 10 January 2010, *The Guardian*.

Chapter 14
1. Scott, Peter and Fisher, James, 1953, *A Thousand Geese*, Collins.

Index